D1378739

THE ATLAS
of
SPECIAL OPERATIONS
of
WORLD WAR II

THE ATLAS
of
SPECIAL OPERATIONS
of
WORLD WAR II

by
ALEXANDER SWANSTON

Skyhorse Publishing

Copyright © 2014 by Alexander Swanston

FIRST NORTH AMERICAN EDITION BY SKYHORSE PUBLISHING, INC. 2014

All rights to any and all materials in copyright owned by the publisher are strictly reserved by the publisher.

First published in Great Britain in 2014 by Pen & Sword Atlas, an imprint of Pen & Sword Books Ltd

All rights reserved. No part of this book may be reproduced in any manner without the express written consent of the publisher, except in the case of brief excerpts in critical reviews or articles. All inquiries should be addressed to Skyhorse Publishing, 307 West 36th Street, 11th Floor, New York, NY 10018.

Skyhorse Publishing books may be purchased in bulk at special discounts for sales promotion, corporate gifts, fund-raising, or educational purposes. Special editions can also be created to specifications. For details, contact the Special Sales Department, Skyhorse Publishing, 307 West 36th Street, 11th Floor, New York, NY 10018 or info@skyhorsepublishing.com.

Skyhorse® and Skyhorse Publishing® are registered trademarks of Skyhorse Publishing, Inc.®, a Delaware corporation.

Visit our website at www.skyhorsepublishing.com.

10 9 8 7 6 5 4 3 2 1

Library of Congress Cataloging-in-Publication Data is available on file.

Jacket design by Dominic Allen
Compass image credit: Jaypee

Print ISBN: 978-1-62873-723-3
Ebook ISBN: 978-1-62914-071-1

Printed in China

CONTENTS

INTRODUCTION

The Second World War was a truly global conflict, involving almost every nation in the struggle to stop the spread of totalitarianism. This meant that battles were fought in all climates and on all sorts of terrain, from the jungle hills of Burma and the Philippines to the snow covered fjords of Norway and the vast desert oceans of north Africa. Technology had also progressed, meaning that war could be fought under the surface of the sea or in the air 40,000 feet above. This unique scenario involving all aspects of the military meant that specialist units bloomed, using the rough ground or unique setting to their advantage.

War was still fought as it had been thousands of years previously. Huge armies moved across continents and large naval units swept the oceans, but unorthodox units could creep through front lines that were thousands of miles long and report on enemy movements or sabotage installations. The evolution of the

aircraft meant that they could carry heavier loads, this could mean delivering a 22,000lb 'earthquake' bomb that literally shook the target to destruction or meant the carriage of parachute troops.

The use of the parachute soldier, or paratrooper, was prolific during the Second World War. This gave the advantage of flanking the enemy overhead. Initially parachutes had been developed during the previous war, but only as a last resort for pilots or balloon observation units. The US Army had thought of using them for dropping troops behind lines but the armistice resulted in this idea being shelved. The Russians later took to creating battalions of paratroopers but never used them in great numbers in the eventual war to follow. Italy also led the way in the creation of parachute troops, but again these troops were never delivered by air into combat and only fought as ground troops.

The de Havilland Mosquito employed by the RAF was a brilliant fighter-bomber. Constructed almost exclusively from wood and powered by two Rolls-Royce Merlin engines the aircraft could reach speeds in excess of 400 mph. The type was employed during the low-level raid on Amiens prison to destroy the walls surrounding the facility, allowing French resistance prisoners to escape.

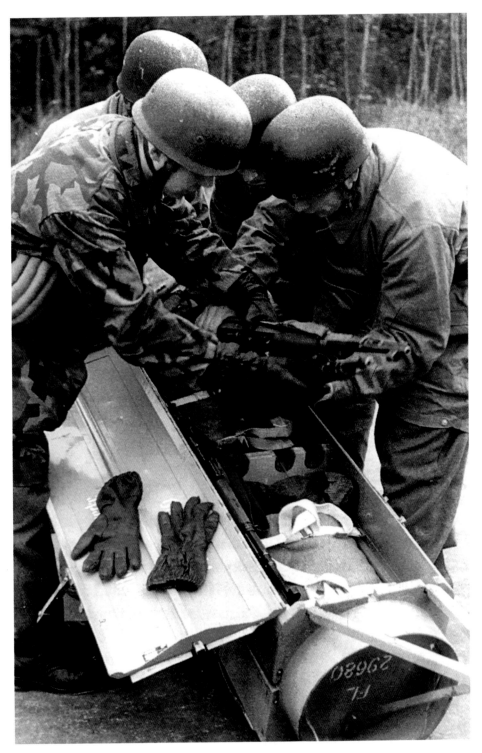

Four Fallschirmjaeger troops unload their kit from an arms container.

It was Germany that was to show the true potential of parachute infiltration. Taking strategic points in their invasions of Norway, Denmark and the Low Countries, coming to a bloody conclusion with their attack on Crete, a pyrrhic victory that led Hitler to never use them again in such a large number.

The Allied armies, particularly the US and Britain, instantly saw the potential and went about activating airborne units. This took time, so only small units saw action during the first half of the conflict, but in the final two years massive air armadas were dropped to aid conventional attacks.

At sea small craft were used to sneak through enemy defences, breathing apparatus meant that 'frogmen' could penetrate harbour defences and cause havoc. The use of aircraft carriers also meant that specialised aircraft could be transported to the vicinity of the target, hitherto comfortable in it's seclusion.

During the Second World War the use of aircraft was staggering, swarms of bombers flew to enemy targets in the hope of destroying factories involved in producing war materiel as well as lowering the morale and will to fight of the opposing country.

This again bred small units that could destroy small targets and structures that would have meant thousands of pounds of bombs and vast amounts of sorties to destroy, such as the Dambusters raid of 1943. The dams supplied much of the power to the Ruhr industrial region of Germany. Instead of sending over waves and waves of bombers to try and demolish these immensely strong structures the RAF took it to train a squadron of men to deliver a bizarre weapon, the bouncing bomb to great effect.

It was not just conventional fighting forces that had been streamlined into these specialised roles. Many men and women were educated in the role of resistance fighters and saboteurs that would work undercover in occupied territories. These men and women would then report on the enemy and train more units. This took great courage as discovery meant almost certain death.

This book hopes to cover a wide range of special operations during the Second World War covering the formation of certain units, why and how they were employed and the outcome of their various actions and how these affected the wider picture.

A wounded Commando is helped back to a landing craft during the raid on Vaagso, Norway. Small raids such as these by specialist troops helped raise morale, gain intelligence and denied the enemy valuable resources.

A member of the French resistance is joined by an American Lieutenant during the liberation of Paris. He is armed with a Sten gun supplied by the British via RAF air drops.

BRANDENBURGERS

A Brandenburger is outfitted in local dress for an operation in Poland. Brandenburgers infiltrated Poland in the days before the invasion on 1st September 1939 to seize communications centres and spread panic in the rear of the enemy.

Hauptmann Theodor von Hippel, a German intelligence officer, had the idea of utilising bilingual troops to infiltrate ahead of regular forces in order to gain control of strategic targets such as bridges, communications hubs and spread panic in the rear of the enemy. He took this idea to the regular army, the Wehrmacht, but was rejected out of hand. He then approached Admiral Wilhelm Canaris, then head of the Abwehr, (German military intelligence). The idea was green-lit and fluent Polish speakers were formed into the first company and given the innocuous title of 800th Special Duties Construction Company.

The men were infiltrated into Poland in civilian dress, posing as coal miners or construction workers just ahead of the main German invasion forces in late August 1939. They then seized communication hubs and important river crossings as well as preventing demolition of railway tunnels important to the main German advance. Even though these missions on the whole were carried out with great success, the company was disbanded shortly after the Polish capitulation.

Hippel persisted and this time a battalion strength unit was formed ready for the invasion of Denmark and Norway the following April. Again using civilian disguise the men were able to infiltrate and capture strategic points.

The battalion was again used in the German invasion of France and the Low Countries in May 1940. Men dressed in Dutch police uniforms approached the Gennep bridge over the Meuse River supposedly escorting captured German prisoners. When the Dutch sentries let down their guard the Brandenburgers leapt into action, pulling out hidden weapons and capturing the bridge intact. However, this ruse did not work on other bridges in the area as the Brandenburgers were caught and shot as spies.

These operations were carried out all along the path of the invasion, securing anything that could hinder the rapid advance of the Nazi Blitzkrieg with such success that after the campaign the battalion was enlarged to regimentals size. The Regiment now recruited men that could speak all the Balkan languages and most importantly Russian. These were the areas now in the sights of the German war machine.

Again the men of the Brandenburgers were infiltrated ahead of the main advance in order to secure a rapid advance. This time men posed as river boatmen on the Danube river in order to stop the scuppering of large ships therefore blocking the important river route.

With the opening of Operation Barbarossa in June 1941 the Brandenburgers adopted the dress of the NKVD, the Soviet secret police. This allowed the men free reign to countermand orders given to the defending troops. The Soviet troops, already lacking sufficient communications equipment were left in disarray.

In North Africa the Brandenburgers attempted to carry out missions behind enemy lines, disrupting supply and communications to the Allied

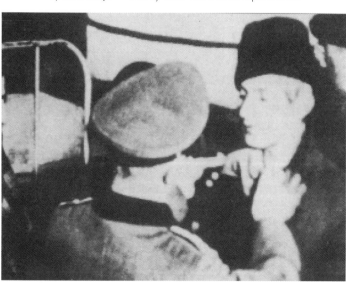

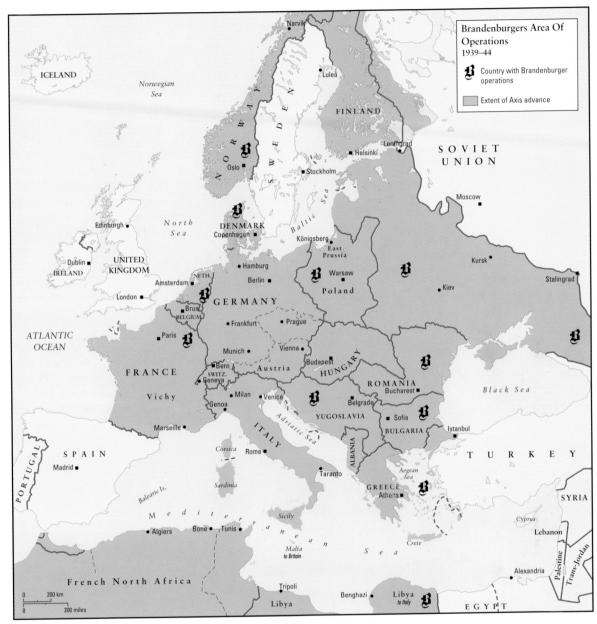

Brandenburgers Area Of Operations 1939–44

𝔅 Country with Brandenburger operations

▨ Extent of Axis advance

armies. Lack of investment in these units led to most being captured. They did not have the same amount of success that the Allied Long Range Desert Group and SAS were to have.

Due to political infighting the Brandenburgers were eventually disbanded in late 1943, most of the troops joined other special forces units within the Wehrmacht, even so, they had proven that with skill and deception, major victories could be achieved by small, specialised units, even though these tasks had been carried out flaunting the 'rules of war' by adopting the uniforms of the opposing armies.

The Brandenburgers fought on all fronts during the war before their disbandment in late 1943.

INVASION OF NORWAY AND DENMARK

The Junkers Ju 52 was the workhorse of the Luftwaffe. Used extensively on all fronts during the Second World War it was nick-named 'Iron Annie' by the crew and troops who flew in her. After the capture of key airfields in Norway fleets of Ju 52s brought in follow up troops to consolidate positions.

Scandinavia was a major supplier of raw materials that was required for the Nazi industrial machine that drove the expansion of the Reich. Neutral Sweden in particular held vast iron ore deposits and these were exported to other nations via the Norwegian port of Narvik in the north of the country just inside the Arctic Circle. Adolf Hitler and his general staff saw the importance of securing these supplies and concluded that the invasion of Norway was required before the Allies could make a preemptive occupation of the country. In order to facilitate this Denmark would also have to be invaded.

Denmark had a very small army and it was thought that the capture of strategic points around the country along with the royal family would produce its rapid capitulation. These points were the fort at Madneso and the airport of Aalborg in the very north of the country. The capture of these points was given to the Fallschirmjaeger, the German parachute division.

Formed in 1938 on the orders of Hermann Goering, head of the Luftwaffe, the first unit, the 7th Flieger Division was commanded by General Kurt Student. A former First World War fighter pilot, Student believed that the use of airborne forces could make an impact disproportionate to their size. This was to be proven correct when his men were

dropped on Madneso and Aalborg in the early hours of 9 April 1940, quickly securing them, the airport being of particular importance to the plan as it was to be a staging post for the follow-up invasion of Norway.

As Denmark fell airborne troops of the 7th Flieger Division were dropping on the airports of Oslo and Kristiansand in southern Norway, along with the air station at Sola. The latter was the only defended airfield but was eventually taken by the paratroops. Waves of Junkers Ju 52 transport aircraft, staging through the captured Aalborg airfield, began disembarking thousands of troops to begin the occupation of Norway.

The Norwegian government soon left Oslo and fled into the interior of the country, King Haakon VII giving the command of the defence to Major General Otto Ruge. Ruge decided to fight a delaying action whilst help arrived in the form of an expeditionary force from Britain. This was to land in the port of Trondheim, but was soon beaten off by the superior fighting of the Germans.

In the north the Germans had landed around 2,000 mountain troops in the northern port of Narvik. The town was quickly taken and the troops took up positions in the hills surrounding the port as battles between the destroyers of the Kriegsmarine that had landed them there and the Royal Navy took place. The Germans took heavy losses in these engagements and the surviving German sailors salvaged what they could and assisted with the land defence.

British troops were landed to the north of Narvik on the 14 April, followed shortly by French and Polish forces. The Allied commanders were cautious in their

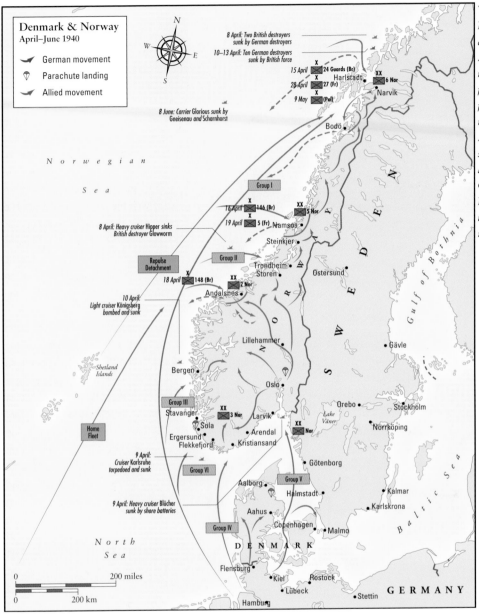

Denmark & Norway
April–June 1940

🕊 German movement

🪂 Parachute landing

🕊 Allied movement

8 April: Two British destroyers
sunk by German destroyers

10–13 April: Ten German destroyers
sunk by British force

15 April ⊠ 24 Guards (Br)

28 April ⊠ 27 (Fr) Harlstadt

9 May ⊠ (Pol) Narvik

XX 6 Nor

8 June: Carrier Glorious sunk by
Gneisenau and Scharnhorst

Bodö

N o r w e g i a n

S e a

Group I

16 April ⊠ 146 (Br)

19 April ⊠ 5 (Fr) Namsos

XX 5 Nor

8 April: Heavy cruiser Hipper sinks
British destroyer Glowworm

Steinkjer

Repulse
Detachment

Group II

Trondheim

18 April ⊠ 148 (Br) Storen

Östersund

Andalsnes

XX 2 Nor

10 April:
Light cruiser Königsberg
bombed and sunk

Lillehammer

Gävle

Shetland
Islands

Bergen

Oslo

Group III

Stavanger

Örebo

Stockholm

XX 3 Nor

Larvik

Lake
Vänern

Home
Fleet

🪂 Sola

Arendal

XX Nor

Norrköping

Ergersund

Kristiansand

Flekkefjord

9 April:
Cruiser Karlsruhe
torpedoed and sunk

Group VI

Götenborg

B a l t i c S e a

Aalborg

Group V

Kalmar

🪂 Halmstadt

9 April: Heavy cruiser Blücher
sunk by shore batteries

Karlskrona

Aahus

Copenhagen

Malmo

Group IV

N o r t h

S e a

D E N M A R K

0   200 miles

Flensburg

Kiel

Rostock

0   200 km

Lübeck

Stettin

Hamburg

G E R M A N Y

The invasion of Norway and Denmark commenced on 9 April 1940 combining maritime, air and land forces successfully for the first time in military history. The Allied response to the situation was slow and weak, leading the Germans to capture Norway completely in a little under two months.

advance on Narvik due to the difficult terrain and adverse weather. However, by 28 May the port had been re-taken and the Germans were forced into the mountains. However, the situation by this time had changed significantly for the Allies, the invasion of the west had begun and the British and French forces were ordered to evacuate. On 7 June King Haakon and his government left for England and exile. The Germans had successfully captured Norway in just under two months. Crucially the Germans suffered heavy losses, over 5,500 men and 260 aircraft and two major warships.

EBEN EMAEL

The German plan in the West was to lure the Allies into a defensive line in northern Belgium whilst the weight of their attack took place through the heavily wooded Ardennes region. The panzers would then rush north to the coast, effectively cutting off the British expeditionary force from its French ally.

The Fort of Eben Emael was the largest in a string of defences along the Belgian-German border. The fort defended the city of Liege, to its south, and the numerous bridges that crossed the Albert Canal. Construction was completed within four years in the mid-thirties, utilising the Albert Canal along its eastern boundary as an extra defensive barrier. Armament consisted of two 120mm cannon in turrets, supplemented by 16 75mm cannon placed in retractable cupolas with 360° traverse. These were protected by machine gun and anti-tank bunkers, everything was connected via tunnels under a thick concrete roof impervious to all airborne bombs at the time. The fort itself was garrisoned by 1,200 men under the command of a major.

The Germans assigned the 7th Flieger Division and the 22nd Airlanding Division for the preliminary stage of the invasion of the Low Countries. From these units Sturmabteilung

Koch under the command of Hauptmann Walter Koch was assigned the job of neutralising the fort at Eben Emael and capturing three bridges over the Albert Canal. Training took place in complete secrecy, men not being able to wear their unit badges assaulted replicas of the fort deep inside of Germany. They familiarised themselves with flamethrowers and the new shaped charge. These cone-shaped devices concentrated the power of conventional explosive, allowing them to cut through thick steel emplacements.

Just before 3 am on the morning of 10 May 1940 the eighty-five men of Group Granite, the force that was to assault the fort, clambered aboard their DFS 230 transport gliders. Tugged to the border of Germany and Belgium and released. During this period two of the gliders were released early from their tugs and landed well inside of Germany. On board one of these aircraft was the force commander Oberleutnant Witzig. Due to strict radio silence the rest of the unit were unaware that they were to land under strength and without their commander.

The nine remaining gliders landed on the roof of the fort with no loss, the troops disembarking and immediately going about their pre-ordained tasks, all cupolas being disabled with the use of shaped charges apart from one that had to be engaged by air support, Stukas being called in. After this attack it took no further part in the battle. All exits and entrances were secured by the airborne troops, effectively trapping the defending Belgians in the fort with no means to escape.

Witzig then arrived on the fort after arranging for another Ju 52 to tow his glider to the target, by now the Fallschirmjaeger were assaulting secondary targets and readying for the inevitable counter-attack. This came within an hour of their arrival but was successfully held. Reinforcement in the shape of German ground troops was to arrive in a matter of hours, but this was stymied by blown bridges. Relief came early on 11 May, the Belgians eventually surrendering the fort at 12.30 that day, casualties amounting to over 100 with over a 1,000 captured. The Germans lost six men in the attack.

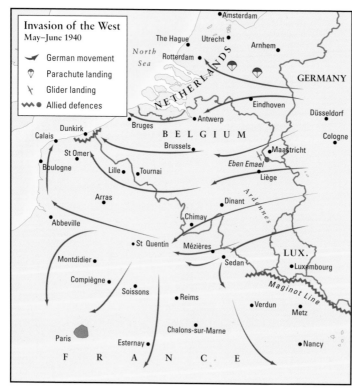

Invasion of the West
May–June 1940

- German movement
- Parachute landing
- Glider landing
- Allied defences

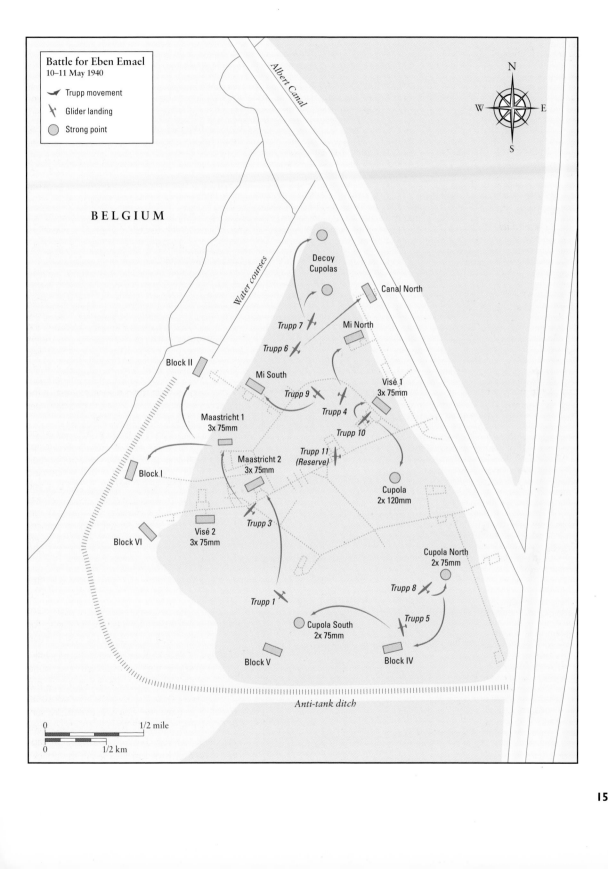

Battle for Eben Emael
10–11 May 1940

Trupp movement

Glider landing

Strong point

BELGIUM

Albert Canal

Water courses

Decoy Cupolas

Canal North

Trupp 7

Mi North

Trupp 6

Block II

Mi South

Visé 1
3x 75mm

Trupp 9

Trupp 4

Maastricht 1
3x 75mm

Trupp 10

Block I

Maastricht 2
3x 75mm

Trupp 11
(Reserve)

Cupola
2x 120mm

Visé 2
3x 75mm

Trupp 3

Block VI

Cupola North
2x 75mm

Trupp 8

Trupp 1

Trupp 5

Cupola South
2x 75mm

Block IV

Block V

Anti-tank ditch

0   1/2 mile

0   1/2 km

FORMATION OF THE COMMANDOS

After the withdrawal of the British Expeditionary Force from the beaches of Dunkirk and with the skies dark with the Luftwaffe ceaselessly bombing RAF installations, Britain's Prime Minister, Winston Churchill, issued an order for a unit to be created that would raid the enemy coast and leave, 'a trail of German corpses behind'. This unit was to become the Commandos.

One man was already ahead of Churchill, Lieutenant Colonel Dudley Pound had drawn up a proposal for a clandestine raiding unit to the then Chief of the Imperial General Staff, Sir John Dill, who immediately green-lit the project. Volunteers were hastily assembled and an action was put in place as soon as possible with a night assault on the French coastline near Boulogne. Very

A Commando scales a cliff during training, slung over his back is the ubiquitous Thompson Sub-machine gun.

little was actually achieved with only two unlucky sentries falling to the Commandos, later another raid on the occupied island of Guernsey, codenamed Ambassador was of little consequence with poor intelligence and heavy seas causing more problematic than the enemy. Nevertheless lessons were learned such as the acquisition of dedicated landing craft in the form of the Thornycroft LCA (Landing Craft Assault). This was an excellent vessel that would be used for the entire conflict in Europe and Asia, the Commando had a love hate relationship with it as it gave moderate protection, but being a flat-bottomed boat, in the open sea led to seasickness.

By November 1940 over 2,000 men had volunteered for the Commandos and were duly formed into the Special Service Brigade, in turn coming under the command of Combined Operations Headquarters commanded by Sir Roger Keyes, himself a veteran of amphibious assault having been involved in the Zeebrugge raid in April 1918.

Training was carried out in Scotland with emphasis on self reliance. The potential Commando was billeted with a local family and was required to make his own way to training and look after himself, rather than living in barracks. Less emphasis was placed on the parade ground and more on cliff scaling, beach assault and demolitions. Rank became less of an issue, with everyone expected to make decisions if the need arose.

Weapons proficiency was a top priority, with the units having a higher proportion of automatic weapons than a regular unit. These included the standard light machine gun for the British Army, the Bren gun. Firing the .303in round it was a fantastically reliable and accurate weapon, perhaps its only draw back was the thirty round magazine meaning it had to be reloaded more often than the German equivalent, the MG.34 which relied on a belt feed. The Commandos also acquired the Thompson Sub-machine gun. Made famous by the gangsters of the thirties, this weapon was heavy but packed a heavy punch with its .45in round and was a favourite amongst the troops.

Another weapon synonymous with the Commandos was the Fairbairn-Sykes fighting knife. Developed by William Fairbairn and Eric Sykes, both ex policemen from Shanghai, they created a 'stilletto' style blade that was perfect for penetrating the ribcage of an enemy sentry. The men trained ceaselessly until they were completely comfortable with the blade in their hands. This weapon would also be issued to SAS troops as well as agents dropped into occupied Europe.

Units would be supplied and trained on support weapons such as 2in motors and later the PIAT (Projector, Infantry, Anti-Tank) as well as evolving their personnel kit to match their operations, discarding the steel helmet of regular units, replacing it with a woollen cap comforter as well as wearing rubber-soled boots as opposed to the iron studded standard boots that could potentially give away their position.

By 1941 there were twelve Commando units each of 500 men, No. 10 (Inter-Allied) Commando being made up of foreign troops from France, Netherlands, Belgium and Poland, that had managed to escape from occupied Europe.

A Commando with blackened face poses with a Fairbairn-Sykes fighting knife in his teeth. Developed by two ex-policemen from Shanghai it would become the unofficial symbol of the Commandos.

FORMATION OF THE LRDG

The vast open deserts of North Africa had been little charted in the first half of the 20th Century and was thought impassable with modern motorised vehicles. But in between wars there had been groups of men taking modified motor cars into the Sahara and using their own initiative had developed ways of taming the ocean of sand. At the head of this group was Major Ralph Bagnold. Bagnold solved the problem of navigation by adopting a solar compass and modified standard cars by adding larger tyres with low pressure, all this combined made roaming the desert feasible.

Bagnold came to the end of his time in the British Army just before hostilities were commenced. He quickly rejoined, and in the army's infinite wisdom sent perhaps the best desert explorer of the time to

Kenya. Due to a string of events he never made it to his posting and he ended up in Alexandria. He then set to work on pitching his ideas for a desert patrol. He eventually came to the attention of Field Marshal Sir Archibald Wavell, Commander of the Middle East at the time. He gave permission to Bagnold to raise a small unit for the purpose of infiltrating the flanks of the Italians in Libya and pass back any infomation gleaned. Bagnold first approached Australian units for volunteers, presuming that their more rugged outdoor life would be more suited to the rigours of the mission. Officers were not interested in letting their best men go to such nascent and untried patrol. The New Zealand Division was approached and the commander, General Freyberg, a friend and colleague of Wavell, obliged the transfer of some of his best men to the patrol. The Long Range Patrol was born. The first

The Chevrolet 30 cwt truck was the mainstay of the LRDG. Rugged and reliable the vehicle was retro-fitted with a radiator condenser and numerous weapons for defence.

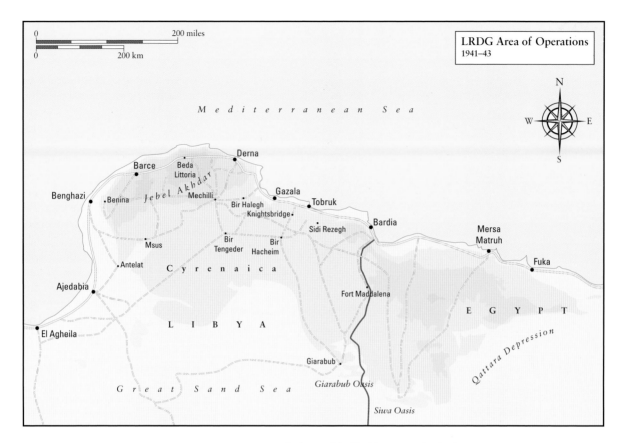

0 — 200 miles
0 — 200 km

LRDG Area of Operations
1941–43

Mediterranean Sea

N
W — E
S

Derna
Barce
Beda Littoria
Benghazi
•Benina
Jebel Akhdar
Mechilli•
Gazala
Bir Halegh
Knightsbridge•
Tobruk
Bardia
Mersa Matruh
Fuka
Msus•
Bir Tengeder
Bir Hacheim
Sidi Rezegh
Antelat•
C y r e n a i c a
Ajedabia•
Fort Maddalena
E G Y P T
L I B Y A
El Agheila•
Qattara Depression
Giarabub•
Great Sand Sea
Giarabub Oasis
Siwa Oasis

reconnaisance was led not by Bagnold, but by Pat Clayton, a former friend from his inter-war expeditions. It was a success and the patrols were quickly expanded. Bagnold could no longer rely on the New Zealand Division as a source for potential troopers so looked to the newly arrived Scots and Coldstream Guards as well as the Yeomanry Divisions. These were segregated into individual patrols. The name was also changed to Long Range Desert Patrol.

The patrols relied mainly on the Chevrolet 30 cwts and Ford trucks for transport on patrols. These were armed with Vickers or Lewis guns for defence from air attack, equipped with camouflage nets, water condensers and wide tyres.

The primary mission of the LRDG was to go on 'Road Watch' patrols. This entailed a wide-flanking patrol via bases like the Siwa Oasis and then penetrate north behind enemy lines and sit for days counting the number of vehicles passing to the enemy front. En route to these missions the men also reconnoitred possible future routes by themselves or larger units as well as charting the previously unsurveyed desert, at the head of this was Ken Lazarus, who commanded a patrol dedicated to this task.

With the introduction of other specialised units the LRDGs skill and capability was called on, SAS troops and intelligence units used the LRDG as a 'taxi' service, using them to be inserted behind enemy lines then whisked back to the relative safety of the Allied lines.

ATTACK ON TARANTO

The Fairey Swordfish, known affectionately as the 'Stingbag' was an aircraft of the first generation, being of wire, strut and fabric construction. However it was ideal for the task assigned to it, being able to fly at exceptionally low speed which aided greatly in the laying of its main armament, the anti-ship torpedo.

At the beginning of Second World War the Regia Marina, the Italian Navy, exerted the concept of the fleet in being. This meant a strong naval force was in place to impose power over a certain area without ever leaving port. This had been foreseen by Admiral Dudley Pound and secretly before the start of hostilities the Royal Navy had made plans for an aerial strike on the Italian fleet based in Taranto, on the 'heel' of Italy. This would entail a force of aging Fairey Swordfish torpedo bombers making a surprise attack on the fleet at anchor. The Swordfish was an anachronism, being a biplane with wires and struts in an age of new sleek all-metal monoplanes. Yet it was ideal for the job, being able to fly at remarkably slow speeds, aiding in the laying of torpedoes on targets.

HMS *Eagle* was chosen for the job of launching the aircraft 200 miles short of the Italian harbour. The Swordfish themselves were modified with extra fuel tanks, this came with the loss of the third crew member in the aircraft. The torpedoes that were to be used in the attack were given sensitive contact fuses and altered slightly to prevent 'bottoming out' in the shallows of the harbour. Due to a fire aboard the *Eagle* and subsequent damage to her fuel systems the force was transferred to the new carrier, HMS *Illustrious*. The crews and aircraft for the attack were drawn from 813, 815, 819 and 824 Naval Air Squadrons, Fleet Air Arm, under the command of Lieutenant-Commander Williamson. The Naval task force consisting of *Illustrious* and her escort of cruisers and destroyers came under the command of Rear Admiral Lyster, who had been instrumental in the planning of the attack.

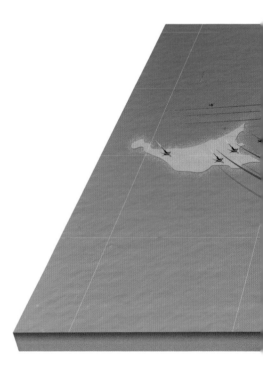

Prior to the attack various reconnaissance flights flying out of Malta had overflown the harbour to check the fleet had not sailed, followed on the afternoon of the 11 November by a Sunderland flying boat making a final pass. This led to the harbour defences being alerted to a probable attack, but was essential in confirming the Italian fleet was still there. The target was to be six battleships, seven heavy cruisers, two light cruisers and eight destroyers.

The attack was to be in two flights, the first being led by Williamson consisting of twelve aircraft took off just after 2,100, followed an hour and a half later by nine others, one turning back with fuel pump difficulties.

The first wave approached the harbour in two formations after losing sight of each other in a cloud bank. Nevertheless the attacks went in, with oil tanks to the west of the harbour being set ablaze by bomb-armed Swordfish and Williamson putting in a successful attack on the battleship *Conte di Cavour*, holing her. She would never see action again. Neither would Williamson and his crewman, being shot down soon after and then taken prisoner.

The second wave flew in an hour after the first, again against substantial anti-aircraft artillery. the battleship *Littorio* suffering heavy damage in the attack. The second wave lost another aircraft, this time the crew perishing.

The attack put out of action three battleships, effectively ending the Italians 'fleet in being', the remainder fled to the safer harbours of north-east Italy. Naval planners from all nations studied the attack with great interest, especially the Japanese, the attack being highly influential in its development of the attack on Pearl Harbour just over a year later.

The attack on Taranto Harbour on the night of 11–12 November 1940. The first wave were split into two formations and attacked from the west, one unit torpedoing targets in the harbour whilst the other bombed installations. The second wave, arriving approximately an hour later flew in from the north.

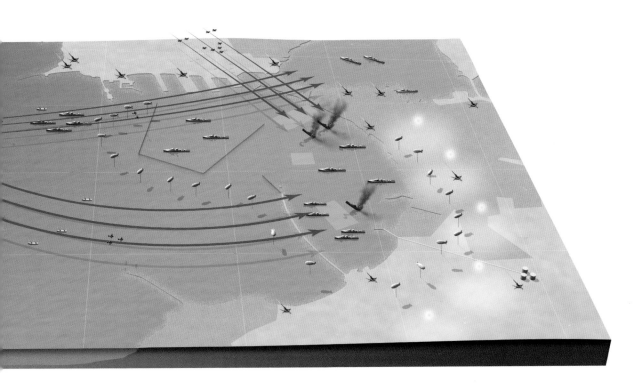

COMMANDO RAIDS ON NORWAY

After the small scale raids of 1940 the policy of the Combined Operations was to greatly increase the size of the force attacking the enemy coast. This was instigated by the arrival of Combined Operations new commander, Admiral Sir Roger Keyes. Keyes had been involved in the failed Dardenelles campaign and in planning of the raid on Zeebrugge towards the end of the First World War. This meant a ramping up in the scale of operations that were to be given to the Commandos, along with an expansion of the Commandos and the acquisition of suitable craft to carry out these tasks.

First target for the Commandos in 1941 was to be the Lofoten Islands off the coast of occupied Norway, just above the Arctic Circle. On these islands were major cod and herring-oil factories, this product being used extensively by the Germans for the production of explosives. The tasks for the Commandos was to destroy the factories, sink any vessels involved in the production, neutralise any German resistance and bring back any Norweigian volunteers.

A Special Service Brigade was created by No. 3 and No. 4 Commandos along with a number of Royal Engineers. Under the command of Brigadier J. C. Haydon, they were to be transported by two infantry landing ships and escorted by five destroyers of the Royal Navy under the command of Captain C. Caslon.

Due to the nature of the approaches to the ports on the islands the destroyers could only give very limited fire-support if required, so two destroyers scouted ahead to check there were no enemy vessels in the vicinity. Enemy resistance was unknown so the Commandos were issued with 48-hour rations and plenty of ammunition.

Surprise was complete as the Commandos approached their embarkation points off the islands. The four ports which were to be targeted; Stamsund, Henningsvaer (No. 3 Commando) and Svolvaer and Brettesnes (No. 4 Commando) were lit up in the early morning of 4 March, making their navigation that much easier. The Commandos were embarked upon their landing craft and got ashore without any enemy opposition being encountered. Instead their arrival was greeted with great enthusiasm by the local Norwegians, even though the destruction of the factories meant many of them losing their only source of income. Volunteers to accompany the Commandos back to the UK was immense, with over 300 opting to return.

The number of prisoners captured during the raid numbered over 200, along with the destruction of eleven factories, oil tanks and the sinking of five ships all for no loss amongst the Commandos.

A similar raid was carried out in June to the Spitzbergan Archipelago. This time the troops involved were from Canadian units that had been schooled at the Combined Operations training centre. They were to destroy the mining facilities on the islands to deprive the Germans of its use now that they had begun their campaign against Soviet Russia and evacuate the population. This was carried out with great success and no loss.

During October of 1941 the head of Combined Operations was changed again. This time Captain the Lord Louis Mountbatten took charge, a position he would hold for the next two years. His first job as Chief was to formulate a plan to raid the Norwegian coast

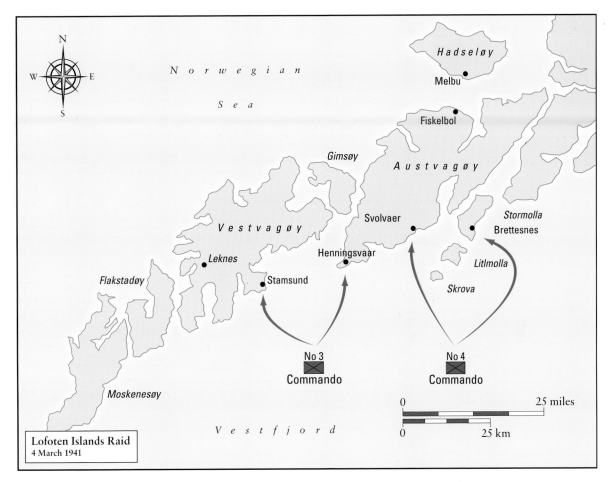

Lofoten Islands Raid
4 March 1941

once more with similar objects as the one on Lofoten, this time along the south-west coast on the islands of Maaloy and Vaagso. These tasks included destroying any German installations and shipping, disrupting fish-oil production and killing or capturing the German defenders.

The town of South Vaagso on Vaagso Island was an important harbour for the Norwegian fishing fleets, being a sheltered port the ships would use this as a stopping-off point to await fair weather before venturing northwards. Opposite the town was the small island of Maaloy. This was a natural defensive position, being in the centre of the fjord and the

Germans built coastal batteries along the south coast facing Vaags Fjord.

The Commandos trained exten-sively for the raid and set sail on Christmas eve 1941. They reached their starting point for the raid by Christmas Day but due to heavy seas the raid was post-poned, allowing the men to enjoy their Christmas dinner in the wallowing sea. By the evening of Boxing Day the force of ships, led by the cruiser HMS *Kenya*, had crept up the fjord.

The following morning was to be the day of the assault.

Just before 09.00 on 27 December the guns of *Kenya* opened up, firing starshell to light up the dark morning. This lit the target for the destroyers as well as the RAF bombers that had arrived overhead to lay down a smoke screen.

The landing craft then made their way to their targets, the Germans were taken completely by surprise. The men from No. 2 and No. 3 Commando with additional units from No. 4 and No. 6 Commando were split into five groups. Group 1 were to land on the south of Vaagso Island at the village of Hollevik. They were to secure the village then move northward to the outskirts of South Vaagso and remain as reserve. Group 2 was to attack the town of South Vaagso, eliminate resistance and destroy any military or economic targets. Group 3 was to assault the small island of Maaloy capture it and destroy four coastal artillery batter-

ies emplaced there. Group 4 was to be a floating reserve, whilst Group 5 was to be taken by destroyer up Ulvesund and cut communications between South and North Vaagso. The force commander was to be Brigadier J. C. Haydon once again.

Group 1s task was accomplished with great ease as there was little resistance, a stronghold being knocked out. These men then moved around the coast to South Vaagso to reinforce the landing by Group 2.

Group 3 were next to go in with their assault on Maaloy. As the landing craft approached the island the bombardment from the destroyers was lifted and the RAF bombers flew in at low level to lay a smokescreen to cover the last leg of the journey, one aircraft being shot down in the process. The men landed as the Germans were still getting over the concussion of the naval bombardment, the

A Commando points to the destruction of a village during a daytime attack on Norway.

Commandos quickly rounded up the surviving defenders and found that the bombardment had destroyed three of the four coastal batteries, the last one was hastily commandeered by the Commandos and used to engage a flak ship. The island was captured in twenty minutes, and the men were tasked with searching for intelligence. Part of Group 3 was then moved over the water to South Vaagso to reinforce Group 2 which had met substantial resistance.

Group 2 landed just to the south of the town, as they advanced they were met with a hail of accurate fire. By now the German defenders were fully alert and as it transpired later the garrison was reinforced by fifty crack troops being rested from the Eastern Front. House to house fighting then took place with heavy sniper fire from the Germans taking its toll on the Commandos. As this was happening a section of Group 2 was taken further north of the town where they successfully destroyed a herring-oil factory.

Group 5 fared better, landing to the north of the main battle where they blew craters in the road to block any potential reinforcement and destroyed the telephone exchange at Rodberg.

By 10.00 the southern part of South Vaagso had been taken with the help of the floating reserve but with heavy casualties, reinforcements arrived in the shape of Group 3 from Maaloy and Group 1 from Hollevik. This weight of men swung the balance in favour of the Commandos, the Germans eventually capitulating. The Germans suffered 150 killed along with ninety-eight captured. A number of Norwegian Quisling, Nazi sympathiser, were also captured. All demolition tasks were completed with factories and a power station being destroyed as well as the coastal batteries.

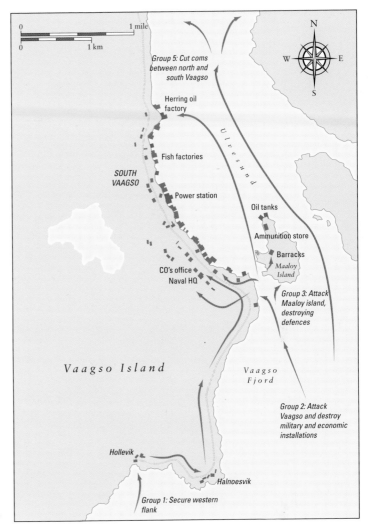

The Commandos began their withdrawal at 13.45, the losses being nineteen killed (including Royal Navy personnel) and fifty-nine wounded, many of these being officers due to the earlier sniping.

This was to be the first time all three arms had combined in an attack on German occupied Europe, and laid the foundations for future assaults. It also led to Hitler reinforcing his northern flank and therefore spreading his already stretched forces even thinner.

OPERATION MERCURY

With Hitler's success in northern Europe and with Britain's defence of its islands running into stalemate, his attentions turned eastward. Hitler saw the invasion of Russia as necessary in order to capture the vast farmlands of Ukraine that would feed his 1,000-year Reich. In order to commit to the invasion the southern flank had to be secured from Allied intervention. The task of invading Greece was passed to Mussolini, who with the assistance of Albania invaded on 28 October 1940. This ill conceived and poorly executed attack initially pushed the Greek defenders back, but counter attacks forced the Italians and the Albanians back over the border. The Allied command also decided to reinforce the Greek peninsula with troops from North Africa.

Hitler, exasperated by his Italian counterparts failure, decided to order a German led campaign in the region. This would secure Yugoslavia, which had been taken over by an anti-fascist coup, and the Greek peninsula, thus securing his southern flank in time for the planned invasion of Russia in June 1941.

On 6 April 1940 a massive air raid was launched on Belgrade, as troops entered Yugoslavia from the surrounding countries of Bulgaria, Rumania and Hungary. As this attack went in the Germans crossed the Greek border with Bulgaria and effectively outflanked the German defensive positions around Salonika. Within days the defensive lines were breached as the combined armies of Germany and Italy could not be stopped by the Greek or Commonwealth forces entrenched in the mountains, Blitzkrieg was again proving to be a very effective tool.

Despite a heroic defence by 21 April the Allied high Command had decided to evacuate all remaining forces to the island of Crete.

Crete lay to the south of Greece in the eastern Mediterranean and was a powerful strategic position. If held by the Allies it could be used as an effective airbase for bombers, particularly for the potential to hit the Ploesti oilfields so important to Hitler's war machine. It had to be taken.

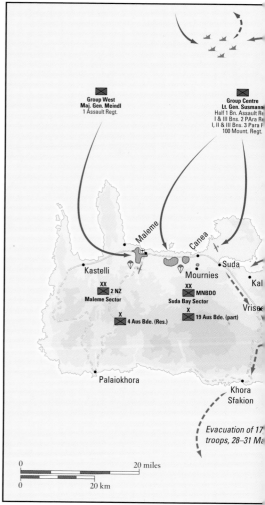

Colonel General Kurt Student, commander of the XI Fliegerkorps came forward with a solution. A drop along the northern coastal strip of the island to capture the four main strategic points on the island; Maleme for its airfield, Canea for its port facilities and the two other major towns of Rethymnon and Heraklion. Once captured the defenders would have little option as the majority of the island is very mountainous, they would have to be either evacuated or surrender as their supplies ran low.

The defenders of the island were made up of around 9,000 Greek troops that had been evacuated from the mainland, supported by Gendarmerie. They were poorly equipped but ready to fight for their lives and their nation. Allied support was in the form of 25,000 troops drawn from the New Zealand 2nd Division, Australian 9th Division and the British 14th Infantry Brigade. Command of these units fell under Major General Bernard Freyberg, a New Zealander who had fought in the First World War, fighting at Gallipoli and later winning a VC on the Western Front. He was given command

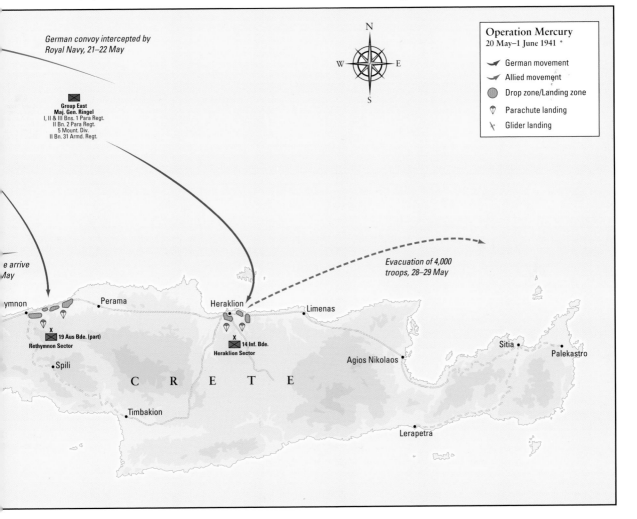

German convoy intercepted by
Royal Navy, 21–22 May

Group East
Maj. Gen. Ringel
I, II & III Bns. 1 Para Regt.
II Bn. 2 Para Regt.
5 Mount. Div.
II Bn. 31 Armd. Regt.

Operation Mercury
20 May–1 June 1941 *

German movement
Allied movement
Drop zone/Landing zone
Parachute landing
Glider landing

e arrive
May

Evacuation of 4,000
troops, 28–29 May

ymnon
Perama
Heraklion
Limenas

19 Aus Bde. (part)
Rethymnon Sector

14 Inf. Bde.
Heraklion Sector

Spili

C   R   E   T   E

Timbakion

Agios Nikolaos

Sitia
Palekastro

Lerapetra

An injured Fallschirmjaeger paratrooper in Crete being carried away from the battlefield by a donkey.

on 30 April and immediately implemented a better organisation of the defences, as the Allies anticipated an attack thanks to ULTRA intercepts coming from Bletchley Park.

By 20 May the New Zealanders were in place around Maleme and Canea, with the Australians near Suda, supported by some aging British tanks. The British were tasked with the defence of the eastern towns of Rethymnon and Heraklion.

The German forces were massed around the airfields of southern Greece and Athens. The units to be employed were the 7th Flieger Division made up of three regiments who would make the initial assault, to be supported by the 5th Mountain Division which would be flown in after the capture of the airfield at Maleme. In total the amount of troops available for the assault numbered 25,000.

Just before dawn the first of the Ju-52 transport aircraft took off towing DFS 230 gliders behind them. The gliders landing around Maleme had some initial success, capturing a bridge over the river Tavronitis and then taking up positions around the airfield. As this was happening the Fallschirmjaeger began jumping out of their transports. They were dropped over the New Zealand and Australian positions and were badly mauled whilst they were hanging defenceless from their parachutes and also when they hit the ground, as Fallschirmjaeger did not drop with their rifles, these having to be picked up from accompanying containers.

Further east things were not going to plan for the Fallschirmjaeger, as they were pushed back by fierce fire from the defenders they formed small pockets as they waited for the rest of the paratroops to come in as they had been widely dispersed, the only objective being completed was the destruction of some anti-aircraft guns and the capture of the small town of Agia. The Germans also faced aggressive Greek defences, the local inhabitants aiding the local military and police forces.

In the late afternoon the second wave of the German assault began with drops on both Rethymnon and Heraklion. Defending the area was the 14th Infantry Brigade augmented by Australian and Greek battalions. The Germans succeeded in entering the town of Heraklion, with the hope of capturing the important port for reinforcements to flow through, but were soon pushed out by the tenacious Greeks. The next day the town was heavily bombed by the Luftwaffe but the defence stood.

By the end of the first day none of the German objectives had been completed and things were looking bleak for the Fallschirmjaeger. In the early hours of 21 May their luck was to change when an error led to the New Zealanders defending the hill over-looking the airfield at Maleme were ordered to withdraw. With this strategic position secured by the paratroops the way was open for the Ju-52 transports to start landing reinforcements. These aircraft landed under incredible conditions, with artillery fire landing all around, however, this was to be the tipping point as elements of the 5th Mountain Division began to stream in.

From this point on the Germans had an established bridgehead, troops could be bought in and sent straight to the front a few hundred metres from were they deplaned. The New Zealanders attempted a night time assault to retake the field, but by this time the defences were strong and the attack failed, the Allies were now fighting a rearguard action.

All was not going to plan for the Germans on the sea however when the Royal Navy intercepted a force of Germans utilising Greek Caiques, a trad itional eastern Mediterranean fishin vessel, to make the crossing to Crete Without defence and lightly escorted, these vessels were no match for Royal Navy destroyers and after a few were sunk the attempt was halted.

By the 25 May the Allies were in full retreat towards the south of the island in order to be evacuated by the Royal Navy. Rear guard actions were fought with great ferocity and on the evening of the 26 May a Commando force was landed at Suda Bay. This force was made up of men from No. 7 and 8 Commando and named Layforce after its commander, Colonel Robert Laycock. The men were ordered to drop all heavy equipment and just retain their small arms. They made their first position along the main road that led to Sphakia, the area where most troops were now headed for evacuation. The the next four days saw them fight a series of battles against the advancing Germans who now had heavy equipment such as motorcycle sidecars with MG-34s and constant air support from Ju-87 Stuka Dive-Bombers.

The Commandos, reinforced by New Zealanders and Australians fought with immense bravery, carrying out numerous bayonet charges in order to cover the evacuation of their comrades. This allowed the Royal Navy to evacuate through Heraklion and Sphakia over 16,000 troops, though many of the rearguard had to stay and face eventual capture.

In total the Germans managed to capture over 12,000 troops, however, the Germans had lost nearly 7,000 killed. The losses alarmed Hitler so much that he went on to cancel any airborne operation involved in the invasion of Russia and Germany was never to use Fallschirmjaeger in such numbers again for the rest of the conflict.

BIRTH OF THE SAS

Lieutenant-Colonel David Stirling was originally an officer in the Scots Guards, going on to serve in No. 8 Commando in the Middle East before creating the legendary unit, the Special Air Service.

The Special Air Service was the brainchild of an ex Scots Guards officer, David Stirling. He had joined the army just before the outbreak of the war and had gone on to serve in the newly created Commandos. Having served with No. 8 Commando in the Middle East the unit was disbanded. This left Stirling aggrieved, seeing that a small raiding force could be of great tactical use in the vast open deserts of North Africa.

He wanted to form a small unit made up of a few officers and about sixty men. Knowing his ideas would be brushed off by his immediate superiors he decided to go straight to the top. Convalescing in Cairo with an injury from a previous parachute training operation, Stirling entered the Middle East Headquarters for the British Army intent on meeting its commanding officer, General Claude Auchinleck. Following a brief scuffle with the military

police, Stirling sought shelter in an office, the office belonged to Auchinleck's deputy, General Neil Ritchie. Impressed by the young Scotsman's brio, Ritchie organised a meeting with the Commander in Chief and Stirling got his unit.

The unit was given a deliberately misleading name: 'L' Detachment Special Air Service Brigade and was given the use of a training ground at Kibrit Air Base east of Cairo. The unit was initially made up of five officers and sixty other ranks. Training consisted of forced marches, shooting and parachute familiarisation. With a lack of resources and assistance from the RAF, moving trucks were used to simulate what it would be like to hit the ground when parachuting, men leaping from the rear onto the sand. After a number of snapped ankles this practice was soon halted.

The units first action came with the launching of Operation Crusader in November 1941. The SAS were tasked with being dropped behind enemy lines and attack known enemy airfields and destroy as many aircraft as possible. High winds led to the unit being scattered and resulted in many injuries. A third of the force was either killed or captured, twenty-two men being lost. The first mission for the SAS had been a disaster.

But Stirling soon recruited replacements and seeing the aerial insertion at night to be unmanageable and unpredictable, Stirling looked to fellow small unit operators, the Long Range Desert Patrol. This unit had been penetrating behind the enemy lines for some time and were familiar with the territory. Working in unison the LRDG would insert the SAS to within marching distance of the target area then fall back. The SAS would then fulfil the mission and rendezvous with the LRDG later for extraction.

This worked well for their second mission when the LRDG took them in to attack the three airfields of Sirte, El Agheila and Aqedabia. Sixty enemy aircraft were destroyed on the ground, utilising the Lewes bomb, created by a member of the SAS, Jock Lewes. The bomb was a combination of plastic explosive and diesel oil and on ignition created the maximum damage to an airframe. Working with the LRDG in this way led to the SAS re-naming their colleagues the 'Libyan Desert Taxi Service'.

Raids of this sort continued into 1942, by then the SAS had started to acquire the Willy's Jeep, a new military vehicle from the USA, which was ideal for driving over the rough terrain of the North African desert. Adapted by the LRDG and the SAS with a simple condenser on the front grill to stop overheating and with machine guns and spare fuel bolted to every available surface, these vehicles greatly increased the SAS's ability to strike the enemy. They allowed the units to get in close at speed, take them by surprise then withdraw before the enemy had time to react. Perhaps the SAS's most famous raid was the night attack on the German airfield at Sidi Haneish where eighteen Jeeps swept through the airfield driving in a V formation and firing incendiary rounds from their twin Vickers K machine guns. The unit managed to destroy twenty-five enemy aircraft.

The SAS, along with the LRDG, took advantage of the US-made Jeep. Strapping extra fuel and mounting heavy machine guns onto the vehicle made it a formidable attack platform.

DECIMO FLOTTIGLIA MAS

The idea of inserting a man along with an explosive charge into an enemy harbour had been mooted since the US Civil War of the 1860s. However it was Italian divers who were first to succeed during the First World War. Without breathing apparatus two sailors from the Italian Regia Marina managed to infiltrate Pula harbour on the coast of Croatia, which was then the Austro-Hungarian Empire. They managed to sink two vessels, including a battleship before they were captured. This was a great leap forward, two men and some explosive had sunk a massive fighting ship, long odds, but the Italian navy thought it was worth pursuing.

With the outbreak of the Second World War diving had become popular in Italy, with men experimenting with gear originally designed for escaping submarines whilst under water, this led to the development of oxygen tanks, fins and wetsuits and thus the frogman was born. This led the Regia Marina to create the Decima Flottiglia MAS, a force divided up into three units, one utilising the basic frogman skills, one using the manned torpedo, known amongst the divers as 'maiale' or 'pig', and the third group used fast motorboats loaded with explosive. These would be aimed at an enemy vessel and at the last minute the man guiding the motorboat would leap off the back, hoping the machine would go on to ram the target and explode.

Initial attempts at using the maiale were scuppered when four being carried by its 'mother' sub the *Iride* were spotted by Allied aircraft off Gibraltar. They were duly attacked and sunk. Their attempts were foiled two more times by intercepting destroyers or aircraft. However,

by October 1940 an attempt was relatively successful when a team penetrated Gibralter harbour and slightly damaged HMS *Barham*, two men being captured and four men managing to escape through neutral Spain.

More success followed in March 1941 with the launching of six 'Barchini' or 'little boats' at targets in Suda Bay, Crete. The men sped to their intended targets, one being the heavy cruiser

September 1941 – *3 Ships*
July 1942 – *4 ships*
September 1942 – *1 ship*
May 1943 – *3 ships*

Decimo Flottiglia Raids Throughout the Med
1941–43

⚓ Raid

HMS *York*. Two boats struck the cruiser and she sank to the bottom in the relatively shallow harbour, along with a Norwegian tanker *Pericles*. All the boat men were captured after the raid.

A large scale raid on Valetta harbour on Malta ended in disaster in July 1941. Two maiale and ten assault boats were launched against the harbour but were detected early by the Radar installations along the coast. The force was decimated by coastal gunfire, fifteen men being killed and eighteen captured.

In December of 1941 a raid was launched on Alexandria which was to be the most famous of the Decima Flottiglia's history. Three maiales, each with a crew of two were launched against the heavily defended harbour at Alexandria, Egypt. One team targeted the battlehip HMS *Valiant*, successfully attaching their mines before trouble with their breathing apparatus forced them to the surface where they were soon discovered. They were then placed under guard in the section of *Valiant* where they had just mined. Not being able to hold their nerve too long they asked to

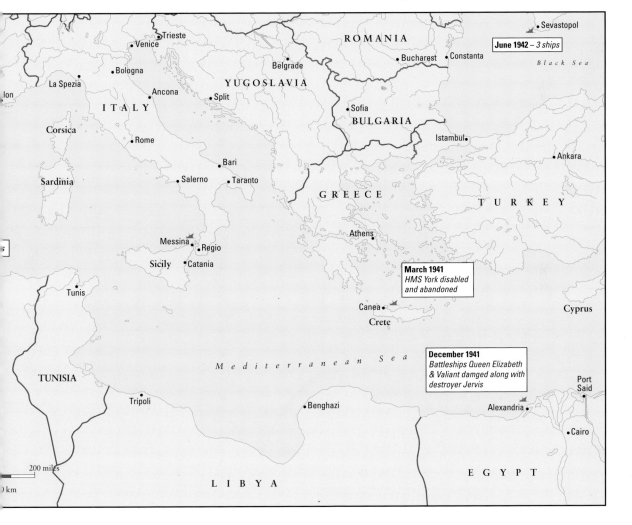

June 1942 – 3 ships

March 1941
*HMS York disabled
and abandoned*

December 1941
*Battleships Queen Elizabeth
& Valiant damged along with
destroyer Jervis*

see the commanding officer, where they notified him of the impending explosion but offered no more information. Luckily on the way back to their incarceration the explosion occurred, badly damaging *Valiant*. Meanwhile another crew had mined below the keel of the battleship *Queen Elizabeth*. They had more luck and managed to exit the harbour, only to be captured two days later. The resultant explosion severely damaged the old warship, which was out of com-

SHIPS SUNK	DATE	PLACE
HMS *York* *Pericles* (Tanker)	March 1941	Suda Bay
Denby Dale (Tanker) *Fione Shell* (Tanker) *Durham* (Motorship)	September 1941	Gibraltar
HMS *Queen Elizabeth* (Repaired, back in action July 44) HMS *Valiant* (Repaired, back in action May 43) HMS *Jervis* (light Damage) *Sagona* (Tanker)	December 1941	Alexandria
2x Russian Transports 2x Russian Submarines	June 1942	Sebastopol
Meta (Steamship) SS *Empire Snipe* (Repaired, back in action Oct. 42) *Shuma* (Steamship) *Baron Douglas* (Steamship)	July 1942	Gibraltar
HMS *Eridge* (Damaged, used as base ship)	August 1942	El Daba
Raven's Point (Steamship)	September 1942	Gibraltar
Ocean Vanquisher (Steamship) *Berta* (Steamship) *Armatton* (Steamship) *Empire Centaur* (Tanker) *N.59* (Military Transport)	December 1942	Algiers
Pat Harrison (Steamship) *Mahsud* (Steamship) *Camerata* (Steamship)	May 1943	Gibraltar
Orion (Motorship)	July 1943	Alexandretta
Kaituna (Motorship)	July 1943	Mersina
Fernplant (Motorship)	August 1943	Alexandretta
Harrison Gray Otis (Steamship) *Stanridge* (Steamship) *Thorshovdi* (Tanker)	August 1943	Gibraltar

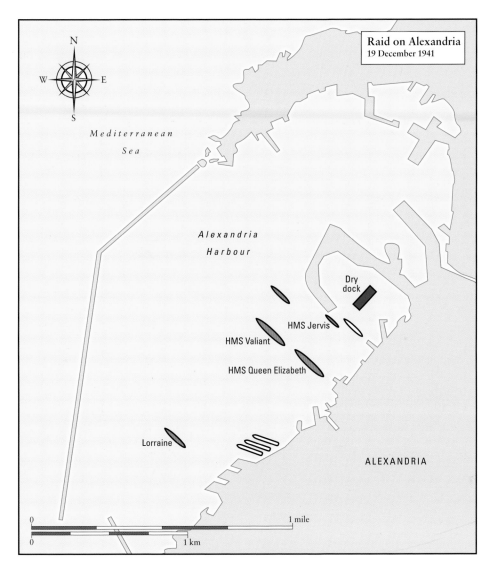

Raid on Alexandria
19 December 1941

N
W E
S

*Mediterranean
Sea*

*Alexandria
Harbour*

Dry
dock

HMS Jervis

HMS Valiant

HMS Queen Elizabeth

Lorraine

ALEXANDRIA

0   1 mile

0   1 km

mission for nearly a year. Two other vessels were also damaged in this raid, but all the crews were captured.

The attacks by the Decima Flottiglia continued right up until the Italian armistice of 8 September 1943. Some of the men stationed in the north of Italy decided to remain with the Axis forces, but did not take part in any further maritime action. Those men from the unit in the south joined with Royal Naval men who had been following the units progress and copying its practices. The Royal Navy had a unit devoted to frogmen activities, whilst they had also produced a similar device to the Italian maiale and were used successfully against Japanese targets in the Far East as well as targets in the European theatre of operations.

ALLIED OPERATIONS IN NORTH AFRICA

Special operations in North Africa continued with great aggression as the success of such units were greatly applauded by the high command. However, not all operations went to plan, this was illustrated well by operation FLIPPER, the infamous 'Rommel Raid'.

Intelligence sources supplied information that the Desert Fox was headquartered at a small house at Beda Littoria and plans were made to either kidnap or kill the Africa Korps' commanding officer along with destroying communication facilities in the area. Two groups, commanded by Lieutenant Colonel Robert Laycock and Lieutenant Colonel Geoffrey Keyes were to be landed by two Royal Navy submarines, *Torbay* and *Talisman*, at Hamma, 20 miles from the target house. There they would separate, one unit attacking the communications target and the other assaulting the house.

Severe weather during the transfer of the commandos from the submarines to rubber boats meant that by the time the force landed it was already depleted. Laycock remained at the landing beach whilst the rest of the men separated into two groups, one heading for the house led by Keyes. On arrival at the house Keyes led the way, unfortunately opening the door to a room full of German troops, who then proceeded to kill Keyes and pursue the remainder back to the landing beach. All were either killed or captured, apart from Laycock and a sergeant who managed to escape overland to the British lines.

Afterwards it was realised that Rommel had never stayed at the house and had been visiting his frontline at the time of the raid, Keyes was awarded the Victoria Cross posthumously for his actions during the raid.

Around this time a force was being established by one of the wars great eccentrics, Lieutenant Colonel Vladimir Peniakoff. Born of Russian parents in Belgium, he was educated

Members of Popski's Private Army take a moment to relax during their epic advance through the North African desert.

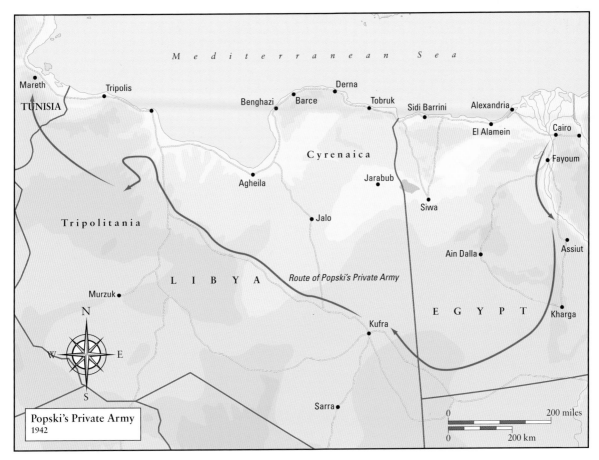

Popski's Private Army
1942

at Cambridge and was well versed in desert exploration, as well as learning to fly. Initially refused entry into the British Army due to his nationality at the out break of war he was posted to command the Libyan Arab Force Commandos. This unit recruited Arabs that worked in Italian mess halls who would then relay intelligence gleaned thanks to the Italian's cavalier attitude to operational security, often assuming those who served them could not speak Italian.

Acting on this intelligence Peniakoff along with his commandos created chaos behind the lines with sabotage and raids. Returning to Cairo in 1942 he was ordered to create a small raiding force along the lines of the LRDG and SAS. Thus he recruited five officers and eighteen men and acquired four Jeeps

and two lorries. The unit was to be officially named No. I Demolition Unit, unofficially it was named Popski's Private Army. Popski deriving from the British troops difficulty in pronouncing Peniakoff's name.

This unit would roam through the western desert mush like his other special forces contemporaries, inflicting lightning raids on enemy installations and gathering intelligence either themselves or through Peniakoff's legion of informants.

By 1943 Peniakoff's force had driven all the way through Libya to Tunisia where the unit was very nearly disbanded, thankfully the resourceful Peniakoff had many contacts in the upper echelons of high command and his force continued its work in Italy.

COASTWATCHERS IN THE PACIFIC

Coastwatchers in the Pacific were used as covert look outs stationed all over the Solomon Islands, the Gilberts, Fijian islands as well as Papua New Guinea. These men would observe enemy movement by sea or air, report these movements to an HQ in Townsville, Australia who would in turn alert the relevant units to respond.

These men were made up mainly of Australian and New Zealand military personnel, though not exclusively. These men would in turn recruit local men from the islands they were stationed on, who they would live with and be assisted by.

Armed with little other than a personnel weapon, a pair of binoculars and a radio these units aided the Allies in spectacular fashion, alerting them to major attacks and allowing the Allies to put into motion preparations or spoiling attacks, issuing weather reports as well as helping downed airmen or sailors whose vessel had been sunk. If caught, however, these men would be faced with summery execution.

Two particular men stationed on Bourgainville, an island in the north of the Solomon Island archipelago, assisted the U.S. Navy to a great extent. Jack Read and Paul Mason were on the northern tip of the island reporting on Japanese naval movements as well as operating as an early warning system for incoming air raids on the American beachhead on Guadalcanal. With the help of these men the US navy could take action to intercept Japanese troop convoys attempting to reinforce and resupply positions already on Guadalcanal. Admiral William Halsey, in overall command of the Guadalcanal campaign, praised the men who lived the solitary lives they did in order to swing the balance of power back into Allies hands.

During the Guadalcanal campaign of 1942–43 there was a chain of coastwatchers along the Japanese main supply routes reporting on movements, air raids and general intelligence, without which the campaign could have ended differently.

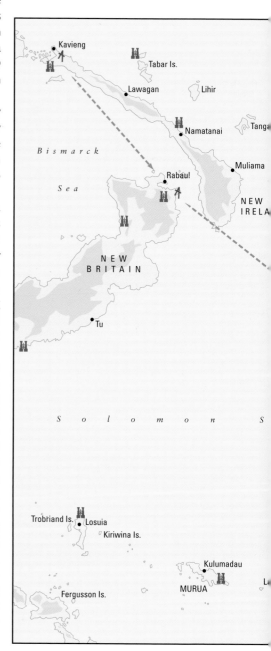

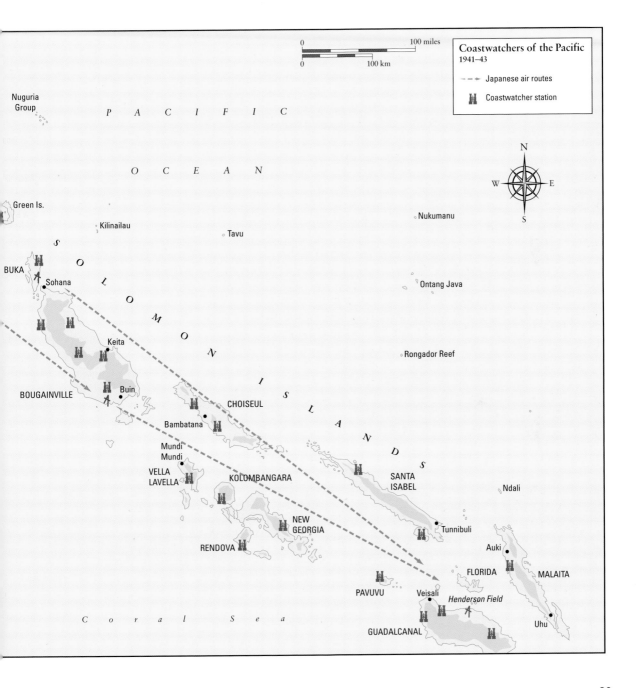

Coastwatchers of the Pacific
1941–43

- - - - Japanese air routes

Coastwatcher station

BRUNEVAL RAID

A reconnaissance photograph of the Wurzburg radar installation and the villa near Bruneval taken by a low flying RAF Spitfire some months before the raid took place.

By late 1941 the only way Great Britain could take the offensive to the Germans was via aerial bombardment at night utilising the RAF's heavy bomber force. The Germans countered this threat by establishing a chain of Radar stations from Norway to the Spanish border. These would then send information of an incoming raid to the waiting night fighters and anti-aircraft sites, readying them to intercept. The radar the Germans used, the 'Wurzburg', could be confused with counter-measures, but British scientists would need information from the apparatus itself in order to know what wavelength to jam. This would require a specialist getting near enough to the radar installation in order to study it and take parts off and bring back for study. A suitable target was found by photographic reconnaissance Spitfire in the north of France on the channel coast at Bruneval, twelve miles from Le Havre. A plan was drawn up by Combined Operations Headquarters to use the newly formed 1st Airborne Division, under the command of Major General 'Boy' Browning. They would be transported by converted RAF Whitley bombers then drop on the target, carry out what was necessary at the installation then withdraw from the coast courtesy of the Royal Navy.

The 1st Airborne Division had only recently been formed, being trained at Ringway near Manchester. For the mission to Bruneval C Company from the 2nd Battalion was chosen, commanded by Major John Frost. Training was carried out in great secrecy on Salisbury Plain as well as in Scotland for training to make night embarkation to landing craft. The men of C Company were under the impression that it was for a showcase operation in front of the top brass. It was not until a few days before the actual mission did they become aware that they would be dropping behind enemy lines. During this time a specialist arrived to train with the unit from RAF intelligence, this was Flight-Sergeant Charles Cox, who had never flown in an aircraft, let alone jumped out of a perfectly serviceable one.

The plan was to drop the 120 men of C Company about half a mile inland from the radar site. They would then split into four sections; one under the command of Lieutenants Rose and Charteris were to cover the exit to the beach. Two sections under Frost and Lieutenant Curtis would approach the radar site, one peeling off to deal with the small villa next to the site whilst the other dealt with the installation. The remaining section would be in reserve and serve as a blocking force against any German counter-attack. On collecting what intelligence they could they would leave charges to destroy what was left then make their way to the beach to rendezvous with the Royal Navy landing craft.

The men assembled next to their aircraft at RAF Thruxton in Hampshire on the evening of 27 February and thus began operation BITING. The aircraft were over the French coast after an hours flying time just after midnight, flak causing Charteris' section to be landed some miles from the drop zone. On realising this they soon orientated themselves and made for their mission at the double, encountering a German patrol along the way which they dealt with without loss.

Frost's group landed as planned and immediately started out for the installation. Frost, blowing a long blast on his whistle to signal the start of the attack, entered the villa. Finding only one defender who was quickly dealt with he went to see how things were going at the radar site. Here he found that the defenders had been neutralised apart from one soldier, who upon interrogation explained that there were 100 troops in the area. At this point the Germans sprang into life laying machine gun fire from the area of La Presbytare. Frost pulled his men out of the villa and along with the reserve set up a

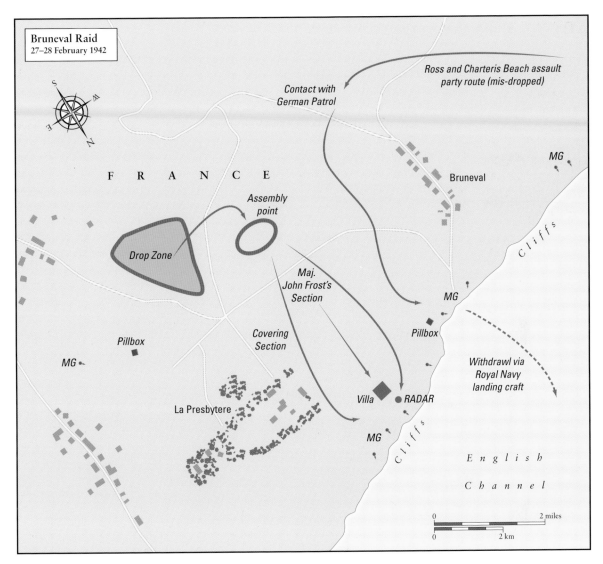

Bruneval Raid
27–28 February 1942

Ross and Charteris Beach assault
party route (mis-dropped)

Contact with
German Patrol

MG

F R A N C E

Bruneval

Assembly
point

Cliffs

Drop Zone

Maj.
John Frost's
Section

MG

Covering
Section

Pillbox

Withdrawl via
Royal Navy
landing craft

Pillbox

MG

La Presbytere

Villa ● RADAR

MG

Cliffs

English

Channel

0   2 miles

0   2 km

defensive line whilst Cox worked on the radar. Frost then saw headlights approaching, assuming this to be reinforcements for the Germans already engaged he decided to fall back to the embarkation point. As the men approached the draw to the beach a pillbox opened up on them. The men laid down suppressing fire but their escape was essentially blocked. It was at this time that the force that had landed some miles away arrived, the airborne men charging the pillbox and neutralising it with grenades.

The Royal Navy ships offshore had witnessed the melee on the cliffs but had been keeping their distance due to enemy E-Boat activity. On the sighting of a Very light fired by Frost the landing craft closed with the shore, picking up the wounded, a few prisoners and the captured pieces of the radar first. The rest of the paratroops were then embarked. All were accounted for except for two killed and six missing. The operation had been a total success and was proof that combined operations were viable.

OPERATION CHARIOT

Late 1941 and early 1942 saw Britain's darkest hours, pushed back in the Western Desert and with its eastern empire crumbling to Japanese aggression, the country stood alone with only the Atlantic convoys keeping the country afloat. These convoys were threatened by one of Germany's greatest weapons, the *Tirpitz*, a battleship that far outclassed anything in the British armoury. The sheer size of the ship limited it to only a few ports where it could be repaired if it were to be damaged, a dry dock of immense proportions would be required, the only one that could be accessed from it's main hunting ground, the Atlantic Ocean, was at Saint Nazaire, in western France. Originally constructed for the ocean liner '*Normandie*', the dry dock was itself an impressive structure and an impossible target to destroy from the air. A force would have to be landed and destroy it with explosives, this was the task handed to the chief of Combined Operations, Lord Louis Mountbatten.

A force of Commandos was to be taken six miles up the Loire estuary to Saint Nazaire aboard an antiquated destroyer packed with explosives and modified to resemble a German destroyer. The vessel would 'bluff' its way past the many german defensive positions using captured recognition codes, the destroyer would then ram the dry dock gates, set a fuse and disembark the Commandos who would set about various sabotage tasks. This force was to be escorted by eighteen small motor launches, who would then embark the Commandos and withdraw. It was an impossible task, perhaps the only chance of success was the Germans would never imagine the British to carry out such an audacious raid.

The ship chosen for the one way voyage was the aging HMS *Campbeltown*. Built in 1919 for the US Navy as USS *Buchanan*, it was acquired by the Royal Navy in 1940. She was modified with extra armour around the bridge and along the foredeck for the protection of the crew and Commandos, as well as the removal of two of her four funnels in order to make her appear similar to a German torpedo boat. A 12-pounder cannon was also added along with 20mm Oerliken cannons and numerous smaller calibre machine guns. She was lightened to give her as much speed as possible and had 4 tons of high explosive placed in her bows, she was commanded by Lieutenant Commander Stephen 'Sam' Beattie and with a skeleton crew and sailed to Falmouth, the staging post for the raid, on the evening of 24 March.

Awaiting the destroyer at Falmouth were two escort destroyers and the men of the raiding force. The force was drawn mainly from No. 2 Commando, supplying 172 men, with ninety-two additional men coming from 1, 3, 4, 5, 9 and 12 Commando, all under the command of Lieutenant Colonel Charles Newman. These men would be split into three groups, the first two would travel aboard the motor launches whilst the third party would be aboard *Campbeltown*. Group one would be landed and secure the old mole, destroy anti-aircraft and machine gun positions, destroy the power station, locks and quay then move into the old town and prepare for any counter-attack. Group 2 were to land at the old entrance to the basin, again blow bridges and quay, destroy gun emplacement and prevent counter attacks from the direction of the submarine pens. Group 3 would disembark from *Campbeltown*, under the command of Major Bill Copeland and go about destroying the pumping house, gate opening station and fuel tanks. On completion of these tasks the men would fall back onto the old mole where they would re-embark the motor launches and rendezvous back in the Bay of Biscay with the escort destroyers.

Early afternoon on 26 March 1942 the attack force left Falmouth harbour, with HMS *Tynedale* and *Atherstone* as it's escort heading

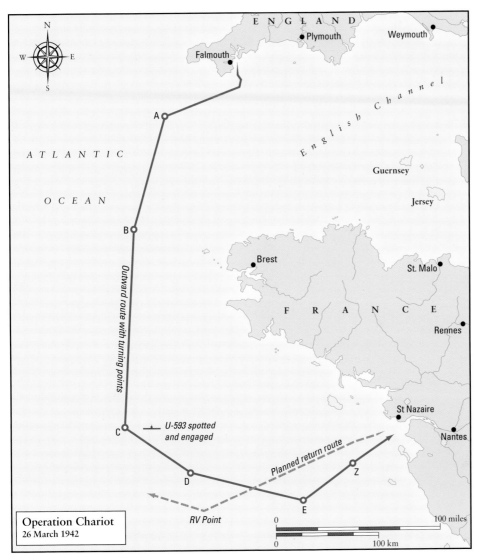

Operation Chariot
26 March 1942

U-593 spotted and engaged

Outward route with turning points

Planned return route

RV Point

south for the Bay of Biscay. The rest of the day was uneventful, but early on the morning of 27 March a German U-Boat, *U-593*, was spotted by the destroyer escort and immediately engaged to no effect. It would be a disaster for the attack force to be recognised for what they were. Two French trawlers were also sighted, with the fisherman aboard the destroyers the vessels were duly sunk, no chances could be taken of the force being compromised.

At around 21.00 that evening the

attack force carried onto the target alone, leaving the escort and heading for a rendezvous with the submarine HMS *Sturgeon* which would signal the route to the Loire estuary with her navigation beacon. With this sighted the force took up the approach formation, with three launches in the van followed by *Campbeltown* and the rest of the launches in two columns either side and behind her.

At the same time as their approach was made a raid by RAF bomber command was also

During the Raid on St. Nazaire five Victoria Crosses were awarded as well as eighty-four other decorations for bravery. Two of them were awarded post-humously. Sergeant Thomas Durant, who manned a Lewis gun aboard ML 306, having been wounded several times he did not stop firing on the enemy, including an attacking German Torpedo boat, firing at the bridge until overcome by his wounds. Able Seaman William Savage manned a 2 pounder 'Pom Pom' cannon, which engaged shore targets allowing for his compatriots to go about their tasks, all the while himself being exposed to incoming fire. He was killed at his post.

taking place, severe cloud cover seriously inhibiting their sight lines. Instead of distracting the German defenders it put them on high alert, thinking that a parachute landing might take place. At the point of no return the Kreigsmarine ensign was raised on the mast of *Campbeltown*, the attack had begun, *Campbeltown* and seventeen motor launches, one having been abandoned due to engine trouble, steamed straight into the lion's den.

Just after 01.00 the force was spotted by shore parties and recognition was demanded, followed shortly with a warning shot being fired across her bows. A german speaker on board flashed back the message that they had been in an engagement and were seeking repair in the docks. This seemed to placate the defenders for a few

minutes before all hell was let loose. Every gun of every calibre on either side of the estuary opened up on the raiding force and the Commandos and Navy personnel duly returned the favour. With the cover blown the German ensign was lowered and the British Ensign raised, along with the speed of *Campbeltown*. Several of her helmsmen were killed directing her to her target but just after 01.30 *Campbeltown* tore through the anti-torpedo net and crashed into the dry dock gates, jamming the bow of the ship 30 feet on top of the gate.

Commandos poured ashore from *Campbeltown* and went about their tasks, many falling to the machine gun nests surrounding the area. All but a few of the motor launches were set afire or sunk by the incoming enemy fire, never-

theless Copeland and Newman were both ashore and directing fire to protect the demolition teams. When it was realised that most of the launches had been destroyed and chance of escape was reduced to nil Newman gave orders for the Commandos to keep on fighting until all ammunition was spent, and even then not to surrender but to try an escape back to England via neutral Spain.

Back on the estuary a few launches had survived and were engaging targets on the water as well as on land, having taken on survivors from the *Campbeltown* and with little else to achieve a few launches made for open water and escape, all the while firing on the enemy.

The men stuck on land fought until the end of their ammunition and were even-tually rounded up and taken prisoner, five men evading capture and making it back to Britain via the Spanish route. Of the men aboard the four motor launches that managed to escape the estuary, one was captured by a German torpedo boat and the others managed to rendezvous with the destroyers.

Campbeltown's explosives detonated at noon that day, killing a party of German officers that were touring the wreck at the time, the explosion put the dry dock out of action for the rest of the war.

In total five Victoria Crosses were awarded for bravery during the raid which came to be known as 'The Greatest Raid of All'.

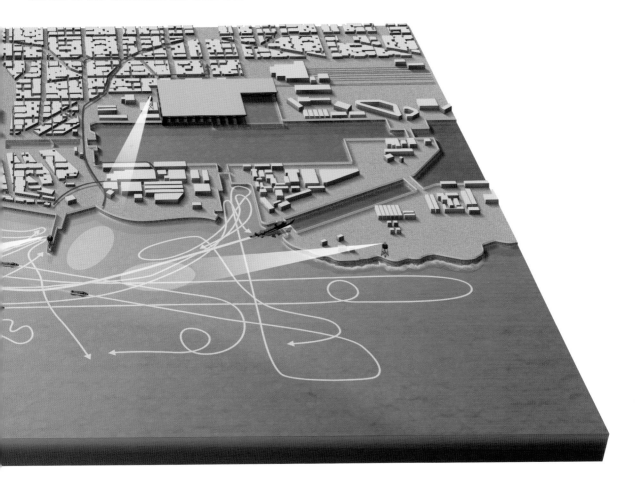

BATTLE OF BIR HAKEIM

Following the Allied operation Crusader, the Afrika Korps, commanded by the great tactician General Erwin Rommel, and it's Italian ally had been pushed back to El Agheila where they promptly turned and faced the now exhausted Allied advance. Lengthy supply lines meant that the attack petered out, leaving the Axis forces to strike back. The Allied 8th Army, under the command of Lieutenant General Neil Richie, fell back onto a defensive line that stretched from Gazala near the Mediterranean coast southward to Bir Hakeim, a small fort near an oasis. This line was made up of thick minefields connecting a series of 'boxes', with about a brigade strength in each. However, much of the Allied strength was focused along the coast road, as this is where the Axis advance was expected to come, leaving much of the line southward thinly defended, without interlocking fields of fire. The Free French forces were given

the unenviable task of anchoring the southern flank of this defensive line at Bir Hakeim.

After a heavy preliminary artillery bombardment on the area directly west of Tobruk on 26 May 1942, two Italian corps were launched towards the line. This was to be a feint whilst the bulk of the Axis force, made up of two Panzer divisions, an Italian armoured division, supported by two motorised divisions, made flanking advances on the Allied line to the south.

At Bir Hakeim were the Free French 1st Brigade, under the command of General Marie Pierre Koenig. Koenig had 3,700 men consisting of two battalions of Foreign Legion troops, one battalion of colonial troops along with marines, sappers and artillery support. They were equipped with over fifty 75mm artillery pieces, various other calibre anti-tank weapons, motors and machine guns. The area around the fort was heavily mined and had a multitude of slit trenches interconnected around it's perimeter.

On 27 May came the first attack on the French enclave. The Italian Ariete Division, an armoured unit supported by trucked infantry, swept around the fort to the south and attacked it from the south east. This attack was met with withering artillery that forced the infantry to retreat. The advancing armour, utilising the Italian M13/40 tank, was isolated and became stuck in the French minefield. They were then easy prey for the French artillerymen. The Italians then tried an attack from the north but were again halted by the extensive minefields and beat a hasty retreat. Elsewhere along the Allied line troops had been forced to retreat towards El Adem, leaving the French completely surrounded.

The next few days was relatively quiet, with the Italians probing the French perimeter and testing the defences, only a lack

General Marie Pierre Koenig, commander of the Free-French forces defending the southern Allied flank during the battle of Gazala.

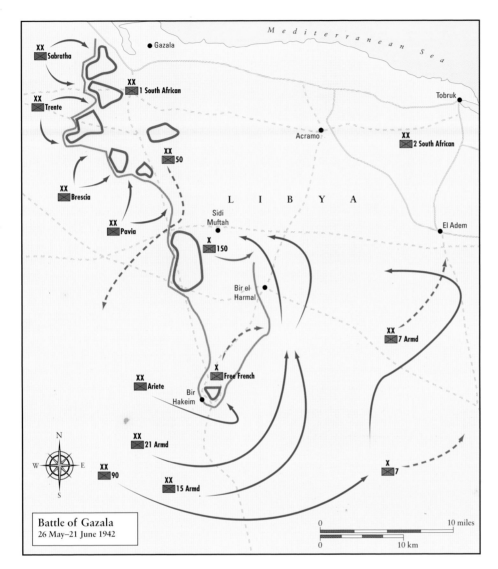

Battle of Gazala
26 May–21 June 1942

of water now threatened the defenders. This was resolved by arrival of re-supply trucks that managed to break through on 31 May.

As Rommel advanced further west the fort at Bir Hakeim became more and more a threat to his line of supply as the French sent out raiding parties to destroy tanks and support vehicles. Rommel had the fort bombed from the air then sent the Italian Trieste Division to attack from the north whilst the German 90th Light Division engaged from the south. Koenig

was approached by the Italians to surrender the fort with honour, this was declined. What followed was intense bombardment from both the air and artillery, but with the aid of the RAF attacking enemy movement and the fantastic skill of the French artillerymen as well as the defending infantry, the fort held out.

On 6 May the troops of the 90th managed to clear a path through the minefield to allow German infantry to approach within 500 metres of the fort. The Legionnaires, in

*Map, opposite:
The Free French man-
aged to hold the fort
on the southern flank
of the allied line for
some sixteen days.
Whilst some of the
Axis forces simply
bypassed the position,
a significant number
of troops and armour
were left behind in an
attempt to break the
defenders.*

trenches fought off this assault again aided by RAF air attacks.

By 8 May the ammunition and water levels were at a critical position for the French, despite the RAF's best attempts at re-supply from the air. Bombardment was constant on the fort and Koenig decided that it was time to evacuate the position, having fought an outstanding defence and held up German and Italian forces that could have done even more harm to the Allied front elsewhere. Thankfully a thick fog fell on the area during 8 May and a re-supply column managed to successfully reach the fort, right under the noses of the aggressors.

On the morning of the 10 May an all out attack was made by the Germans on the north perimeter of Bir Hakeim, this was barely held off and the Germans re-grouped for yet another assault the following morning, little knowing that the French had used up the last of their ammunition. That night Koenig ordered a path to be cleared through the minefields to

the south west. As the sappers were clearing the path they were spotted and illuminated by the enemy. With no choice, Koenig ordered a general withdrawal before the enemy could mobilise, although vehicles were destroyed by their own mines and by enemy action, by 08.00 11 May the evacuation had been completed, leaving behind only 500 wounded men. Over 2,600 men managed to escape with the majority of their equipment.

Their task was complete and had helped the British stave off absolute disaster, had Rommel's supply lines not been disrupted by the French the outcome of the battle could have been very different. Rommel was eventually halted along the line south of Mersa Matruh, this did however mean that Tobruk once again came under siege. The defence of Bir Hakeim was a great incentive to the Free French who had lost favour from the Allies because of the loss of France in 1940 and the subsequent Vichy government. They had proved themselves in crucible of battle.

*Free French troops
advance under fire in
the Libyan desert near
Bir Hakeim.*

MAKIN ISLAND RAID

After the Japanese attack on Pearl Harbour on 7 December 1941 the Japanese carried out a rapid expansion of territory. This covered much of South East Asia and many of the Pacific islands. In order to maintain control over this vast area the Japanese constructed seaplane bases on small atolls to establish a chain of communication and defence. A plan was drawn up to raid one of the smaller islands to gain intelligence and prisoners for interrogation. The island chosen was Makin in the Gilberts chain. The raid would also draw Japanese attention away from a major landing that would be made by the US Marine Corps on the island of Guadalcanal in the Solomon chain south of the Gilberts.

The unit chosen for the task was the 2nd Raider Battalion. This unit had been the brainchild of Lieutenant Colonel Evans Carlson. Carlson had served in the Army during the First World War and in Mexico and then joined the Marines in the 1920s, rising through the ranks and gaining much knowledge and experience. He approached training differently, with all the men in his unit on equal terms, regardless of rank. He also taught his men 'ethical indoctrination', this explained fully the reasons why the men were fighting specific battles and its effects on the war as a whole. He also implemented changes to the layout of his squads, with them being made up of ten men rather than the usual eight, with one leader and three three-man fireteams.

For the raid two US Navy submarines were tasked with transportation duties, USS *Argonaut* and USS *Nautilus*. Because of the limited space on board only two reduced companies from the battalion were taken, 120 aboard *Argonaut* and nine-ty aboard *Nautilus*. On Makin was a garrison of around eighty Japanese personnel under the command of a sergeant-major, they were centred around the middle of the tiny island.

The men cast off from their submarine transports just after midnight 17 August 1942 in rubber boats. They were due to split into two formations landing east and west of the Japanese positions. Bad weather and strong tides led Carlson to alter his plans en route, ordering his entire force to land to the south west of the enemy, all but one of the boats getting the message. This stray boat, under the command of a Lieutenant Peatross carried on to its original landing point.

On making the beach the men hurried ashore, securing and camouflaging the boats to await their withdrawal. Carlson led his men inland in order to attack the Japanese from the north-east. Shortly after sunrise the attack was put in, initially against strong opposition and casualties mounted from accurate sniper fire from the Japanese. The enemy commander then decided to launch a banzai charge, the men running with bayonets fixed. These men were easily dispatched by the gunfire of the Marines and therefore drastically reduced the defence of Makin.

Mid-morning saw Lieutenant Peatross and his twelve men in position behind the defending Japanese positions, they duly attacked and inflicted many casualties, including killing the commanding Sergeant-Major. Unable to break through to join Carlson and the rest of the Raiders and with casualties himself Peatross withdrew to his boat and returned to the waiting submarines.

By the early afternoon word had

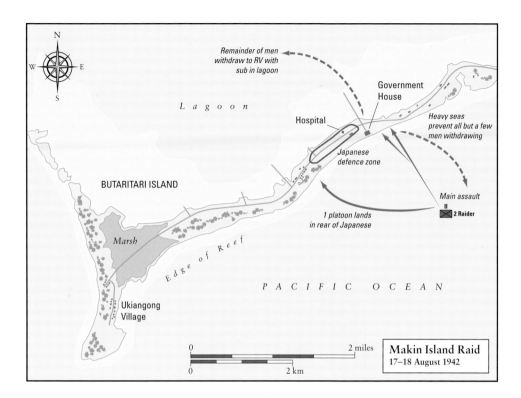

Map labels:

Remainder of men withdraw to RV with sub in lagoon

Government House

Hospital

Heavy seas prevent all but a few men withdrawing

Lagoon

Japanese defence zone

BUTARITARI ISLAND

Main assault

II 2 Raider

1 platoon lands in rear of Japanese

Marsh

E d g e   o f   R e e f

P A C I F I C   O C E A N

Ukiangong Village

0 — 2 miles

0 — 2 km

Makin Island Raid
17–18 August 1942

been passed to the Japanese that an attack had been made on the Makin Island base and reinforcement was sent in the form of a company of men aboard two flying boats with a fighter escort. By this point the Japanese positions on Makin had been neutralised and the men of the Marine Raiders could concentrate all their firepower on the flying boats as they attempted to land on the lagoon north of the island, both transports were destroyed. However the escort did strafe the US positions but to no effect.

What remained was for the Raiders to gather as much intelligence material as possible then return to the subs. However high seas that evening prevented almost half the men from reaching the comparative safety of the subs. The next morning saw another attempt, again high sea did its best to scupper the withdrawal and only a few made the subs, seventy-two

men still remained on the island. A third attempt was made but the submarines had to suddenly crash dive when attacked by Japanese aircraft. Carlson then decided to haul the remaining rafts to the north of the island and using what little resources he had and a little ingenuity constructed a raft that could take the men over the relatively calm water of the lagoon where they rendezvoused with the waiting submarine. In all the Marine Raiders inflicted well over 100 casualties but lost nineteen men killed and eleven taken prisoner, these men having been split from the main party and subsequently missing the evacuation. They were later executed. The raid itself achieved little, having captured no prisoners to interrogate and gained little intelligence, however it had proven the effectiveness of small unit raiders to the military high command and was a boon for morale when the United States had little to celebrate.

DIEPPE RAID

Due to political pressure from Soviet Russia and with a real need for a victory in the dark days of 1942, Combined Operations Headquarters came up with a plan to attack and hold a port on the occupied French coast for a short period of time. The attack was to test the strength of the German defenders and how they reacted to an amphibious assault as well as destroy enemy installations and capture troops for intelligence purposes. The target chosen for this assault was the medium sized fishing port of Dieppe in the Seine-Maritime department of France on the channel coast. The predominant force to be used in the assault was to be Canadian under command of Major General John 'Ham' Roberts, reinforced by a tank regiment and two commando units.

Initial landings on either flank early in the assault by the Commandos would silence two large coastal batteries that could interdict the main amphibious force at Varengeville and Berneval. Then landings were to be made on two villages just to the east and west of Dieppe, The South Saskatchewan Regiment at Pourville and the Royal Regiment of Canada at Puys. These missions would neutralise any enemy positions on the cliffs that rose above Dieppe. The main force would then make a frontal attack on the port itself, infantry landing shortly followed by its armoured support. The armoured element would be drawn from the 14th Tank Regiment equipped with the new Churchill tank, the infantry being made up of the Calgarys, 4th, 5th and 6th Infantry brigades, all Canadian units, supported by A Commando Royal Marines.

The armada, made up of 230 ships left harbour in England in the late evening of 18 August. The journey went well until the eastern flank force, made up of 3 Commando mostly in LCP (Landing Craft Personnel), ran into a German convoy. The convoy included armed trawlers which proceeded to engage the landing craft. Several were sunk and the rest scattered. Losing the element of surprise many LCPs turned back but a few pressed on. Landing at the designated point the few Commandos remaining made their way to the coastal battery just outside of Berneval. The force was too weak to effect an all out assault so resorted to

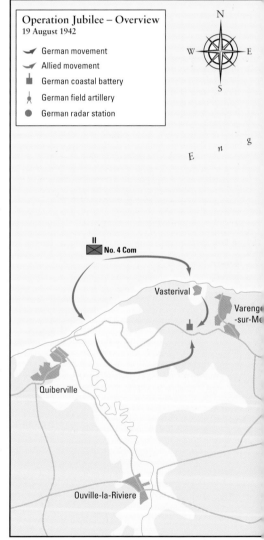

Operation Jubilee – Overview
19 August 1942

⤜ German movement
⤜ Allied movement
▪ German coastal battery
⚓ German field artillery
● German radar station

No. 4 Com

Vasterival

Vareng-
-sur-Me

Quiberville

Ouville-la-Riviere

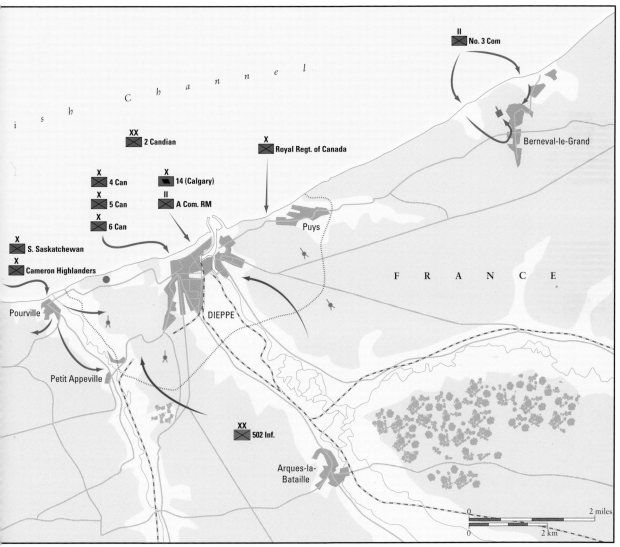

sniping at the gun crews serving the weapons. Thanks to this the fire from the battery was ineffective and no ship was lost during the assault as a result.

Next to No. 3 Commando were the Royal Regiment of Canada. Due to the run in with the German coastal convoy the German defences on the beach at the village of Puys were fully alerted. Most of the men made it to shore only to be held under intense machine-gun and cannon fire. Unable to get off the beach the force was completely destroyed, 200

men being killed and almost all the remainder being taken prisoner.

No. 4 Commando under Lord Lovat was on the opposite flank of the main assault and had a similar task to carry out, making an assault on 'Hess' battery and silence her. The commandos were separated into two groups, Group one commanded by Major Mills-Roberts would land on Orange Beach 1, climb the cliff and blow holes in the barbed wire. They were then to establish a reserve and set up a firebase to lay fire from mortars

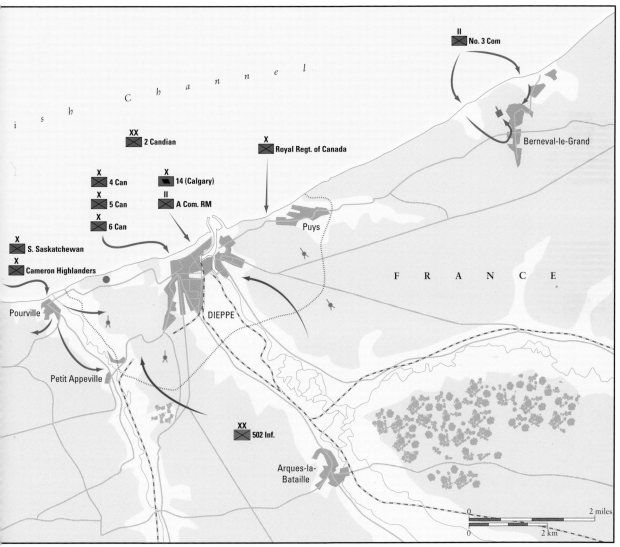

and machine-guns onto the battery from the north. Meanwhile Lord Lovat's Group Two would land at Orange beach 2 and swing south of the battery and line up ready to assault. On the morning of 19 August all went to plan, with all the troops in position. The attack was commenced in conjunction with an attack by low-flying RAF fighter-bombers, units assaulting the battery buildings and the artillery positions themselves. After brief firefights both positions were taken, the artillery being disabled and intelligence material being captured from the buildings. The assault group then fell back through the support teams positions towards Orange Beach 1 where all the Commandos were successfully lifted from. The men were back in England by nightfall. This was to be the

The Commando attack on the right flank of the assault was to be the only real success of the entire action. Lord Lovat led his troops in the assault on Hess Battery and successfully put it out of action.

only successful part of Operation Jubilee.

At Pourville the South Saskatchewan Regiment came ashore along with the Cameron Highlanders of Canada. Most of the force found themselves on the wrong beach which was west of the river Scie. This meant they had to cross the river and there was only one bridge. The Germans realised this and set up a strong defensive postion. Repeated attempts to cross the bridge ended in failure. With massive casualties the commanding officer, Lieutenant Colonel Merritt, had little choice but to withdraw to the beach where 300 men managed to embark, the remaining men were left to surrender.

After the initial landings had gone in the main assault on Dieppe then commenced.

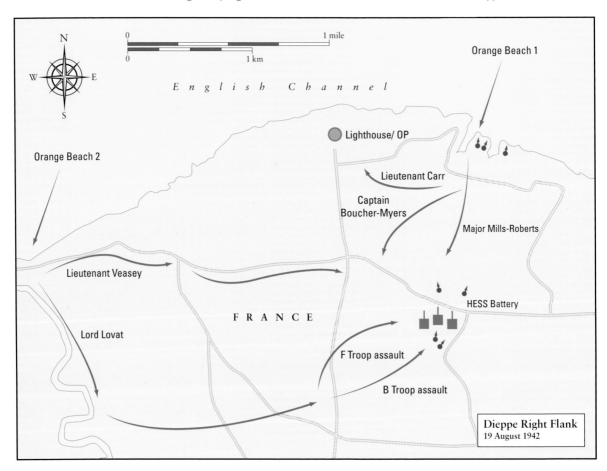

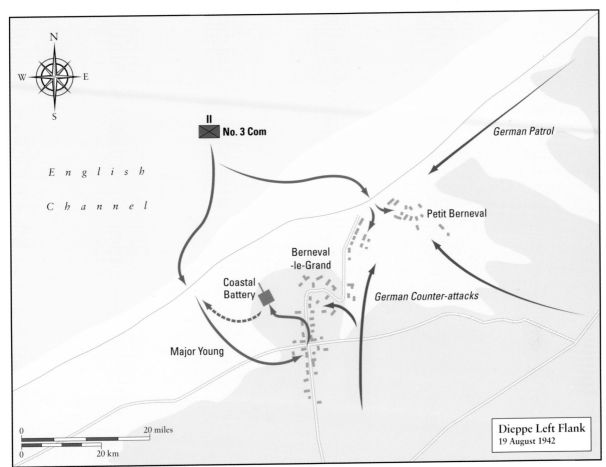

No. 3 Com

N. 3 Com

German Patrol

E n g l i s h

C h a n n e l

Petit Berneval

Berneval
-le-Grand

Coastal
Battery

German Counter-attacks

Major Young

0   20 miles

0   20 km

Dieppe Left Flank
19 August 1942

It was preceeded by bombardment from Royal Navy ships and fighter-bombers from the RAF. As the first infantry units approached under a smoke screen they realised that their armoured support was not with them, landing nevertheless they came under heavy enemy fire from the cliffs surrounding the port. As casualties mounted the armour arrived in the form of the 14th Tank Regiments Churchill tanks. Some almost immedietely sank in the breakers and many more foundered on the shingle that covered the beaches. These became easy targets for the German gunners and were picked off one by one. Of the twenty-seven tanks landed fifteen made it off the beach only to be halted by thick wire and anti-tank obstacles in the town. With the attack losing energy the reserves were com-

mitted by Roberts in the form of the Fusiliers and the Marines. This did little to help and ended with more slaughter. By late morning defeat was eventually realised and what was remaining of the troops on the beach were lifted off and completed by 14.00.

Casualties amounted to 3,367 killed, wounded or taken prisoner. The Royal Navy lost a destroyer and over thirty landing craft, the RAF losing over 100 aircraft. German casualties were 591 and forty-eight aircraft. Lessons were learned from the fiasco, such as the need for heavy bombardment before amphibious assault and firm beaches for tanks to climb, but the attack was not planned thoroughly enough and was pushed through to relieve political pressure rather than achieve any strategic advantage.

No. 3 Commando were severely depleted when they landed on the coast of France. Not having enough troops to carry out the planned assault the troops lay down fire on the battery which distracted the German gunners enough not to hit any of the main force. They then withdrew successfully.

OPERATION FRANKTON

Operation Frankton was the brainchild of Major Herbert 'Blondie' Hasler, a canoeing specialist in the Royal Marines. He proposed the plan to the Combined Operations chiefs that a small group of men could paddle canoes up the River Gironde to the port of Bordeaux and place explosive charges on enemy shipping without compromise. The targets would be 'blockade runners', ships that were too fast for Allied submarines to intercept taking important electronic technology out to the Far East and returning with other vital war material such as rubber. The then commander of Combined Operations, Admiral Louis Mountbatten, gave the go ahead in mid-October, for the operation to take place in the first weeks of December.

Blondie Hasler had taken command of the innocuously named Royal Marine Boom Patrol Detachment in July of 1942. The name referred to the men who inspected and repaired the anti-submarine boom in Portsmouth harbour, but in actual reality it meant that a selected few Marines could train in canoeing, diving and underwater demolitions. The men were initially based in Southsea and used the Folbots of the Special Boat Section. These were ideal for river operations but were found wanting in coastal waters, the area where the men would launch from a submarine to avoid detection. As a result the Mk II was born, of Hasler's own design. It was a semi-rigid two-man canoe that could be collapsed for ease of stowage, still having enough room for personnel rations and weapons, along with explosives and spare paddles.

As the date for the launch approached, a 'dress-rehearsal' was carried out, launching from Margate with the aim of getting as far as Deptford, along the Thames, undetected. Only Major Hasler, along with his number two, Marine Sparks made it. The prospects for the team did not look good. The team then moved up to the Clyde for further training, forced marches and familiarity with submarines.

On the 1 December 1942 the men and the canoes were loaded onto the T-Class submarine HMS *Tuna* commanded by Captain Raikes. The final team consisted of six canoes each of two men: *Catfish*, Major Hasler and Marine Sparks. *Crayfish*, Corporal Leaver and Marine Mills. *Conger*, Corporal Sheard and Marine Moffat. *Cuttlefish*, Lieutenant MacKinnon and Marine Conway. *Coalfish*, Sergeant Wallace and Marine Ewart and *Cachalot*, Marine Ellery and Marine Fisher. Hasler had been asked to stay behind as the casualties for the raid were expected to run at 100 per cent, but he insisted he lead the men he had spent months arduously training, he did not expect his men to do anything he would not do himself. Once on board the men started to speculate as to where they were headed, the concensus was Norway, for a crack at *Tirpitz* maybe. All were shocked and excited on hearing their target was to be Bordeaux, almost sixty miles down the tidal River Gironde. They then learnt that they were expected to lay their charges then withdraw some way back up the river, scuttle their boats then make their way to Spain by foot. Not a single man faltered at this high risk enterprise.

HMS *Tuna* surfaced off the coast of France in the Bay of Biscay on the 7 December, the men immediately setting about their task of unloading the canoes. Disaster struck almost immediately when one canoe, *Cachalot*, tore her hull. The men, diappointed, would have to stay with the sub whilst the rest continued.

As they approached the mouth of the Gironde the men had to negotiate the tidal races of the river. The first took its toll, with *Coalfish*, containing Ewart and Wallace, being reported

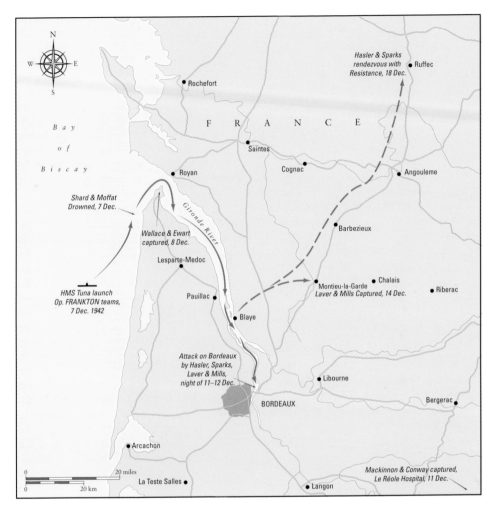

Hasler & Sparks
rendezvous with
Resistance, 18 Dec. • Ruffec

F R A N C E

• Rochefort

Bay

of

Biscay

• Saintes

• Royan

Cognac •

• Angouleme

Shard & Moffat
Drowned, 7 Dec.

Gironde River

Wallace & Ewart
captured, 8 Dec.

• Barbezieux

Lesparte-Medoc •

HMS Tuna launch
Op. FRANKTON teams,
7 Dec. 1942

Pauillac •

Montieu-la-Garde   Chalais •
Laver & Mills Captured, 14 Dec.   • Riberac

• Blaye

Attack on Bordeaux
by Hasler, Sparks,
Laver & Mills,
night of 11–12 Dec.

• Libourne

BORDEAUX

Bergerac •

• Arcachon

0   20 miles

0   20 km

La Teste Salles •

Mackinnon & Conway captured,
Le Réole Hospital, 11 Dec.

• Langon

missing. (Later captured). Regardless the men had to press on. A second tidal race was hit this time capsizing *Conger*. Hasler and Sparks retrieved the two marines and towed them to as near the shore as possible, then had to make the devastating decision to leave them to their almost certain deaths. *Cuttlefish* also capsized, with the men being taken to shore by the remaining canoes and left to fend for themselves. The two remaining canoes managed to sneak past three patrolling German frigates and enter the Gironde river. There they made it 20 miles inland before holding up for the daylight hours near St. Vivien de Medoc. The two crews continued on their slow advance against the river's ebb tide for the next three nights before the attack was set for the night of 11/12 December.

Hasler and Sparks took the west side of the harbour whilst Laver and Mills took the east. A total of sixteen limpets were placed on six vessels, including the patrol boat *Sperrbrecher*. The two crews then retired back down the river, this time with the tide and reached St Genes de Blaye before daybreak. Here they scuttled the canoes and left in their separate groups for the Spanish border. Several days later Mills and Laver were captured, they would later be shot.

Hasler and Sparks were to have better luck, managing to make contact with the resistance and after an epic journey over the Pyranees and through Spain to Gibralter, would make it back to Britain. All the other crews were shot or drowned in the initial insertion.

NORWEGIAN HEAVY WATER RAIDS

After the invasion of Norway the Germans took control of all aspects of Norwegian production, with one major coup being the capture of the hydroelectric plant at Vermork next to the Rjukan waterfall. This plant specialised in separating hydrogen molecules in water in order to produce ammonia, which could then be used in the production of fertilisers, a by-product of which was heavy water, which in turn could be used by the Nazi war machine in it's Plutonium production. With a nuclear weapon the Axis powers would be unstoppable so a plan was put into action to knock out the plant and destroy all the heavy water that had already been produced.

Luckily for the Allies an engineer from the plant, Einar Skinnarland, was on a month-long sabbatical from the plant and managed to escape to Britain. Here he gave valuable information to the SOE who decided to return Skinnarland to Norway before his break was over so as not to arouse suspicion and to help lead a sabotage attack against the plant. RAF bombing of the plant was thought to be too costly as the weather was unpredictable in the mountainous region as well as the plant being a formidable construction, many many bombs would have to be expended before any tangible results were to be seen.

With Skinnarland successfully dropped back into Telemark, it was decided to send an advance party made up of four Norwegians familiar with the region. This would be known as Operation Grouse. These men were; Jens-Anton Poulsson, the leader, Knut Haugland, Claus Helberg and Arne Kjelstrup. They had undergone intensive training in the wilds

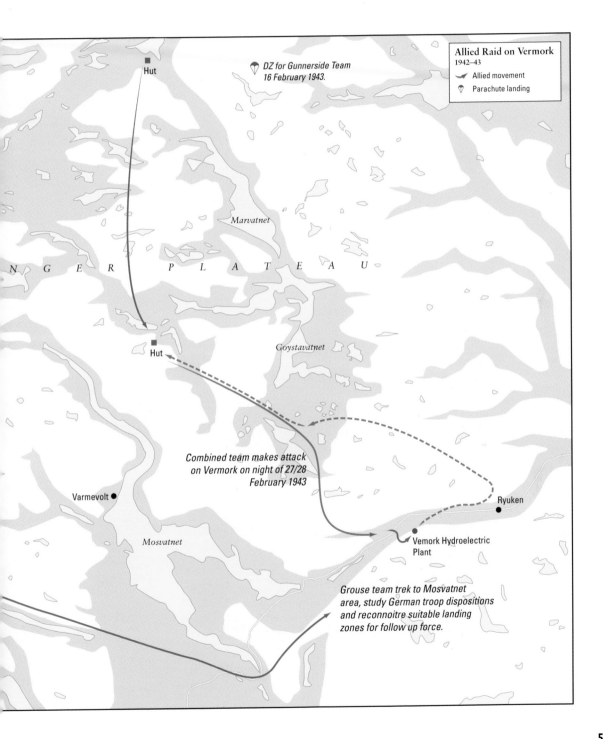

DZ for Gunnerside Team
16 February 1943.

Allied Raid on Vermork
1942–43
Allied movement
Parachute landing

Hut

Marvatnet

N G E R P L A T E A U

Goystavatnet

Hut

Combined team makes attack
on Vermork on night of 27/28
February 1943

Varmevolt

Ryuken

Mosvatnet

Vemork Hydroelectric
Plant

Grouse team trek to Mosvatnet
area, study German troop dispositions
and reconnoitre suitable landing
zones for follow up force.

of Scotland courtesy of the Commandos, learning invaluable skills such as sabotage, unarmed combat and extreme weather survival. After several attempts, which were aborted due to inclement weather the team was finally dropped on the Hardanger Plateau on 18 October 1942. They landed well west of any German garrison and it took them several days of trekking and cross country skiing to make the rendezvous at Mosvatn, where they met with Skinnarland's brother. They immediately set about reconnoitering the area for a suitable landing zone for the gliders that would bring in the Commando assault team. This was found and reported back to London via radio. The men also sent back information gleaned by Skinnarland and his brother that the Germans had placed around twenty-four low grade troops to guard the dam and plant area, but with reinforcements within easy reach to repel any attack. The plant itself was perfectly protected, being in a steep valley with the approaches mined and guarded by machine guns.

With all the details assessed it was decided by Combined Operations to send in thirty-four sappers drawn from the Royal Engineers that were attached to the 1st Parachute Division, known as Operation Freshman. These men would be towed by Halifax bombers in two Horsa gliders, they would then land on a area 3 miles from the plant and rarely patrolled by the Germans. The men would then be escorted by the men of the Grouse Team to attack and destroy the plant and all heavy water.

On 19 November 1942 the operation was launched, even though the weather was far from perfect. The operation did not go to plan as the first combination of Halifax and Horsa could not locate the beacon set up by the Grouse team. Due to heavy ice the tow rope snapped, leaving the Horsa to crash land in south-

ern Norway near Fyljesdal. Seventeen men were on board, eight being killed in the crash with many of the others badly injured. These men were found by locals but soon after the Germans located them and took them into custody. The other combination fared even worse, both the Halifax and the Horsa crashed, with no crew surviving aboard the Halifax. Aboard the Horsa seven men were killed and the rest injured. The men managed to make contact with th locals but again were discovered by the Germans and taken to a prisoner of war camp.

Unbeknownst to the Glider men Hitler had decreed the Commando Order a month previously, that all commandos should be shot immediately on capture. All the survivors of the two glider crashes were summarily executed. Along with this hideous war crime a map was found amongst the wreckage plotting Vermork as the target for the raid, the Germans increased security of the plant immediately.

With the failure of the operation the men of the Grouse team now had to retreat into their mountain hideaway, a small ski cabin high on the plateau north of the plant and exist on meagre rations, even resorting to eating lichen, until further on into the winter a reindeer was spotted and butchered.

On the evening of the 16 February 1943 a further six men were dropped on the plateau to supplement the Grouse team, known as Operation Gunnerside, these men were also Norwegian nationals who had been trained by SOE and the Commandos. Bringing with them much needed supplies and sabotage equipment the night of 27/28 February was chosen for the attack. Due to the discovery of the documents amongst the Freshman raid German security had been substantially raised, especially the bridge linking to the plant. It was decided that the team would descend into the valley and climb the opposite side then follow a rail line into the plant. Thanks to intelligence gleaned from workers inside the plant the men were able to gain access to the plant without alerting the German guards. However a caretaker was disturbed but he was happy to let the men continue their sabotage mission. Charges were placed and a British sub-machine gun was purposely left behind to show that it had been a Commando raid and therefore reduce local reprisals.

The men escaped without discovery and the machinery and stocks of heavy water were destroyed. Four of the raiding party decided to stay in the area to monitor the German response and act accordingly whilst two men moved to Oslo to continue work with the Norwegian underground, whilst the rest headed east to neutral Sweden.

Within two months the plant had been restored to full capability and this was relayed to SOE back in Britain. The chance of another raids success was minimal now that the Germans had increased the protection of the plant, but by early 1943 the USAAF had started to arrive in numbers in Britain, so a daylight raid, carried out by over 140 bombers was flown in November when the weather permitted a reasonable chance of target acquisition. However many of the bombs fell without result and the machinery itself was easily protected by the heavy concrete construction of the plant. However this caused the Germans to fear further raids and decided to transfer what stocks of heavy water they

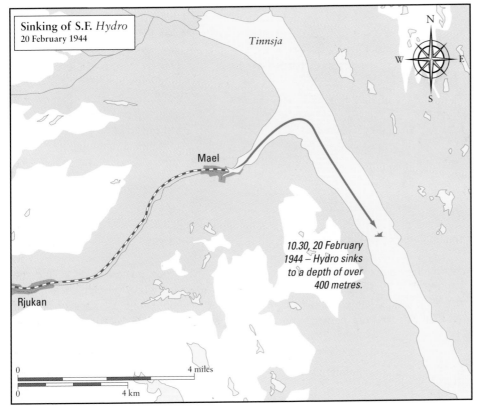

Sinking of S.F. *Hydro*
20 February 1944

Tinnsja

Mael

Rjukan

10.30, 20 February 1944 – Hydro sinks to a depth of over 400 metres.

0 — 4 miles
0 — 4 km

Norwegian operative aimed to sink the SF Hydro at Lake Tinnsjo's deepest part. The operation was successful, however sadly some Norwegian locals were killed in the attack.

SF Hydro *at the rail dock on Lake Tinnsjo. She would be later sunk by Norwegian operative in order to deny the Germans heavy water from the plant at Vermork.*

had produced and the machinery to a safer location in Germany. In order to transfer the remaining heavy water to the coast for transport to Germany it first had to travel a short distance from the plant to Mael. Here it would be loaded on to the steam ferry SF *Hydro*. Four men of the Norwegian resistance decided to sabotage the vessel whilst it was over the deepest part of lake Tinnsjo and deny the Germans the heavy water. The Germans decided to move the stock on a Sunday, lucky for the saboteurs as this would reduce any Norwegians travelling on the *Hydro* too.

The men snuck aboard the ferry on the evening of Saturday 19 February 1944 and proceeded to place an explosive charge in the bows of the ship. With the timers set the men withdrew.

The ferry left the station on time and by 10.30 am it was over the required area and the explosives blew as hoped. The ship started to list almost immediately, with those on deck managing to clamber aboard lifeboats or stumble over the side, however eighteen people were killed, including three Norwegian passengers, seven crew and eight German guards. The rest were picked up by locals using nearby boats to drag them out of the freezing water. The *Hydro* itself sank to below 400 metres, well beyond salvageable depth. The German Atomic programme, although never advanced, had taken a massive blow and would never recover.

Elsewhere in Norway, particularly in the south and especially in and around Oslo, there quickly formed a strong resistance movement, the men and women of the country having a strong patriotic streak and being disappointed by how quickly their country had fallen to the Nazi oppressor joined in droves. With the leaders of what became known as 'Milorg' making contact with the government in exile, based in London, the resistance grew and grew.

At first underground papers were the only course of action these groups could take, counteracting the strong bias of the local press and the propaganda that abound through all sources of media. Nearly 300 such papers were founded but would only appear at random intervals as the men and women of the publications played a cat-and-mouse game with the Gestapo and their Norwegian counterparts.

To assist the Norwegian underground the SOE set up what would become known as the Shetland Bus. This was a group of Norwegian trawlers that were tasked with infiltrating and bringing back agents from occupied Norway. Using fishing trawlers they were ideally camouflaged and only lightly armed. They still ran the risk of having to cross the North sea at night, in winter under the constant threat of discovery, however they were extremely successful right up to the end of the war.

Armed resistance and sabotage in Norway itself posed other problems, with any act of sabotage usually met with harsh reprisals by the occupies. However, members of the Norwegian Independent Company No. 1 were highly successful, notably Max Manus, a veteran who had fought in the Finnish campaign of 1939–40. Having seen his country capitulate to the Germans in 1940 he actively worked in underground propaganda. He was then caught and injured trying to escape custody. He then dramatically escaped the hospital he was being treated in and arrived in Scotland for Commando training following an epic journey through Sweden, Soviet Russia, Africa and eventually to Canada.

Following training he was dropped into Norway along with a friend Gregors Gram. They were tasked with attacking shipping in Oslo harbour using Limpet mines, a small explosive charge, attached below the waterline of a ship by magnets.

The first raid was carried out on the evening of 28 April 1943, where they successfully sunk two transports and damaged a third.

In January the following year the decision was made to attack the large troop carrier *Donau*. This vessel had previously been used to transport Norwegian Jews to Germany where they were then sent onto concentration camps. This time canoes could not be used to approach the ship at night as security was high by the wharf. However, with great audacity Manus and his companion, Roy Nielson, entered the docks dressed as workmen. Whilst a colleague distracted the gate guards the two men were only given a cursory security check and proceeded to a small area beneath a lift where an insider had left a dinghy. The men took off their boiler suits to reveal full British uniform, so if they were captured reprisals would be reduced to the local populace. The explosives were placed and the men withdrew without any attention. At ten o'clock that evening the charges blew, and although the captain of the *Donau* tried to beach her, she was lost.

During Crown Prince Olav's return to Norway Max Manus was tasked as his personal bodyguard in admiration for the heroic work he had done during the occupation.

FORMATION OF THE US ARMY RANGERS

Major William O. Darby was given the task of raising the 1st Ranger Battalion, originally from Arkansas he was admired by his men and led from the front.

The Rangers have been noted in history as first appearing in the colonial wars of the 17th and 18th Centuries, working as scouts for the controlling British colonists that were not used to fighting in the heavily wooded and mountainous terrain of the American north east. These men combined their knowledge of Indian and european warfare to reconnoitre in advance of the British Army and relay information on incoming raids or carry out spoiling attacks of their own. Using the terrain to their advantage much like the native Indians, they were able to live off the land and not have to rely on long lines of support.

A British Commando lights a cigarette for his comrade in arms, a US Ranger after the Dieppe raid, August 1942.

The Rangers appeared again in the history of American warfare during the Civil War. A Colonel Mosby commanded a battalion of Rangers for the Confederates and was used as a raiding force attacking the Union's lines of supply and communication, making swift attacks or lying in ambush, creating as much destruction and chaos as possible then making a swift withdrawal, many of the attributes that would be used by special forces and resistance groups during the Second World War.

On the United States entry into the conflict it was decreed that a unit should be created following the lines of the British Commandos. As of 19 June 1942 Major William Darby was given command of the 1st Ranger Battalion, made up of 600 men, they would enter training in Achnacarry, Scotland alongside their Allies, the Commandos. Their training officer would be Lieutenant Colonel Charles Vaughan, a veteran of the raids on northern Norway at Lofoten and Vaagso. One hundred men were weeded out under intense training that included live-fire exercises and rigorous assault courses, all well known to the Commandos that were training them.

Darby, a West Point graduate, went through all the training alongside his men. Originally an artilleryman, he would not expect his men to do anything that he was not prepared to do himself, leading from the front. During this training period fifty Rangers were chosen to go on the first major combined arms assault on the occupied coast of France, the raid on Dieppe on 19 August 1942, known as Operation Jubilee. It

was thought that a small cadre of the Rangers would be given some real battle experience which they could then relay back to the main unit, it would also provide a propaganda coup, illustrating that American men were involved with the war effort and fighting on the frontline alongside their British and Canadian allies. Many of the men relished the chance for some action and were dispersed amongst the raiding units of 4 Commando, who were on the right flank and 3 Commando on the left flank. No. 3 Commando was under the command of Lieutenant Colonel Dumford-Slater and was ordered to destroy batteries 5 miles east of Dieppe whilst 4 Commando was commanded by the great Lord Lovat and were tasked with destroying the coastal battery at Varengeville, capable of firing on the main assault group landing two miles away at Dieppe.   To the west the Commandos and Rangers climbed

up off the beach facing little initial resistance and moved inland to flank the batteries from the west and south. Most of the Rangers were attached to the supporting units during the actual assault on the battery providing covering fire. On the East the assault fell into disarray and little was achieved as most of the raiding party did not reach the battery, only harassing fire was brought down on the crews before withdrawal was required. During this raid the commander of the Rangers for the raid, Captain Roy Murray, recorded that seven men had been either captured or killed. These men would be amongst the first, but not the last, casualties suffered by US land forces in the European theatre of operations. However, the Rangers had proven themselves capable and had earned the respect of their opposite numbers in the British Army.

Training at Achnacarry in Scotland was intense, using live fire and forced marches, the men of the Rangers were soon hardened into a tough fighting unit.

RANGERS IN NORTH AFRICA

Far right: Rangers of the mortar company haul a utility cart loaded with their 81mm mortar and ammunition through the streets of Arzew.

By the end of October 1942 the Rangers were fully equipped and trained and prepared to board three converted ferries at Glasgow for the journey south to the Mediterranean where they would take part in the Torch landings along the coast of North Africa. The men would form the eastern most part of Centre Task Force, under the overall command of Maj. General Lloyd Fredendall's Centre Task Force. The Task Force's main objective was the capture of the Algerian port of Oran. On 8 November the rangers would land at the smaller town of Arzew, some miles east of Oran, where they were to destroy two Vichy French coastal batteries that could interdict the main landing at Oran. This was a classic role for the Commando-trained Rangers.

Darby separated his forces into two groups, the main force, which he would lead, would land north of the main battery, Batterie du Nord, whilst the other force, named Dammer Force, would assault the Fort de la Pont and the harbour itself further to the south. The two assaults would go in simultaneously.

Darby to the north landed without discovery and soon took positions ready to assault with a mortar team covering the battery. After cutting the wire and after a few cursory shots from the defenders, quickly silenced by the mortar team, the battery was seized. A similar story was apparent to the south at Fort de la Pont as all objectives were taken with minimal casualties. Darby then turned his attention to the massive Fort du Nord and after a few shots the fort capitulated.

Over the next few months the majority of the Rangers were kept in the rear to continue training and pass on amphibious

assault techniques to other units.

They were then deployed into the mountainous regions of western Tunisia where they were tasked with deep penetration missions to reconnoitre enemy dispositions and put in spoiling attacks, whilst the main Allied thrust was built up in the north of the country, a role for which they excelled.

The final task the Rangers were given were the capture of the mountain towns of El Guettar and Djebel el Ank, these were important positions as they overlooked the entire Axis positions strung out along the eastern seaboard of Tunisia. This they achieved with great initiative and flair. The men were then withdrawn and prepared for the assault on Sicily.

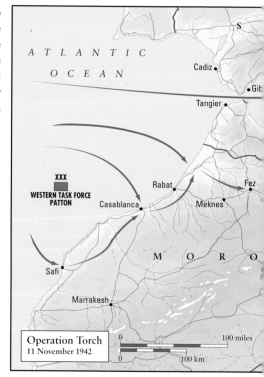

ATLANTIC OCEAN

Cadiz

Gib

Tangier

XXX
WESTERN TASK FORCE
PATTON

Rabat

Fez

Casablanca

Meknes

M O R O

Safi

Marrakesh

Operation Torch
11 November 1942

0   100 miles

0   100 km

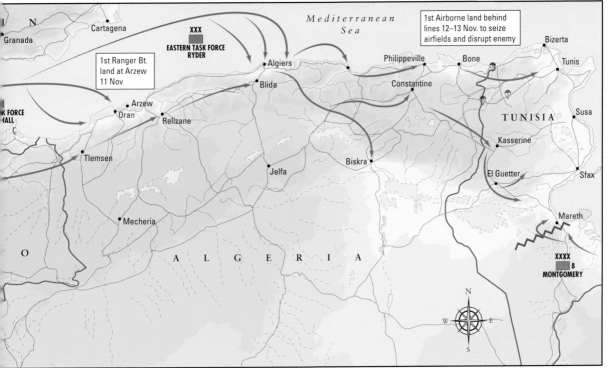

1st Ranger Bt. land at Arzew 11 Nov

EASTERN TASK FORCE RYDER

1st Airborne land behind lines 12–13 Nov. to seize airfields and disrupt enemy

DAMBUSTERS RAID

In the years running up to the Second World War the Air Ministry of Great Britain started to identify potential targets within Germany that would weaken its industrial output should hostilities break out. One of these targets was the destruction of the dams in and around the industrial area of north west Germany called the Ruhr. These dams supplied much of the power to the steel mills that were intrinsic to the German war machine. However, the dams were also noted as potential targets by the Germans, conventional bombing would be incredibly wasteful and bear little damage, whereas a torpedo attack may cause enough structural damage for the dams to fail. The Germans duly ran anti-torpedo netting along the length of the dams on the reservoir side.

Barnes Wallis, Chief designer at Vickers, and famous for designing the Wellington bomber, took it apon himself to discover a way to deliver a bomb accurately, missing the netting. His idea was to skip the bomb over the netting by launching the bomb at a very low altitude and with a heavy backwards spin. This spin would not only assist in the skimming but would also help the bomb 'walk' down the side of the dam iteself before detonating with a hydrostatic fuse. After initial doubts by the Air Ministry, tests were made with scale models before moving up to full-scale bombs. The bomb was at first shaped with a wooden curved shell, but this was found to disintegrate on contact with water, it was found that the straight-sided 'mine' worked just as well but had to be launched

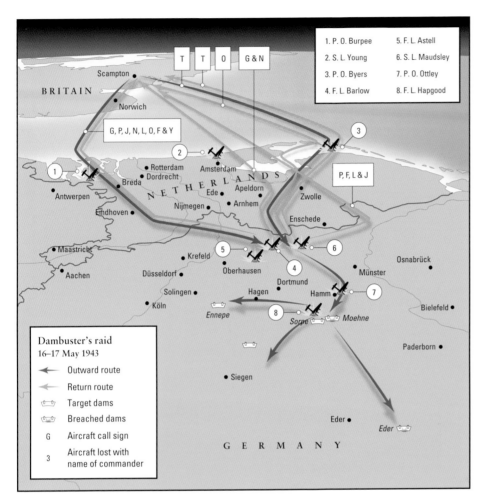

1. P. O. Burpee	5. F. L. Astell
2. S. L. Young	6. S. L. Maudsley
3. P. O. Byers	7. P. O. Ottley
4. F. L. Barlow	8. F. L. Hapgood

Dambuster's raid
16–17 May 1943

← Outward route

← Return route

⬚ Target dams

⬚ Breached dams

G Aircraft call sign

3 Aircraft lost with name of commander

at a very specific speed, height and a certain rpm to the spin. This would require highly-trained aircrew, flying the relatively new Avro Lancaster, emphasis now moved to training these aircrew.

No. 5 Group, RAF were tasked with creating a new squadron made up of veterans and newly passed out crews. It was to be led by the 24-year-old Wing Commander Guy Gibson, an old hand having flown 170 missions. Based at RAF Scampton in Lincolnshire, Gibson soon pressed his men into training at extreme low-level, at first during daylight then during the hours of darkness, at no time

were the crews made aware of what their mission was to be, many suspecting a low-level attack on one of Germany's pocket battleships.

The targets were chosen as the Mohne, Eder and Sorpe dams, the latter being of an earthen construction, the bombers were to fly along the length of the dam and drop the mine directly on to it. It was therefore thought that this was the least likely to be breached. The others were to be approached dead on, at a height of 60 feet and at an approximate speed of 240mph. This was all to be done whilst under intense ground fire.

The newly designated 617 Squadron was to be split into three sections for the raid. The first group, led by Gibson himself and made up of nine aircraft, would attack the Mohne dam and if there were any mines remaining move onto the Eder. The second, with five aircraft would attack the Sorpe and the third section, taking off an hour behind would act as a reserve and move to continue attacks on the main dams in the event that none were breached, or otherwise attack three smaller dams at Lister, Ennepe and Diemel.

The First and second waves took off after 9 pm on 16 May 1943, with the third wave leaving just after midnight. En route to the dams two aircraft had to turn back, one flying too low and losing its bomb to the wave tops, the others radio being damaged by flak, these two returned without incident. Three other aircraft in the first two waves were lost before reaching the dams, either to flak or colliding with powerlines. On arrival at the Mohne dam Gibson made the first run. It was a successful attack but did not breach the dam. The second aircraft's bomb exploded above the dam, causing the aircraft

to lose control and crash. There followed three more runs by the squadron, whilst Gibson flew his Lancaster low over the dam to draw the flak. After the fifth bomb was dropped the dam broke, flooding the valley below, Gibson led the remaining crews to the Eder.

The Eder was a particularly difficult target due to the steep valleys surrounding the reservoir, the first aircraft making six abortive runs before having to take a rest. Of the following two runs one bomb struck the top of the dam and the second successfully blew below the waterline. The third bomb proved to be the one that would breach it. Follow-up attacks were made on the Sorpe and Ennepe dams but with no result.

The raid was a great success, severely hampering German production in the region and forcing the enemy to send resources that could be used elsewhere to defend the dams from further attack. Out of the nineteen aircraft sent on the raid eight would not return. For his role in the raid Gibson would be awarded the Victoria Cross.

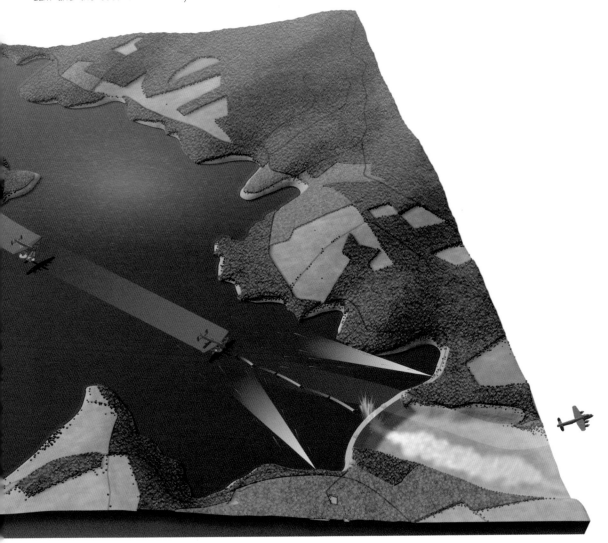

FORMATION OF THE US AIRBORNE

Lieutenant General James 'Jumpin' Jim' Gavin of the 82nd Airborne Division. He started the war commanding the 505th PIR before commanding the entire 82nd. Loved and respected by his troops he gained his nickname by always jumping in the first wave of all the assaults the division took. He was one of the most outstanding leaders of the Second World War.

The use of parachutes in warfare had been around for some time, the Germans in the First World War being the only country to supply their airmen with one as a means of escape from a doomed aircraft. The Allies only reserved the use of parachutes to Balloon observers, thinking that aircrew would use them as a means of escaping any impending action. This was counter-productive as it often meant that a highly-trained pilot would have to go down in flames with his aircraft rather than escape and fight another day.

The parachute's use as a means of placing troops en masse towards the enemy rear was mooted by the US aviation pioneer Colonel Billy Mitchell, who approached the commander of the American Expeditionary Force in France, General Pershing, in 1918 with such an idea. However, the war came to an end shortly after and the idea was shelved.

From the mid-1930s the Italians, Germans and the Russians all started equipping and training large airborne units. It would be the Germans who would display the full potential of airborne insertion during the first half of 1940 with the capture of Denmark and Norway preceded by airborne coup de main operations as well as the invasion of the west with critical points such as bridges and forts being captured before the main thrust arrived via more traditional methods.

This stirred the the US president himself, F.D. Roosevelt, to push for the development of an airborne force for the US Army. By June 1940 a test platoon was created to experiment with various equipment and training methods. Emphasis was immediately placed on physical exercise and aggressive tactics, as well as landing techniques and uniform variations. By the end of the year a full battalion had been created and trained, the 501st Parachute Infantry. This would form the basis for all US parachute units.

By mid-1942 it was decided to make the established infantry division, the 82nd 'All American', the first airborne division. This unit had been training under Omar Bradley at Camp Claiborne in Louisiana, Major General Matthew B. Ridgway taking command of the division whilst half of the division was moved to the newly created 101st Airborne Division under the command of Major General William Lee.

The 82nd would shortly thereafter move to a larger training facility at Fort Bragg, Georgia whilst the 101st 'Screaming Eagles' remained in Louisiana. Both the divisions would include parachute infantry battalions as well as Glider infantry. The choice of glider was the CG-4 'Waco'. The Waco Aircraft company produced well over 13,000 of these aircraft, which were made from a metal and wood frame with fabric stretched over. The aircraft had seating for a pilot and co-pilot, who would then become infantry on touch down, as well as space for thirteen fully equipped troops or a jeep/75mm howitzer and crew.

The method the paratroops went into battle meant that they were light infantry, very lightly armed and behind enemy lines. This dictated what type of tactics to utilise. The individual soldier might be dropped separately from his parent unit so he would have to be extremely self-sufficient and capable of making his own decisions under stress. The paratroops primary role would be one of sabotage and destruction, operating in small units, creating confusion and panic in the enemy rear whilst the main frontal assault proceeded. The paratrooper had to expect and to be 'comfortable' with being surrounded and not relieved for several days. This required a certain type of person, so all paratroopers were volunteers, with the extra incentive of double the pay of an average infantryman. This obviously attracted the adventurous and wild men of the United States, with the weak and unsuitable weeded out very quick-

ly after basic training commenced. This included a month of extreme physical training as well as weapons and orienteering, followed by the fifth week with five jumps from a USAAF C-47, which had to be made in order to gain the much coveted jump wings.

The men of the 82nd were dispatched to North Africa to take part in the invasion of North Africa in mid 1943, whilst the men of the 101st would transfer to Great Britain to continue training for the upcoming invasion of north west Europe. The men of the two units would become some of the best fighting men that would see action during the Second World War. Led from the front by inspirational leaders of men, including Colonel (later Lieutenant General) James M. Gavin, who commanded the 505th PIR in Italy before taking command of the 82nd Airborne Divsion later in the war. Loved by his men he preferred to carry a trusty M1 Garand rifle into battle rather than a pistol.

82ND AIRBORNE IN SICILY

Unfortunately due to high winds over Sicily on the night of 9–10 July 1943 the troops of the 82nd Airborne RCT did not find their designated drop zones. This did not impede the effectiveness of the force however.

With victory in North Africa the eyes of the Allied commanders were drawn northward to what Churchill called 'the soft underbelly of the Axis'. The choices for invasion were Southern France, the Greek peninsula or Italy. It was decided that Italy would be the best option as the defeat of this nation would completely open up the Mediterranean Sea once more to Allied shipping, allowing supplies to reach the Middle and Far East unimpeded. The first step in the invasion would be the capture of Sicily, the largest island in the Mediterranean and defended by two corps from the Italian 6th Army reinforced by the Hermann Goering Panzer Division and 15th Panzergrenadier Division.

Command for the operation, known as 'Husky', was given to US General Dwight D. Eisenhower, with British General Alexander as his number two. The Allied plan was to land two armies along the south eastern corner of the island, one British, commanded by General Montgomery, and one American, commanded by General Patton. It was decided that airborne troops were to be utilised for the first time in a major invasion, employed to drop just beyond the beachheads to secure bridges, destroy enemy strongholds and slow down any attempt by the Axis to reinforce the beach defences.

The US 7th Army was to land on the beaches around the southern Sicilian town of Gela, General Matthew Ridgway, commander of the US 82nd Airborne Division was given the task of securing beyond the beachhead.

The number of aircraft in the Mediterranean was severely limited, it was decided that the British airborne would get the bulk of the gliders, making the American mission a pure parachute assault. The number of transports available to Colonel James M. Gavin, chosen to lead the combat team, limited the amount of men he could employ, 504th and 505th Parachute Infantry Regiments along with their support troops were chosen for the assault and numbered 3,400 in total.

Training was carried out in Tunisia around the town of Kairouan. Mock ups of the pillboxes the troops would face were assaulted with live rounds until every man was confident of the task he had been given. The troops themselves were not told where they would be dropped until the last moment.

On the evening of 9 July 1943 the troops began to enplane their transports for the flight to their dropzones, this was flown via Malta at low level just behind the British lift. As the transports gained height the weather took a turn for the worse with heavy winds making formation flying in the dark near impossible. As a result many of the sticks were widely scattered, very few men making their designated DZs.

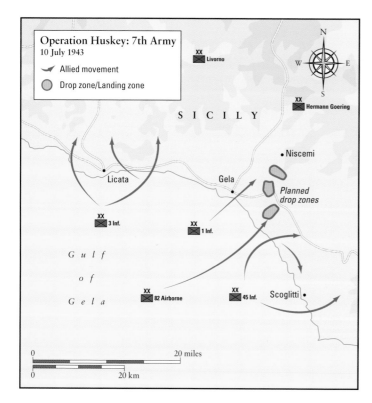

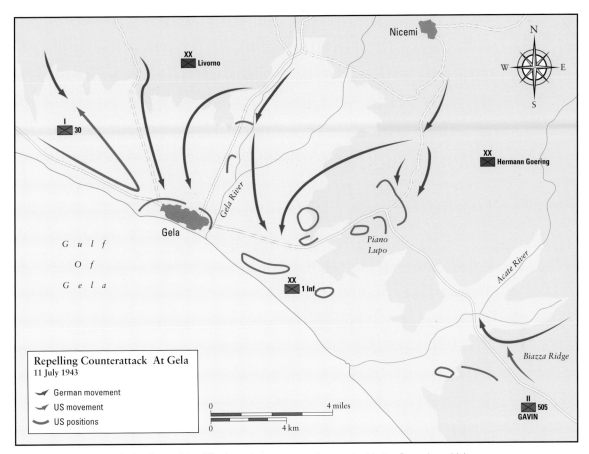

Repelling Counterattack At Gela
11 July 1943

German movement
US movement
US positions

0   4 miles

0   4 km

The weather also made landing safely difficult, resulting in many landing injuries.

Despite this the paratroopers went about causing as much confusion as possible, the scattered troops causing the defenders to think they were being attacked by a much larger force. Pillboxes and important road junctions were captured, aiding greatly to the follow up seaborne invasion getting a much needed toe-hold on the Sicilian coast. Consolidation of the positions the 82nd had occupied followed very quickly as counter-attack was imminent.

On the morning of D+1 the Hermann Goering Division started to move south to attack the 45th Infantry and push them into the sea. Between them stood Gavin with about 250 men along the Biazza Ridge. Facing Tiger tanks with supporting infantry, the amer-icans were only armed with the Bazooka, which was ineffective against the German behemoth, and a single pack howitzer. After heavy losses on the American side the attack was halted, with help from naval gunfire called in by the airborne troops. Only a few German tanks made it through to the beaches and these were soon withdrawn.

Even though the drops had been disastrous in terms of how far and wide the men of the 82nd were scattered, this did not diminish from the massive effect they had on the outcome of the battle. With troops apparently everywhere, the Axis were confused and intimidated into taking immediate action and thanks to the heroic defence of the beachheads by so few men the invasion was able to grow in strength and succeed.

BRITISH AIRBORNE IN SICILY

A C-47 tows a CG-4 Waco glider into the air. Constructed from wood, steel and fabric they would be used extensively by the Allied airborne armies in the European theatre of operations.

The British Airbornes role in the invasion of Sicily was similar to that of the 82nd Airbornes role in securing behind the beachheads but also included the capture of two major bridges that would speed the advance of the Allies once they had landed. The first bridge was called Ponte Grande just outside of Syracuse, the capture of which would then lead to the eventual capture of Syracuse itself. The second lay further north at Primasole, again the capture of this bridge before it could be destroyed by the Axis was vital.

Due to lack of aircraft in the Mediterranean it was decided that the two attacks would take place on separate nights, the operation against Ponte Grande, codenamed 'Ladbroke' would take place on the night of 9 July, utilising the 1st Airlanding Brigade commanded by Brigadier Philip Hicks, just before the main seaborne landings. Whilst the Primasole mission, codenamed 'Fustian', involving the 1st Parachute Brigade commanded by Brigadier Gerald Lathbury, would take place two nights later.

Training was carried out in North Africa but was limited by the number of gliders that were available and the pilots that would fly them were unfamiliar on the type, the US CG-4 Waco. These gliders could carry up to thirteen fully armed men and would be supplemented by a few British Horsa gliders, with a larger cap-

acity. Training was extremely rudimentary, with few of the men of the Glider Pilot Regiment having more than ten hours of flying time under their belts, none having any actual combat experience.

The Brigade was made up of two battalions, one from the South Staffordshire Regiment and one from the Borders. This was reinforced by a company of sappers as well as a unit of 181st Airlanding Field Ambulance. Two companys of the South Staffs were to be landed near the bridge to capture it in a coup de main operation just before midnight of the 9th. The rest of the brigade would be landed near Syracuse to assist in its capture as well as around the bridge to form a defensive ring.

On the evening of the 9th July the men of the 1st Airlanding Brigade climbed aboard their transports and began the trip to Sicily. During the flight many of the towing aircraft, having seen little action began evasive-manouvres to avoid the Axis flak as well as strong winds preventing exact navigation. This resulted in many of the gliders being released too early from the designated release point. Sixty-five of these gliders had to ditch in the sea, with the loss of of over 250 men. The rest were widely scattered, the result being that only one Horsa glider managed to land within sight of the bridge. This contained a platoon of the South

Staffs, commanded by Lieutenant Withers. He quickly separated his men into two sections, one swimming the river and then assaulting the bridge from both ends. The action was a success and the bridge captured and all demolition charges removed. Men from other gliders slowly made their way to the bridge and by dawn the defenders numbered some 87 troops.

Following a counter-attack by the Italians in the early morning, which was repulsed, a much larger force of two Italian battalions was formed. They attacked the bridge from several directions just before noon, with ammunition low and with only a handful of able- bodied men, the bridge fell to the Italians, many of the men becoming POWs, with a few managing to escape into the Italian countryside. Due to the British disabling the demolition charges the Italians were unable to destroy the bridge before the arrival of the lead unit coming in from the beaches, The Royal Scots Fusiliers. This unit counter-attacked the Italians and pushed them from the bridge, it was now firmly in British hands.

The 1st Parachute Brigade's task, under the command of Brigadier Gerald Lathbury, was to capture the Primosole Bridge and was to take place on the evening of the 12/13 July. This was however delayed by 24 hours due to 8th Army preparations being slow. This bridge over the river Simeto was vital to the Allied plan of advancing up the eastern coast of Sicily to the north eastern port of Messina.

Elements of 1st Battalion were to land to the north and south of the bridge, they were then to move on the bridge from both ends and capture it in a coup de main operation. Sappers attached to the battalion would then make safe any preparations for demolition the Axis had made.

Whilst this occurred the 3rd Battalion of the brigade were to drop some miles north of the bridge and prepare a defensive screen after the destruction of some heavy Italian anti-aircraft artillery. This is where it was thought the main

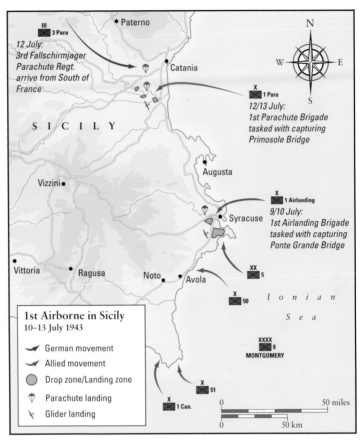

1st Airborne in Sicily
10–13 July 1943

↙ German movement
↙ Allied movement
● Drop zone/Landing zone
⛃ Parachute landing
↓ Glider landing

thrust of any enemy counter-attack would come.

The 2nd Battalion had a similar task to the 3rd but to the south of the bridge, priority being given to the capture of three high points thought to be occupied by Italian artillery and supporting infantry. With the added assistance of air-landing artillery the men of the 1st Parachute Brigade were only expected by the Allied planners to hold out for 12 hours before support came from the lead elements of the 8th Army advancing from the south.

Little did the Allied planners know was that the Fallschirmjaeger Regiment 3, part of the 1st Fallschirmjaeger Division had been moved from their base in the south of France, to Rome, where they were then dropped on the area immediately surrounding Primosole Bridge. These soldiers were hardened veterans of the

Pyrrhic victory on Crete as well as fighting in the extreme conditions of Russia. The Germans had seen the importance of the bridge to the allied advance and were prepared to hold it at all costs.

As the aircraft approached the Sicilian coast they were again set upon by accurate Axis anti-aircraft fire. The American pilots again showed their lack of experience, through no fault of their own, and were widely dispersed. The Pathfinders tasked with marking the landing zones for the gliders were made redundant, some being dropped some eight miles from the designated landing zones.

Due to the highly scattered drops the men of 1st Parachute Brigade spent much of the time fumbling around in the dark trying to attain where they were and where their fellow troops were. The elements of 1st Battalion that were to drop either side of the bridge and attack immediatly failed to land in their required zones. However, fifty men of the Brigade managed to form up and attacked the bridge after a quick reconnaissance saw it was defended by a similar number of Italian troops. These men duly surrended when faced by the paratroopers attack.

Shortly afterwards Brigadier Lathbury arrived at the bridge with a further forty men to reinforce the defence of the bridge and remove the demolition devices. This was followed by the bulk of 1st Battalion arriving under the command of Lieutenant Colonel Pearson.

The 3rd Battalion, who were meant to supply the northern defensive screen to the men of the 1st Battalion on the bridge were the worst scattered during the drop. The commander of the Battalion, Lieutenant Colonel Yeldham only managing to rustle up some thirty-odd men during the night. With this tiny force he decided to join the men of the 1st Battalion, where they were placed some 50 metres north of the bridge to aid in its protection.

The 2nd Battalion to the south of the bridge faired a little better. Their drop was not as scattered and a platoon made up from various units assaulted 'Johnny I', one of three small hills to the south of the bridge, 'Johnny I' being the highest of these. The assault was a success and the men were soon reinforced by follow up troops coming from the DZs, including 2nd Battalion's commander Lieutenant Colonel John

Fallschirmjaeger man an MG42 position in Sicily. The weapon had a fearsome rate of fire, spitting out over 1,200 rounds per minute, it was respected and feared by the Allied armies.

Frost. The men went about consolidating the position and by dawn they started to come under fire from German machine guns on the opposing two features, 'Johnny II' and 'Johnny III', however the Germans could not counter-attack as the Para's hill dominated the area.

By early morning of the 14th July the Germans were starting to make probing attacks on the bridge from the north, whilst in the south sporadic fighting was taking place between the hill features. Further south a raid by men of 3 Commando had captured a bridge to aid the advance of the land forces from the south. It had been a success but the Commandos, suffering heavy casualties had to abandon the bridge as no reinforcement arrived in the shape of the advancing 4th Armoured Brigade, which was in the van of the 8th Army.

Meanwhile the men on 'Johnny I' had managed to raise a British cruiser on the only working radio on the hill. This cruiser immediately started shelling German positions and was instrumental in keeping them at bay. On the bridge the men of 1st and 3rd Battalion had been strafed by enemy fighters before being heavily shelled. This was the overture to several infantry assaults from the north, both of which were repulsed, incurring significant casualties on both sides, the Germans making good their losses, the British being dependant on stragglers still coming in from the widely dispersed drop.

By mid-afternoon another attack was put in by the Germans preceded by a massive artillery barrage. This caused the paratroops to withdraw from the north end of the bridge and take up positions in the Axis bunkers on the southern side as well as along the southern bank of the river. The paras were now desperately short of ammunition and were utilising anything that had been left behind by the retreating Italians. The bunkers were methodically destroyed by German anti-tank guns, and with the arrival of 8th Army not to be seen the British paratroopers position was extremely precarious. By 06.00 Pearson decided the

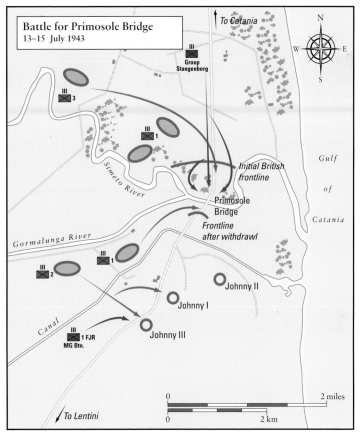

bridge had to be abandoned and ordered his men to join up with 2nd Battalion on 'Johnny I'. This was carried out with minimal casualties. The bridge now lay in enemy hands once more. By early evening the lead elements of the 8th Army started to arrive, but the bulk of the force would not reach the bridge area until midnight.

The following morning an infantry assault by the Durham Light Infantry was put in against the bridge, with heavy loss of life and without success. It was at the suggestion of Pearson that the force be sent across the river by boats some distance up river, this force could then attack the Germans in the flank. This was carried out in the early hours of 16th July, the Germans being taken by complete surprise. The Bridge was once again in Allied hands.

BATTLE FOR SALERNO

Lieutenant General Mark Clark. Commander of Fifth Army during the assault on Salerno and subsequent operations during the Italian campaign.

After the battles for the beach heads and bridges around the south eastern coast of Sicily the Germans continued a successful defensive retreat to the northern port town of Messina. Here the Allies missed a chance at annihilating the Axis forces in southern Italy by allowing the Germans to escape across the straits of Messina with much of their equipment in tow. The fighting in Sicily had also worked to the German's advantage, gifting them time to prepare defensive lines all along the width of the Italian peninsula. For the Allies it was decided to pursue the enemy onto the Italian mainland, with the 8th Army, under General Montgomery taking the shortest route accross the Straits of Messina into the 'toe' of Italy, known as operation Baytown. This would

be supplemented by smaller landings at the 'heel' of Italy near Taranto, operation Slapstick, both of these operations going in on the 3 September 1943. Further north would land the US 5th Army, under Lieutenant General Mark Clark, at Salerno, a wide bay south of the town of Naples on Italy's western coast. This would be the main Allied thrust into Italy with a two corps assault, the US VI Corps and the British X Corps, with 82nd Airborne held in reserve.

The plan was for the US 36th and 45th Infantry Divisions to land to the south of the Gulf of Salerno, whilst north of them would land the British 46th and 56th Divisions. The northern flanks and mountain passes that lead north to the city of Naples would be held by British Commando and US Rangers landing on the northern shore of the gulf around Salerno itself and Maiori. The Allied assault was on a very wide front with the US and British units being separated by the Sele river. Furthermore the Commandos and Rangers were even more isolated from the main landings.

The landings would go in against a prepared enemy, the Germans aware of the Italian moves for an armistice, they had started to occupy the Italian defences in the area. It was also decided by Allied commanders that there would be no preparatory naval bombardment of the immediate landing area. This was to be a major oversight. Another problem facing the invading army was a severe lack of adequate landing craft and ships. This meant that there would be fewer assault troops on the beach at the beginning of the assault.

The German defence of southern Italy came under the overall command of Generalfeldmarschall 'Smiling' Albert Kesselring. Under him the new Tenth Army was activated under General Heinrich von Vietinghoff, consisting of three panzer divisions, two panzergrenadier divisions and 1st Fallschirmjaeger

Division. Reckoning that the main Allied thrust would come in the Naples area or north of Rome the bulk of Tenth Army was held back from the toe of Italy where elements of the 8th Army had already landed. The Germans were well aware of an impending beach assault and were well prepared, wanting to hold the Allies on the beachhead for a relatively short period of time, inflict as many casualties as possible then withdraw to prepared defensive lines that stretched across the Italian peninsula.

At around 3 am on 9 September men of the 4th Ranger Battalion were shuttled ashore by British landing craft. They landed on the beach near Maiori with little resistance, they established flank guards on the Sorrento-Salerno road as the follow up wave of 1st and 3rd Rangers along with the 509th Parachute Infantry Battalion that had become seaborne

troops came ashore. These follow-up units then moved through and successfully took positions covering the Chiunzi Pass. From mountain top positions the Rangers could call down naval fire on any German troop movements from the north coming to support the defences further south. The men of the 4th Battalion then moved north and west, covering the road around the Sorrento peninsula as well as capturing the town of Castellammare on the Gulf of Naples, thus denying the Germans a crucial supply route.

Further to the east at the same time the Rangers landed, the men of 2 Commando and 41st Royal Marine Commando landed at Vietri sul Mare, with the intention of capturing a large Italian Coastal Battery recently taken over by the Germans. This they achieved with little fuss. They then moved in on the town of Vietri,

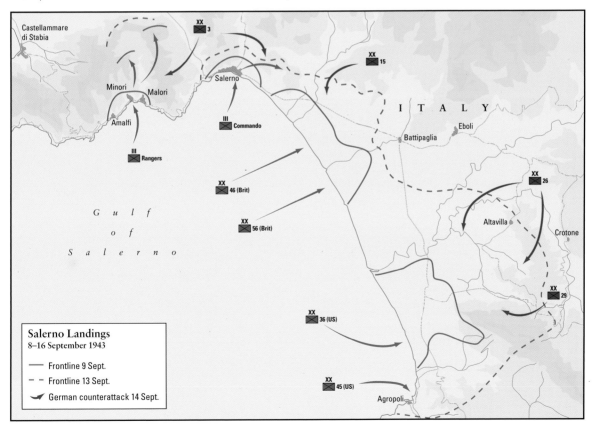

Salerno Landings
8–16 September 1943

— Frontline 9 Sept.
- - Frontline 13 Sept.
✔ German counterattack 14 Sept.

opening up the small port for follow-up troops. The unit then made contact with their American colleagues to the west during the following few days, contributing to the defence of the northern flank, they faced concerted attacks by German Panzergrenadiers as well as Fallschirmjaeger.

To the south of Salerno the two British divisions, the 46th and 56th, faced much more opposition than that of the two special units. However, they managed to push some five miles ashore and establish a beachhead. South of the Sele river the Americans of the 36th Division were facing similar problems. Some units found it difficult to escape off the beaches and advance inland. This led them open to horrific bombardment from German artillery in the hills beyond the beachhead, and if they could not get off the beaches then follow up

forces could not arrive in turn. By the end of the day the initial landing had gone more or less to plan, especially the special forces guarding the northern flank. However, if the allies could not get off the beaches and push inland it would be in vain and Italy would remain in German hands.

The Germans had spotted a weakness with the Allied plan, with the emphasis on the northern part of the Gulf of Salerno, there lay a gap along the Sele river between the US 36th in the south and the British 56th to the north. The Allied build up was slower than that of the Germans, and they were able to launch a counter-attack on 13 September. Whilst the Hermann Goering Division assaulted the British around the area of Salerno the main thrust came from two German battlegroups pushing on the gap between the two Allied Corps. This

British infantry advance past a burning tank in Italy.

assault was only halted in part by the landing of the 45th Infantry Division the previous day and by every available person, be it a cook or a clerk, grabbing a rifle and holding the line. Naval gunfire from the Allied shipping and the Army artillery that had been landed on the beaches contributed greatly too. Had the Germans been able to reach the beach and exploit the gap between the two corps, the whole operation could have failed. With the crisis barely averted it was decided by Clerk to drop 2 battalions of the 504th Parachute Infantry Regiment within the beachhead. These units would then advance up to the frontline. THe following night, 14 September, men of the 505th PIR landed in a similar fashion and quickly moved up to the line. This is all the more incredible as the 504th had only eight hours to prepare for the drop and it illustrated how adaptable and remarkable the airborne forces were, especially under such intelligent command from Ridgway and Gavin. Men of the 325th Glider Infantry Regiment and the 3rd Battalion of the 504th also joined the beachhead fight, but they were delivered via landing craft, the Glidermen and paratroops fighting with the Rangers on the Sorrento peninsula.

On the evening of 14 September men of 2nd Battalion 509th PIR were dropped behind the lines in the mountainous area towards the German rear. The drop was a near disaster with many of the 600 men dropped being widely dispersed. But being Airborne men, and with confidence built from fighting in Sicily, they made up ad hoc units that harassed the Germans in the rear and contributed to the battle by diverting troops that would have otherwise been used on the beachhead fighting.

The Allied air forces also played a major role in holding the Salerno beachhead. Without the bombers, fighter-bombers and fighters interdicting enemy troop movements and destroying artillery emplacements the battle could have turned out very differently. The same could be said for the naval gunfire from the Allied fleet offshore. This was reinforced by the arrival of HMS *Valiant* and HMS *Warspite* on 15 September. The addition of their 15" guns was a boost to morale. However, *Warspite* was targeted by a German Dornier Do. 217 which was carrying a new type of weapon, the Fritz X. A radio-controlled guide bomb with a 700lb armour-piercing warhead. One struck *Warspite* taking out her boiler room and leaving her without power. A second near miss holed her as well. She was quickly withdrawn to Malta for repairs.

With the bulk of 8th Army advancing slowly up the toe of Italy it was decided by von Vietinghoff that the Germans should withdraw from the battle. This they started on 17-18 September, with Salerno on their right flank and swinging their left round to cover over the Apennines to Foggia. With the 8th linking up with American forces on 17 September also, a general advance could start up the 'leg' of Italy.

By 27 September the major airfield complex at Foggia had been captured by 8th Army, a major coup for the Allies as this meant they now had a major airbase on the Italian mainland and thus providing airfields for the Allied air forces to provide tactical cover for the advancing army as well as more easily strike at strategic targets such as the Ploesti oilfields in Rumania.

Naples was eventually captured on 1 October 1943 but by this time the bulk of the German forces had retired behind the natural defensive lines of the Volturno and Biterno Rivers. It would be a hard struggle for the Allies as they slogged up the Italian peninsula, with the high Apennines forming a spine along the peninsula and with many rivers being perfect terrain for the defenders and a nightmare for the attackers, used to open advances with armoured support. Not only the terrain but the withdrawal of some of the best fighting troops, now required to withdraw back to Great Britain to prepare for the imminent allied assault on Normandy, resulted in some of the toughest fighting seen during World War II. A battle that did not end until the end of the war.

GRAN SASSO RAID

A Fallschirmjaeger poses in front of the DFS 230 glider that delivered him to the hotel. Over his arm is slung a FG42. This weapon was specifically designed for the German paratroops and was a precursor to the modern day assault rifle.

By 1942 the tide had turned for Benito Mussolini's Italy. Defeats at El Alamein and all along the North African coast had led to the eventual expulsion of Axis forces from the african continent all together. Followed shortly by the Allied invasion of Sicily in July 1943 and with the people of Italy close to starvation the Italian Fascist government convened along with the monarch, King Victor Emmanuel III, to oust him on 23 July 1943. He was duly arrested and replaced by Pietro Bodoglio.

Not wanting Mussolini to flee to his ally, Adolf Hitler, he was moved around the country to counter any attempt at a rescue. Shortly after Mussolini's expulsion the Italian government agreed an armistice with the Allies on 3 September 1943 near Syracuse which threw Italy into a maelstrom. Bodoglio fled Rome and left his army without orders. The German army swiftly fell on the Italian capital as well as the rest of the nation.

Mussolini's final incarceration was at the Campo Imperatore Hotel high in the Gran Sasso, a mountain in the Apennine range of Italy.

It was decided by Hitler that he could

not leave his ally to the mercy of what would be an angry nation and ordered a rescue mission to be put in place. The task for this was given to Captain Otto Skorzeny who specialised in unconventional warfare, under the supervision of General Kurt Student, head of the Fallschirmjaeger. Based in Rome Skorzeny had difficulty tracking down the whereabouts of the fallen dictator. Eventually a radio intercept relating to security being completed on a mountain hotel led him to believe that was where Mussolini was being held captive.

After personally reconnoitring the hotel Skorzeny planned his assault. Twelve DFS 230 gliders each with ten troops would land on the plateau by the hotel whilst commandos captured the cable car below in the valley. Mussolini, once secured would be taken by the cable car to the valley floor from where he would be flown to Vienna by a Fieseler Storch then on to Berlin.

On 12 September operation Eiche (Oak) was launched, the Fallschirmjaeger's gliders

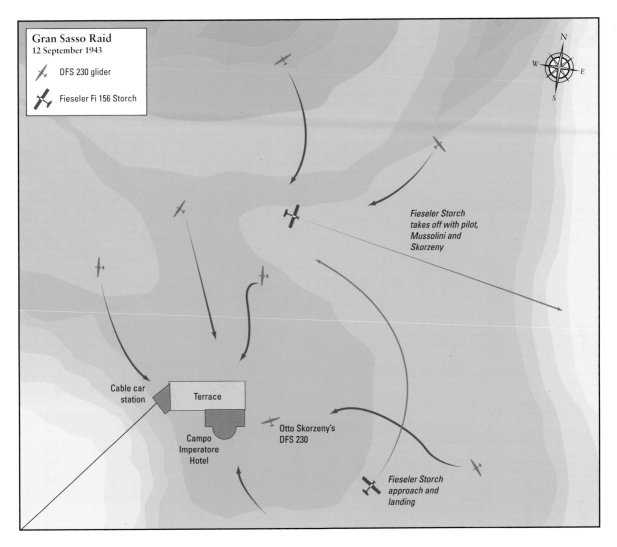

Gran Sasso Raid
12 September 1943

DFS 230 glider

Fieseler Fi 156 Storch

Fieseler Storch
takes off with pilot,
Mussolini and
Skorzeny

Cable car
station

Terrace

Campo
Imperatore
Hotel

Otto Skorzeny's
DFS 230

Fieseler Storch
approach and
landing

landing in the area of the hotel. Surprise was complete with the astonished Italian guards laying down their arms without a shot being fired. Skorzeny confidently strode up to Mussolini pronouncing his mission to come and rescue Il Duce. A problem had occurred with communications with the commandos assaulting the lower station of the cable car. It was decided by Skorzeny to fly Mussolini out directly from the mountain plateau rather than descending the cable car. A Fieseler Fi 156 Storch was brought into land amidst the crashed gliders. Only designed for a crew of two, Skorzeny insisted that he be squeezed in along with Mussolini and the pilot. The raiders watched in muted terror as the aircraft made a slow run down the hillside before plunging down into the valley below, sighs of relief were made as the small aircraft rose and struggled into the sky.

Mussolini was first flown to a north Italian airfield where he and Skorzeny transfered to a He 111. They were then flown to Vienna and a heroes welcome. German propaganda made much of the success of the raid.

OPERATION JAYWICK

At the start of 1942 the Japanese had advanced as far south as Papua New Guinea, east as far as the Solomon islands and west as far as the Indian border with Burma. The Allies were reeling from this ferocious advance but were now in a position to hit back, on the front lines with conventional forces as well as covertly with special units. One such unit that was founded was the Services Reconnaissance Department, better known as the Z Special Unit. This unit was formed mainly from Australian servicemen but also contained men from Great Britain, the Netherlands, New Zealand and from men from the South Asian islands. These men would make long range patrols, reporting back information on the enemies movements as well as perform sabotage missions whenever the opportunity arose.

At first it was thought to use these men on a raid on the main Japanese base in the south Pacific, Rabaul, on New Britain. The men would be taken to within striking distance of the harbour by a ship that could blend in with the craft of the area and then utilise canoes to breach the defence during the hours of darkness and sabotage any shipping that they could. However, this target was scrapped and a new one sought, Singapore would be the new target, deep in enemy territory.

Fourteen men were chosen for the task, four from Great Britain, the rest made up of Australians. The unit was to be led by Captain Ivan Lyon, formally of the Gordon Highlanders and now with the Allied Intelligence Bureau. A craft was found that would not arouse suspicions from the patrolling Japanese, an ex-Japanese fishing vessel named *Kafuku Maru*, was located in India. This ship, twenty-feet long and nine-feet wide was brought to Australia and supplied to the men, it was re-named *Krait*, after a particularly venomous snake from south India. The men trained with the vessel and familiarised themselves with the canoes that were specially flown in from Europe at Broken Bay on the northern tip of Australia. From here the men of what was now named Operation Jaywick sailed to the US Naval base at Exmouth Gulf in Western Australia.

On 2 September 1943 the *Krait* left the safety of Exmouth Gulf and started the hazardous voyage to Singapore harbour. The men stained their bodies brown and wore sarongs in order to look as inconspicuous as possible, their cover being that of local fishermen. They also had as few a men on deck at any one time and maintained strict radio silence at all times.

By 20 September the *Krait* had reached as near to Singapore Harbour as possible and the three canoes, with a crew of two men each were launched. The canoes were of a wood and rubber construction, with compartments for the crew and their equipment, which included Limpet mines, personnel weapons and rations, along with a cyanide capsule for each man in case they were captured. The *Krait* would continue to sail in the region and would rendezvous back with the canoes on 1 October.

The three canoes paddled to a forward operating base on an island opposite the harbour, and on the night of the 24th they attempted to cross the straits to start the raid. Strong currents meant that this raid would have to be abandoned, so the next day the men searched for a better place to launch from. This completed, the men paddled into the harbour on the 26th. The men succeeded in placing mines on seven ships, and eagerly left the harbour still under the cover of darkness. Between the hours of five and six in the morning, the men safely back in their hiding place heard the explosions that would eventually sink nearly 40,000 tons of enemy shipping. The men remained hidden as they watched the Japanese launch sea and air search parties, which were

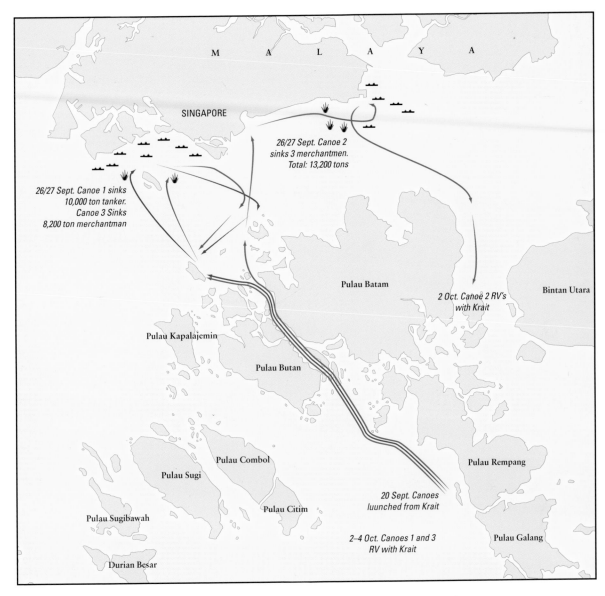

M A L A Y A

SINGAPORE

*26/27 Sept. Canoe 2
sinks 3 merchantmen.
Total: 13,200 tons*

*26/27 Sept. Canoe 1 sinks
10,000 ton tanker.
Canoe 3 Sinks
8,200 ton merchantman*

Pulau Batam

Bintan Utara

*2 Oct. Canoe 2 RV's
with Krait*

Pulau Kapalajemin

Pulau Butan

Pulau Combol

Pulau Rempang

Pulau Sugi

*20 Sept. Canoes
luunched from Krait*

Pulau Sugibawah

Pulau Citim

*2–4 Oct. Canoes 1 and 3
RV with Krait*

Pulau Galang

Durian Besar

never to locate them. After remaining hidden for a few days the men paddled to their rendezvous with the *Krait*. The mission a success the men still had to make the long and slow journey back to Western Australia. Apart from a near disaster when a Japanese destroyer came along beside the *Krait*, but decided against any search, the return journey was uneventful.

The Japanese, unable to locate the source of the attack took grave repercussions out on the local population of Singapore, suspecting local guerrillas of the sabotage.

A similar raid was launched a year later, named Operation Rimau and again led by Captain Lyon. This mission managed to sink a further three vessels, however the men of the raiding party were either killed, or after their capture, beheaded.

OPERATION SOURCE

In order for the defeat of Nazi Germany to become reality it was essential that Great Britain survived. This would be achieved by the supply lines from the USA remaining open, and in turn the convoys to the north Russian port of Archangel. This was against a tide of efficient and brutal U Boats, which hunted the Atlantic in packs. To add to this terrible threat Germany had constructed battleships, that if let loose into the Atlantic could wreak havoc amongst the convoys. One such battleship, the *Bismarck*, was hunted and eventually sunk, but with a cost of one of the Royal Navy's battlecruisers, the HMS *Hood*. *Bismarck*'s sister ship, *Tirpitz*, was an equal threat with eight 15 inch guns and had to be put out of action.

Originally *Tirpitz* had been used as part of the Baltic fleet after being commissioned in February 1941 but was deployed to Norway in order to intercept convoys travelling from Great Britain to Russia in early 1942. Her presence in Norway also acted as a fleet in being, this meant that many of the Royal Navy's assets that could be utilised elsewhere were kept in the area in case the *Tirpitz* broke out into the North Atlantic.

The German high command were wary of the *Tirpitz*'s position and were reluctant to use her in an open fight with the Royal Navy as her sister ship the *Bismarck* had been lost in 1941. However she was used in the shelling of the British weather station on Spitzbergen, the only time that the battleship would fire her main armament, after the attack she returned to her base in Trondheimfjord. Norwegian spies managed to send a message to the British informing them of the *Tirpitz*'s whereabouts. It was thought that a frogman attack, using the 'human torpedoes' of the Royal Navy known as Chariots could be put into action. Using a Norwegian fishing vessel as cover, three were stowed aboard along with seven crew and sailed for the coast off Trondheim. However on their arrival a storm blew up, the Chariots which were now being towed to a release point were lost in the heavy seas.

By September 1943 Norwegian intelligence had notified their British colleagues that the *Tirpitz* was now stationed in Kaafjord, near the town of Alta in the very north of Norway. It was thought that X Craft midget submarines could attack the ship, laying high explosive under her keel and destroy or heavily damage the battleship along with her escorts made up of the pocket battleship the *Lutzow* and the battle cruiser, *Scharnhorst*.

Six X Craft commanded by an Australian, Lieutenant Henty-Creer, left Scotland on the night of 11 September 1943 and were towed by conventional submarines to a point some 100 miles from Kaafjord. Here two of the X Craft were lost in the high seas.

Op. Source Route
20–22 September 1943

X8 scuttled

X9 Lost

X6

X7

X5   Release
X10 points

ARCTIC OCEAN

Route of X Craft & mother subs

SWEDEN

FINLAND

NORWAY

RUSSIA

UNITED KINGDOM

DENMARK

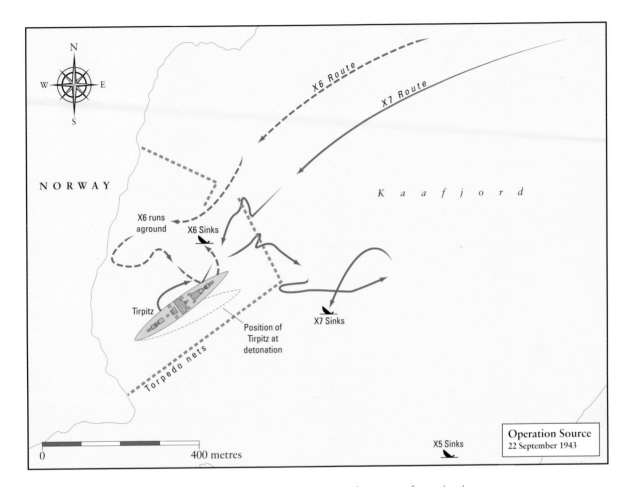

X6 Route

X7 Route

N
W E
S

NORWAY

K a a f j o r d

X6 runs
aground

X6 Sinks

Tirpitz

Position of
Tirpitz at
detonation

Torpedo nets

X7 Sinks

0   400 metres

X5 Sinks

Operation Source
22 September 1943

The remaining four made headway for Kaafjord. On 21 September the attack was ready to begin, but not before the loss of one more of the X Craft due to an electrical fault, however the other three managed to gain access into the fjord without arousing suspicion.

X6, commanded by Lieutenant Duncan Cameron managed to gain access beyond the anti-torpedo nets by shadowing a motor launch inside. Once this had been achieved they went about the attack, however they struck the bottom and had to surface, where they were immediately spotted. Before their capture the crew managed to drop their explosives below the forward part of the ship. X7 had problems when it became entangled in the netting, its crew managed to escape the net-

ting and place two charges, one forward and one amidships. Again X7 became entangled and was spotted by German surface vessels and engaged. The commander, Lieutenant Godfrey Place and one other crewman managed to escape only to be captured, the remaining crew went down with their ship. What happened to Henty-Creer and the crew of X5 remained a mystery, thought it is though that they managed to deploy their charges. Just after 08.00 the charges exploded. A massive breach was made in the *Tirpitz*'s hull, along with damage to her steering gear. She would never put to sea again, however it would be a raid by the RAF which would eventually put her out of action. Cameron and Place both received a Victoria Cross for their leadership during the raid.

SAS & SBS Operations in Italy

After the successes the SAS had in the desert, operations in the Mediterranean continued as the Allies attacked what Churchill called the, soft underbelly of the Third Reich. Unfortunately the commander of the SAS, Lieutenant Colonel David Stirling had been captured in Tunisia by the Germans. Despite escaping from his captors numerous times he would eventually sit out the rest of the war in the apparently escape-proof prisoner-of-war camp at Colditz Castle.

His successor was to be the ex-Ireland rugby player and boxer, Major Robert Paddy Mayne. A man perfectly suited to unconventional warfare, he would often be arrested for fighting whilst off duty, but would lead from the front when in action and was respected by the men he commanded. He oversaw the reorganisation of the SAS into two parts. One would become the Special Raiding Squadron, whilst the other became the Special Boat Section. Whilst the latter would move to operate in the Aegean, under the command of Lieutenant Colonel Patrick Jellicoe, the former would take part in the larger actions involved in the invasion of Sicily and Italy.

Two raids were made in support of Operation Husky, the invasion of Sicily. One was to capture high ground over-looking allied landing beaches whilst the other was to drop behind enemy lines and cause disruption. The first went off without a hitch but achieved little whilst the other was a near disaster thanks to the drop being badly scattered and having little radio communications.

The landing of the 2nd Special Service Brigade at Termoli was perhaps the largest engagement of the SAS in Italy, landing with 2 Commando and 40 (RM)Commando, the SRS captured the 91 town and set up road blocks outside of Termoli whilst they awaited reinforcement from the south.

A machine gun team of the SAS walk along a road in Italy, leaden with ammunition and equipment. The man in the centre carries a Vickers Medium machine gun whilst the man on the left carries the tripod on which it is mounted.

British Special Operations
in Italy
1943–45

AUSTRIA

YUGOSLAVIA

Trieste

Venice

Milan

GALIA TOMBOLA

Genoa
La Spezia

SPEEDWELL

POMEGRANATE

Bologna

MAPLE

Rimini

Pisaro

BAOBAB

Ancona

Florence

Urbino

CANDYTUFT

Fabriano

SAXIFRAGE

Siena

BEGONIA

Ascoli

JONQUIL

MAPLE

Terni

SLEEPY LAD

Pescara

CORSICA

ITALY

Adriatic
Sea

ROME

Termoli

Anzio

Naples

Bari

Salerno

SARDINIA

Taranto

MARIGOLD

Tyrrhenian
Sea

Bagnara

SICILY

Catania

Augusta

Syracuse

Tunis

Pantelleria
Island

Capo Murro
Di Porco

TUNISIA

SNAPDRAGON

Mediterranean Sea

0   100 km
0   100 miles

The Germans counter-attacked and were only just held off by the raiders thanks to six-pounder antitank guns brought ashore with them. Whilst a bridge was repaired by sappers the men held off concerted attacks by the 16th Panzer Division, and only after tanks arrived from the south was the town and its environs consolidated, with great losses to the men of the 2nd Special Service Brigade. The SAS did great work in returning escaped POWs and assisting Italian partisans in the north of the country towards the end of the war, aiding the difficult Allied advance.

First Chindit Raid

In 1942 Brigadier Orde Wingate, a man of with eccentric behaviour, but with a proven track record put forward a plan to organise a group of men to insert themselves in the Burmese jungle, east of the Irrawaddy river. Here they would destroy Japanese lines of communication and supply as well as ambush patrols.

Wingate had already led such groups in Palestine against Arab raiders, as he was a devout Zionist and saw it as his duty to protect the Jewish settlers in the area. At the start of the Second World War he found himself in the Sudan and again led a guerrilla-type force raiding Italian forces that were in neighbouring Ethiopia. Combining with local resistance fighters, his force, made up of British, Sudanese and Ethiopian troops managed to successfully harass the Italian occupation forces to such a degree that they were eventually pushed out of the country within months. Wingate, always outspoken, was extremely critical of his com-

manders and political superiors after the victory and was eventually posted to Rangoon to be alongside one of his close friends and allies, General Wavell, who was then commander in South East Asia. It was here that he suggested putting together a similar unit to the one he had commanded during the Abyssinian campaign.

Promoted to Brigadier, Wingate was given command of Indian 77th Infantry Brigade and immediately set about toughening up all within it to meet what would be an arduous and spectacularly dangerous mission. This would entail marching on foot through the Japanese front lines, traversing the Chindwin and Irrawaddy rivers and then going about their various tasks of sabotage and intelligence gathering, being re-supplied from the air, all whilst in the midst of a hot, wet and unforgiving jungle.

The men of the brigade, now named the Chindits, which was a corruption of a Burmese word, 'chinthe', which meant lion, left

Brigadier Orde Wingate, in his trademark Pith helmet, briefs his men.

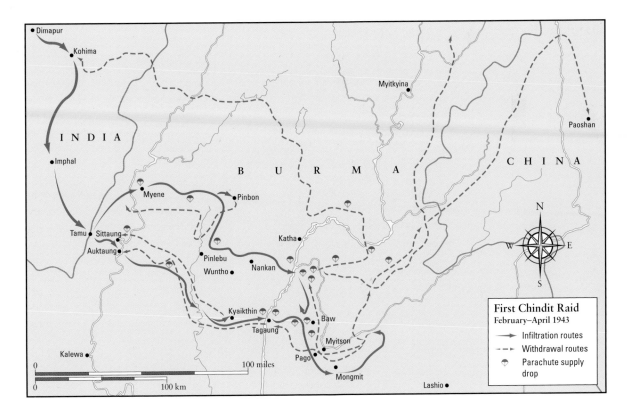

the Allied outpost at Imphal on 13 February 1943. After crossing the Chindwin river they successfully carried out sabotage attacks against several rail bridges, before Wingate ordered the brigade further behind the lines and across the Irrawaddy.

Beyond the Irrawaddy river lay an inhospitable area of the Burmese jungle, with a road network that played in favour of the Japanese. Soon the Japanese had the upper hand by intercepting the air supplies intended for the Chindits, who by now were suffering from malaria as well as extreme fatigue and shortages of food and medical supplies.

Towards the end of March, Wingate ordered that the patrol break up into smaller columns and make good their escape. Some columns were made up of large groups of men whilst some worked in pairs or even on their own. The routes back to the Allied lines varied as well, as the Japanese realised that the force

was retreating and covered any major crossing point of the Irrawaddy and Chindwin rivers, along with confiscating any river vessel that could aid the flight of what was left of the brigade. Men who were wounded in small actions with the enemy, or were too ill were simply left behind by their comrades, left with what little their friends could spare, to be left to the jungle or worse, the enemy.

By the end of April, Wingate had managed to lead a group of his men back to Allied lines, with others joining later as the weeks went by having successfully evaded the enemy. Others took a more circuitous route north via China.

The expedition cost the Chindits a third of their original 3,000 strength. Many of the survivors would be too weak to enter into action again. The patrol was deemed a failure by many but through Churchill's insistence that the British be seen to be attacking the Japanese, another patrol by the Chindits was sanctioned.

SECOND CHINDIT RAID

Following the Quebec conference of August 1943, which Wingate attended with Churchill, American support was given to a second Chindit raid into Burma. This time it would have the full resources of the USAAF behind it, being able to supply the advancing columns from the air, the Chindits would disrupt Japanese supply lines to the north of Burma as the American-led Chinese army advanced on the area, hoping to open up the China-Burma Road in the process.

This time the Chindits would be of divisional strength, being made up of no less than six brigades, numbering a total of 20,000 men. This would be supported by the newly established 1st Air Commando, which included C-47 Dakotas and CG-4 Waco gliders for transport duties, P-51 Mustang fighter-bombers and B-25 Mitchell medium-bombers for air to ground interdiction as well as light planes for the evacuation of the wounded.

The plan was to fly in half of the Chindit force to three landing zones via glider. The men in the first waves would secure the location, the second wave would reinforce the defence as well as bring in engineers who would then go about construction of airstrips that the

Chindits arrive back from their incursion into the Burmese jungle in 1944.

C-47s were capable of landing on. From these positions, named after major roads in London, New York and Calcutta; Piccadilly, Broadway and Chowringhee respectively, the men would go about sabotaging Japanese supply routes to the north and hold down reinforcements that were meant for the fighting in the north. Meanwhile a brigade of the Chindits would be marching into the combat zone from Ledo, they would march south with the aid of mules carrying their heavy equipment. These men would then split into further columns and establish more strongholds in the jungle from which to operate from.

On the evening of 5 March the airborne operation commenced, Piccadilly having to be abandoned as a landing zone due to felled trees. Gliders of 77th Brigade were flown into Broadway, commanded by Brigadier Mike Calvert. During the flight there were heavy losses due to the C-47s towing two gliders at a time. This led to the engines overheating and resulted in many ditching in the jungle. Out of the fifty-two gliders that took off in the first wave some thirty-five managed to land on Broadway and the men immediately set about securing the area and clearing the landing zone.

One month earlier 16th Brigade had left Ledo commanded by Brigadier Bernard Fergusson. These men had a tough time hacking through the thick jungle and had to make many river crossings. They eventually met with the airborne element and set about establishing another stronghold named Aberdeen and created another landing strip.

By now the Japanese had realised what was happening in their rear and flank areas and set about attacking Broadway and Chowringhee. Chowringhee was abandoned soon after but the men on Broadway held off vicious attacks from the ground as well as constant bombardment from the air, with much of the combat hand to hand.

On 24 March Wingate was killed in an aircrash whilst returning from a conference at Imphal. His replacement, Brigadier Joe Lentaigne ceded much of the decision making to US commander Colonel Joe Stilwell, who ordered the

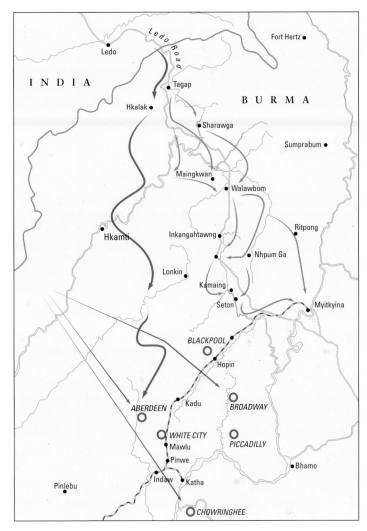

Chindits to capture various Japanese held areas which resulted in high casualties to the the men of 77th Brigade.

By the end of August nearly all the men of the various brigades were suffering from either wounds, malaria, Dysentery or a combination of them all. The force was ordered to evacuate from the region. They had managed to hold down a significant proportion of the enemy that could have swayed the result in the north to the Japanese Army, the cost however, was extremely high to the Chindits.

MERRIL'S MARAUDERS

Major General Frank Merril prepares a meal in the jungle. He commanded the Marauders until he suffered a heart attack and was evacuated.

After the Quebec conference the Americans created their own force based on this unit which would become the 5307th Composite Unit. Volunteers answered the call from units that had operated in Guadalcanal and the Solomon Islands campaign as well as men who had fought in New Guinea. These combat veterans were augmented by men fresh from the United States. Training commenced at the end of 1943 in India, with emphasis on small unit attacks, marksmanship, demolition and the clearing of trees to aid in casualty evacuation. Command was given to Major General Frank Merrill, who would give his name to the unit: 'Merrill's Marauders'. The Marauders would eventually make up three battalions, split into six combat teams totalling 3,000 men, plus mules and handlers for their heavy equipment.

On 24 May 1944 the Marauders entered Burma via the Ledo Road and a march over the Himalayas. The men immediately went about attacking the Japanese supply routes and ambushing patrols and were extremely successful in this role, taking a heavy toll on the Japanese thanks to their expert marksmanship, which had been drilled into them during their extensive training.

Early on in the campaign Frank Merrill suffered a heart attack and in late March was evacuated from Burma, his executive officer, Colonel Charles Hunter, taking command.

General Joseph Stilwell, commander of US and some Chinese forces in the theatre, encouraged by the Marauders success, ordered them further into Burma. He hoped to advance on the town of Myitkina which had the only all-weather airfield in northern Burma. Before the men could reach this target, a march of over 500 miles through thick jungle, the unit would have to fight a defensive battle at the town of Nhpum Ga. An operation for which they were poorly suited as they had no heavy artillery to back them up with, a situation that Stilwell did not fully appreciate. However the men managed to hold off attacks from the Japanese 18th Division and during early May continued their march over the Kuman Range towards Myitkina.

Outside of Myitkina the men, now assisted by two regiments of the Chinese Army assaulted Myitkina airfield. This objective was taken but the town itself was heavily defended and the Marauders were unable to capture it. What followed was a series of attacks and counter-attacks which took its toll on the men, now seriously depleted through death, injury and disease. Every single man suffered malnutrition through lack of proper rations.

Nevertheless the town was taken in early August with only 200 of the Marauders still able to fight. The men had marched over 800 miles and had fought continuously for four months behind enemy lines, the longest for any US unit in the Second World War.

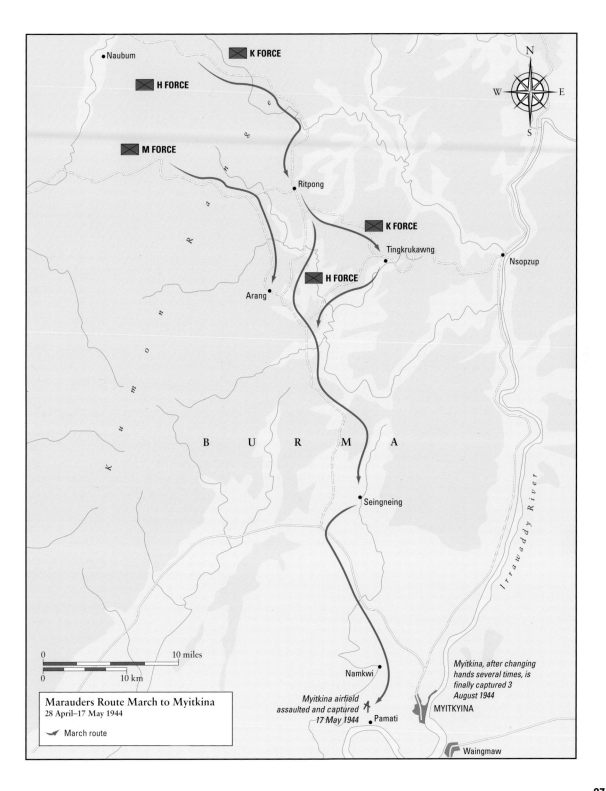

K FORCE

H FORCE

M FORCE

Naubum

N

W   E

S

Ritpong

K FORCE

Tingkrukawng

Nsopzup

H FORCE

Arang

B   U   R   M   A

Irrawaddy River

Seingneing

Myitkina, after changing
hands several times, is
finally captured 3
August 1944

Namkwi

MYITKYINA

Myitkina airfield
assaulted and captured
17 May 1944   Pamati

Waingmaw

0   10 miles

0   10 km

Marauders Route March to Myitkina
28 April–17 May 1944

March route

OPERATION JERICHO

Towards the end of 1943 many of the resistance operatives working in and around the Amiens area of northern France had been betrayed and captured by the German occupying army. These men were incarcerated in Amiens prison and 100 men were due to be shot on 19 February 1944. It was deemed necessary for the British to attempt a prison break, one that was never before, or to be seen again.

Eighteen de Havilland Mk IV Mosquito fighter-bombers were assigned to the mission. Nos. 487 RNZAF, 464 RNZAF and 21 Squadrons, all part of 140 Wing, supplying six aircraft each. Command was initially to be taken by Air-Vice Marshal Basil Embry, but due to his involvement in the planning of the invasion of Normandy, command was ceded to Group Captain Charles Pickard. The aircraft would fly to the target at low level, escorted by Typhoons of 198 Squadron, drop time-delayed bombs on the outer walls, interior walls and barracks area

A shot of Amiens prison taken by one of the attacking Mosquitoes.

of the prison. It was thought that many prisoners would perish in the raid but as they were under a death sentence this was deemed acceptable.

By the beginning of February the squadrons were ready to fly but poor weather conditions kept them grounded. By 18 February the attack could wait no longer as the resistance men were due to be executed the following day. In the morning the men were finally briefed on what their task was to be, they duly walked out to their waiting aircraft, each carrying four 500lb, 11 second time-delay bombs. The aircraft took off, with 487 squadron aircraft in the lead flight, accompanied by a special Photographic Reconnaissance Unit Mosquito equipped with cine cameras to record the event.

Weather conditions were very poor, causing some of the aircrafts crews to lose orientation and were forced to return to base. At just after noon the first aircraft of 487 Squadron approached the target, three aircraft attacking the east wall, followed shortly by two more aircraft from the same unit who hit some of the eastern most buildings.

Two aircraft from 464 squadron then attacked the eastern wall again, as it appeared to have not been breached, followed by two more 464 aircraft which hit the barracks, killing many of the German guards and prisoners alike. On seeing this final attack run, Group Captain Pickard, who had been circling the prison at 500 feet, ordered the reserve 21 Squadron to return to base as he could see men escaping into the surrounding countryside. A few minutes later Pickard and his navigator Flight Lieutenant Alan Broadley would be shot down and killed by a Focke-Wulf Fw 190. Another aircraft would also not make it home.

Of the 700 plus prisoners held captive at Amiens prison, 102 would be killed in the raid, seventy-four wounded whilst 258 would manage to escape. Though this would be short lived as many of the escapees would later be re-captured.

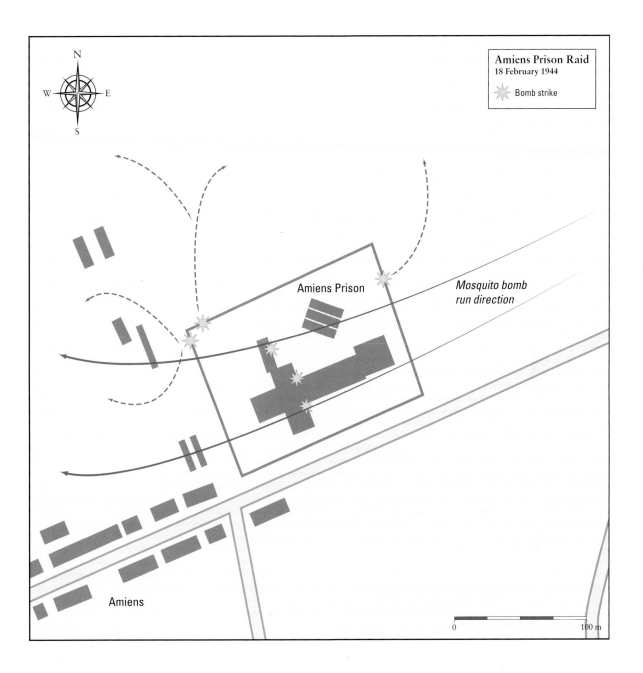

N
W E
S

Amiens Prison Raid
18 February 1944

✳ Bomb strike

Amiens Prison

Mosquito bomb run direction

Amiens

0   100 m

PARTISANS IN YUGOSLAVIA

The German invasion of Yugoslavia came about due to the failure of Mussolini's Italian forces in taking northern Greece in early 1941. Hitler, preoccupied with the impending invasion of the USSR, wanted to secure his southern flank. At first political pressure on Prince Paul of Yugoslavia seemed to work, but following a coup d'etat by the Yugoslav military, invasion was Hitler's only option. Attacking from Austria and Axis Hungary and Rumania on 6 April 1941, the German Army made quick in-roads, aided by the luftwaffe's heavy bombing of the capital Belgrade, which paralysed the Army's command and control structure. By 17 April Yugoslavia was in German hands and quickly broken up into its old divisions, Germany controlling Serbia, Croatia and Bosnia.

Many of the officers and men of the Yugoslavian Army took to the hills of the region and quickly started forming resistance groups, the first major unit of its kind was commanded by Draza Mihailovic, they would become the Chetniks. His plan was to keep down the upsurgence of Communism in the country and eventually restore the Serb-dominated monarchy,

Armed members of the Yugoslav Resistance pose for a photograph.

then after the war take revenge on those that had opposed him, especially the communists.

The Communist faction of the Yugoslav resistance was led by Josip Broz 'Tito'. He had worked for the Comintern before the conflict and was chosen by the Russian government to represent the Communist party in Yugoslavia. A civil war broke out between these two partisan groups, fighting amongst themselves as well as attacking the German occupational forces. However these attacks brought about terrible reprisals on the local population, which only acted to strengthen the resolve of the resistance. By the end of 1941 Tito could boast over 70,000 fighters to his cause. Through 1942 Tito and his forces would fight a fighting retreat into the Balkan mountains, losing many fighters along the way, before establishing a proper command structure as well as schools to teach the art of sabotage, intelligence gathering and patrolling to future officers of the 'People's Liberation Army'.

Following the insertion of SOE agents into the region support for Mihailovic dwindled as it became clear that he had been collaborating with the Germans to destroy Tito's partisans in return for arms. Allied support then quickly switched to Tito, who demanded the upmost discipline within his forces.

In 1943 the Germans launched a force of 120,000 men to hunt down and destroy the Partisans, who were eventually pushed back into the mountains of Montenegro. These partisans managed to fight their way out of the trap thanks to the training Tito had insisted on. The Partisans of Yugoslavia managed to hold down as many as 500,000 German troops that could have fought on other fronts, thanks to these actions they greatly contributed in the shortening of the war. Josip Broz Tito became the first President of Yugoslavia until his death in 1980.

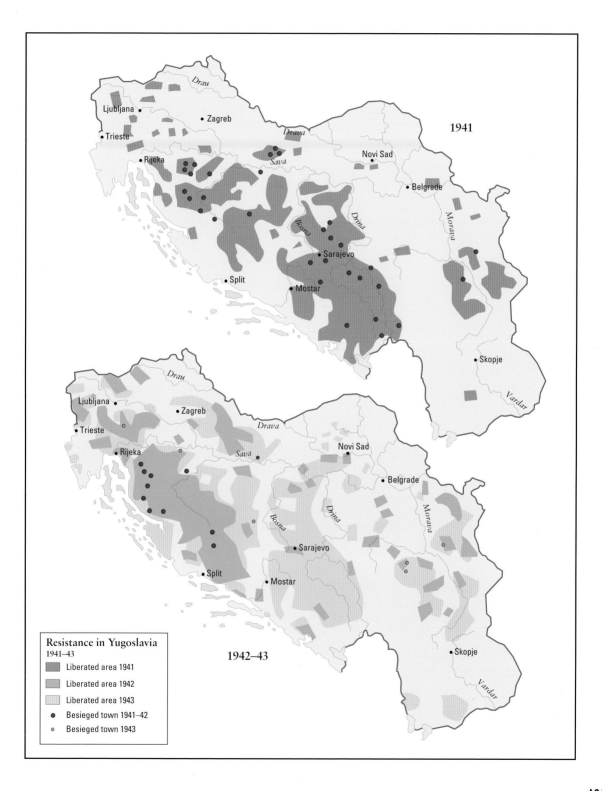

1941

1942–43

Resistance in Yugoslavia
1941–43

■ Liberated area 1941

■ Liberated area 1942

□ Liberated area 1943

● Besieged town 1941–42

○ Besieged town 1943

RESISTANCE AND SOE IN GREECE

The Greek Army had managed to hold off the Italian offensive into the country starting in October 1940. A stalemate had been created along the Greek border with Albanian, and it remained as such until the German intervention of 6 April 1941. The Germans invaded from Yugoslavia and allied Bulgaria, bypassing the Greco-Italian frontline and made a rapid advance down the mountain roads against the gradually failing defence of the Greek and Allied armies. Hitler required the pacification of the region for his upcoming assault on Soviet Russia. He did not want his southern flank left open to pro-Allied nations that could interfere with his assault. The Greeks would not react well to being occupied.

Two major resistance forces would rise from the Greek capitulation, both under differing ideologies. The first would be raised by Athanasios Klaras, an artillery major in the Greek army who had been court martialled down to corporal and sent to the Greco-Italian front. He would fight under the nom-de-guerre: Aris Velouchiotis and was of pro-communist persuasion. His group would become known as ELAS, the Greek People Liberation Army. He would walk into villages asking for their support, and would especially recruit mountain bandits, familiar with the mountainous regions of Greece.

On the other side of the political divide was EDAS, the National Republican Greek League. This was commanded by Napoleon Zervas and was anti-monarchist and pro-social democracy. This unit would operate predominantly in the Epirus region of Greece. Both forces, though fierce rivals, were sceptical of Allied support and involvement in the region.

However this was to change in mid-1942 when both units would be called upon by the SOE to aid in the destruction of a railway viaduct north of Piraeus. The Eighth Army under General Bernard Montgomery in North Africa was building up to its major offensive at El Alamein that would finally push Axis forces out of Egypt. It was thought that any disruption to the Axis supply lines would be advantageous to the assault. The Axis forces were supplied via two routes, through Italy and Sicily or through Greece. The Greek route utilised the main railroad that led through the country from Thessalonika in the north down to Athens. Three railroad viaducts were chosen as potential targets; at Gorgopotamos, Asopos and Papadice and an SOE assault team of twelve men were assembled.

The mission was to be commanded by Lieutenant Colonel Eddie Myers, splitting the group up into three groups of four, each containing a commander, an interpreter, a sapper and a radio man. The men were to be dropped by three RAF B-24 Liberators flying from Cairo on the 28 September 1942, with the hope of contacting the local resistance. Little information could be given on how to contact these parties. This was abandoned as the pre-arranged fires that were to be lit to locate the landing zones could not be found. Two days later the drop went ahead, two of the groups landing near Mount Girona whilst the third would land near the town of Karpenissi, some distance away. All the men once they hit the ground were immediately taken in by the locals and hidden from patrolling Italians, alerted by the low flying bombers.

Contact was made by the Karpenissi group, led by Major John Cooke with ELAS and they were taken to meet Velouchiotis. He was initially reticent about the raid, feeling that the main resistance was to be carried out in the occupied cities, but once he understood the strategic situation he agreed to participate.

Elsewhere a group led by Major Chris Woodhouse, second in command of the oper-

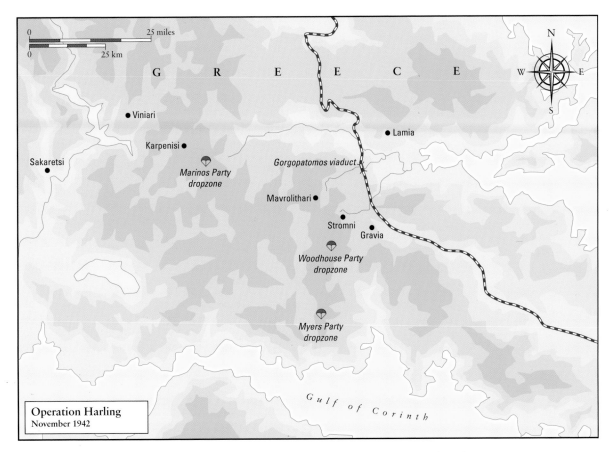

Operation Harling
November 1942

ation, made contact with EDAS and their leader Zervas, who immediately offered support and troops for the attack. Myers meanwhile was taken by local Greek guides to make a reconnaissance of the prospective targets, eventually choosing Gorgopotamos as it had the best route for infiltration and exfiltration, along with the least amount of garrison troops, about 100 Italian troops. After ten days all three groups were reunited, along with their new found allies.

The stage was set for the attack to go in on the night of 25/26 November. The Greek resistance fighters were tasked with assaulting both ends of the bridge to hold down the Italian garrison, this they did just before midnight, throwing grenades into the pillboxes at either end which kicked off an enormous firefight. Whilst this was going on above their

heads the SOE demolition team moved up the valley to the base of the viaduct. Here they attached explosives to one of the main piers. This was ignited at 01.30, causing two of the spans to drop into the valley. Deciding that more destruction could be had the demolition teams went back to attach more explosives to a remaining pier and on ignition dropped a further span. By 04.00 the attack was called off and the men withdrew, with only four wounded as a result. A day later the Italians would retaliate by executing fifteen civilians.

The attack was considered a success as it caused Hitler to move more troops from the fighting in Russia to reinforce his southern frontier, afraid that an Allied invasion may come via the Balkans and threaten his precious oilfields in Rumania. It was also a morale boost not just for the Greek people but also to SOE, proving that resistance and sabotage attacks could be fruitful.

Eddie Myers along with Chris Woodhouse, who could speak fluent Greek, were ordered to stay behind after the raid and remain as the British Military Mission to the country. The pair would again launch a similar attack on the Asopos railway bridge. This time it was a lot harder to approach as it was situated in a deep, vertical gorge and garrisoned now by German troops. With the aid of additional sappers the team of six British engineers crept down the gorge to the base of the bridge. Once here two men climbed the supports and laid the charges. They then stole away and watched with relish the destruction of the bridge. The Germans would repair the bridge in record time, thanks to enforced labour. However the first train to cross would collapse the bridge once more.

Myers would then be pulled out of Greece over political reasons but Chris Woodhouse would remain in Greece as head of the Military Mission.

The resistance on Crete was very much a thorn in the German garrisons side. Here the population were a ferociously proud people and took great offence at the German invasion of May 1941. So much so that during the airborne assault men, women and even some children took up what little arms they had, usually aged rifles or knives, and joined in the defence. This was to little effect as the Allied army was soon pushed off the island. The Cretans would not give up their island so easily though, many of the Cretan soldiers involved in the defence fleeing into mountain hideaways where they would become 'Ardartes'– mountain guerrillas. They would be aided by all of the islands inhabitants despite brutal German reprisals.

The island of Crete was of great strategic importance as it was on the supply route from Hitler's oilfields of Rumania to the battlefields of Northern Africa, this led SOE to send numerous liaison teams to assist the Cretan resistance with supply and planning.

Two such men of the SOE that would become infamous on Crete were Major Patrick Leigh Fermor and Captain Bill Stanley Moss. Fermor could speak fluent greek and was to spend over two years of the war on Crete. In Cairo these two men would meet and hatch a plan that would boost the morale of the occupied islanders whilst simultaneously lowering the morale of the German garrison. They were to capture the German Military Governor on the island, General Friedrich Wilhelm Muller, and spirit him away to Egypt. He had been guilty of committing many atrocities on the island including starving villagers into submission as well as flattening entire towns as reprisal to any attack on German troops.

Leigh Fermor was dropped on Crete on 4 February, Moss being unable to make the drop. He would rejoin Leigh Fermor the following April via motor launch from Egypt. By this time the Military Governor role had been taken by General Heinrich Kreipe, but it was thought that the kidnapping should still go ahead.

On the evening of 26 April 1944 Leigh Fermor, Moss and a kidnap team of five Ardartes set up a road block on the road from Kreipe's villa to his headquarters in Heraklion. Whilst the Cretans hid themselves in the surrounding scrub the two SOE men, dressed as German corporals awaited the arrival of the General's car. As it approached the men casually waved it down for an inspection, much to the annoyance of Kreipe, who had given specific instructions not to stop his car. As soon as Leigh Fermor identified the General, Moss coshed the driver and the Cretans jumped from their hiding places, quickly securing the general in the back. Moss then drove with Leigh Fermor posing as the general, wearing his peaked cap, through numerous checkpoints until they were through Heraklion. The team then took to the mountains in order to lose any pursuers and make the rendezvous on the southern coast of the island with a Royal Navy launch whilst Leigh Fermor

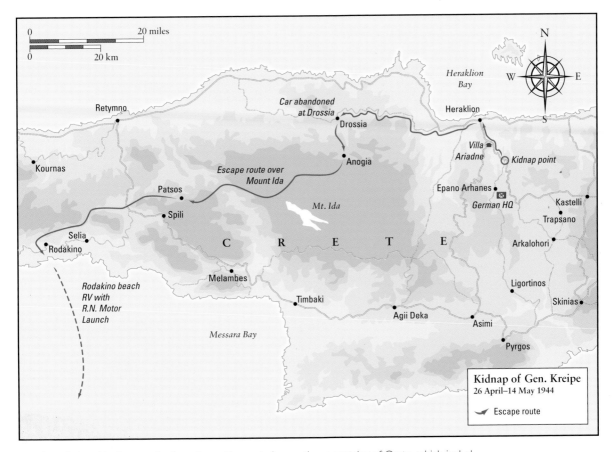

continued on with the car. Further down the road he would abandon it, leaving materials that would lead the Germans to suspect it was a British only raid, therefore averting any reprisals. Leigh Fermor would then rejoin the party in the mountains.

The Cretans supplied the General with a mule to aid his ascent of the steep mountain paths, and Leigh Fermor and Kreipe would bond over their mutual appreciation of ancient writing. As the days went by the team would take shelter near to mountain villages in order to attain supplies, happily donated by the people within them. Thanks to the network of villages the townsfolk would know of their imminent arrival and prepare, even though a large proportion of the island knew of this plan no information was ever given to the Germans in pursuit. On 14 May, after an eighteen-day trek over the mountains of Crete, which included Mount Ida, the team arrived at a beach near Rodakino where a launch picked up the General and the SOE men and took them back to Egypt.

The Germans would never break the spirit of the Cretan people and the Andartes. The Germans were often unnerved by their unwavering bravery even in the face of a firing squad. Thanks to the activities of the resistance on the island a total of 100,000 troops would be garrisoned here, troops that were desperately needed on other fronts. This was achieved at a very high cost in lives to the islanders of Crete.

RESISTANCE IN FRANCE

The German invasion of France and the low countries in May 1940 came as a great shock to the western Allies. France fell to the Germans within a month, some of the army escaping with the British through the Dunkirk evacuations, but many would become prisoners of war or simply return to their family homes. The French capitulation came as a result of political shortsightedness, apathy within the high ranks of the armed forces and an unwillingness to lose another generation of young men in a society still scarred by the conflict twenty years earlier.

After the invasion the Germans installed a puppet government to control the central and southern regions of France whilst they maintained control of the north, especially the English Channel and Atlantic coastlines. The government would become known as Vichy with Marshal Philippe Petain being controlled ostensibly from Berlin. Petain was a highly regarded member of the French government before the conflict, having been an outstanding commander of the French Army during the battle of Verdun in 1916. His government was accepted at first by the people of the French south, however, as they began to see the Vichy heavily collaborating with the Germans, with the expulsion of the Jews and the movement of French people for compulsory work in Germany, anger soon grew. By 1942 the Germans would take control of the entirety of France with the more present threat of Allied invasion from North Africa.

Resistance in France in the beginning of the war was mainly passive, with the printing of underground papers and small scale intelligence gathering and sabotage.

There were many wings of the french resistance, all operating under different political banners. The Communist elements of the french underground did not openly start operating until the German invasion of the Soviet Union in June 1941. After this they undertook several high level assassinations, but these led to harsh reprisals from the German occupiers. There were also left and right leaning movements in the resistance and it was not until late 1942 early 1943 that all these units were brought under the combined operational control of the Free French Forces, with command coming from Generals Charles de Gaulle and Henri Giraud back in Britain.

The main aim of the resistance was the supply of intelligence to the Allies back in Britain, such as troop displacements, unit numbers and prospective targets for the bombing campaign. This intelligence could also be acted on in the form of sabotage, be it with explosives or with strikes in the factories and rail networks for France. The French were also called upon to aid in the escape and evasion of downed air crew and escaped POWs. This would mean the smuggling of men through various resistance cells to the Spanish border where the men could then return to Britain.

In the south of France the Maquis would rise, these units would be made up of men familiar with the high mountain passes of the southern French Alps, who would make strikes on the German occupiers and the french anti-resistance police force that had been created to combat them: the Milice. Milice were made up of Nazi-sympathisers who would act in a similar role to the Gestapo. Investigating and discovering resistance cells then taking out brutal punishments, often resulting in the death of the Maquisard. The men of these units would later be hunted down by the resistance after the war and face reprisals of their own.

The resistance came into its own during the build up of the Allied invasion of Normandy. In the months leading up to the invasion in June 1944 the resistance would relay vast amounts of information to the Allies

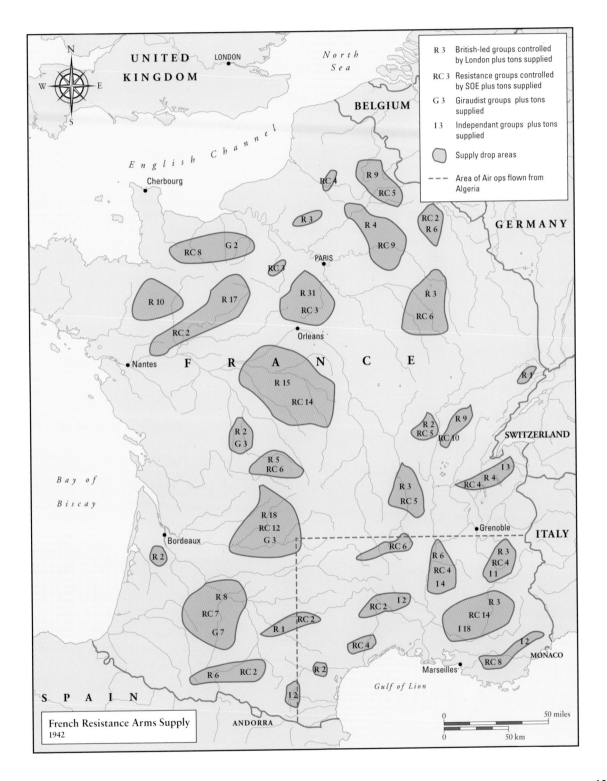

UNITED KINGDOM

LONDON

North Sea

BELGIUM

GERMANY

English Channel

Cherbourg

RC 4

R 9
RC 5

RC 2
R 6

R 3

R 4
RC 9

PARIS

RC 3

RC 8   G 2

R 10   R 17

R 31
RC 3

R 3
RC 6

RC 2

Orleans

Nantes   F   R   A   N   C   E

R 15

RC 14

R 1

R 2
G 3

R 2
RC 5

R 9

RC 10   SWITZERLAND

R 5
RC 6

I 3

R 3
RC 5

RC 4   R 4

Bay of
Biscay

R 18
RC 12

G 3

Grenoble   ITALY

Bordeaux

R 2

RC 6

R 6
RC 4
I 4

R 3
RC 4
I 1

R 8

RC 7

G 7

RC 2

R 1

RC 2   I 2

R 3
RC 14
I 18

I 2

MONACO

RC 4

RC 8

R 6   RC 2

R 2

Marseilles

Gulf of Lion

SPAIN

I 2

ANDORRA

French Resistance Arms Supply
1942

R 3   British-led groups controlled
by London plus tons supplied

RC 3   Resistance groups controlled
by SOE plus tons supplied

G 3   Giraudist groups plus tons
supplied

I 3   Independant groups plus tons
supplied

        Supply drop areas

- - -   Area of Air ops flown from
Algeria

0   50 miles

0   50 km

which would be vital to the success of the assault. This would entail detailed information on the German defences of the Normandy coast that could not be assessed from aerial reconnaissance, as the Germans were superb at camouflaging their strongpoints, particularly in built up areas. This information would be relayed via radio messages sent by pianistes. These men had an extremely dangerous job as the Germans constantly surveyed for radio signals, and if captured they had little chance of survival. Likewise the British and French intelligence commanders would communicate to the resistance through the BBC World Service, using poetry verses as code to warn of upcoming events.

Sabotage was also an important contribution made by the resistance. In the build up to the invasion hundreds of railroad bridges were attacked, rail lines, locomotives and marshalling yards would by destroyed and the communications network brought down. This would all work to stop the Germans from reacting efficiently to the invasion. With communications down the outlook to the high command would be muddled and any hope of reinforcement to the front would be severely hampered.

After the invasion itself the resistance role did not end. They continued to work behind the Allied lines, often in conjunction with special forces such as the SAS, raiding German convoys and continuing to sabotage transport and communications links. On 25 August Paris was liberated by the French 2nd Armoured Division. Aiding its arrival in the capital was the resistance, aggressively attacking the German occupiers, along with the strikes of the Metro and law enforcement. After the Liberation of France General Eisenhower would liken the contribution of the French resistance to the equivalent of fifteen army divisions. It would also stand as a symbol for the French population to be proud of in their fight against Nazi aggression and oppression. and the un-patriotic regime of Vichy France.

A derailed train as a result of resistance activity.

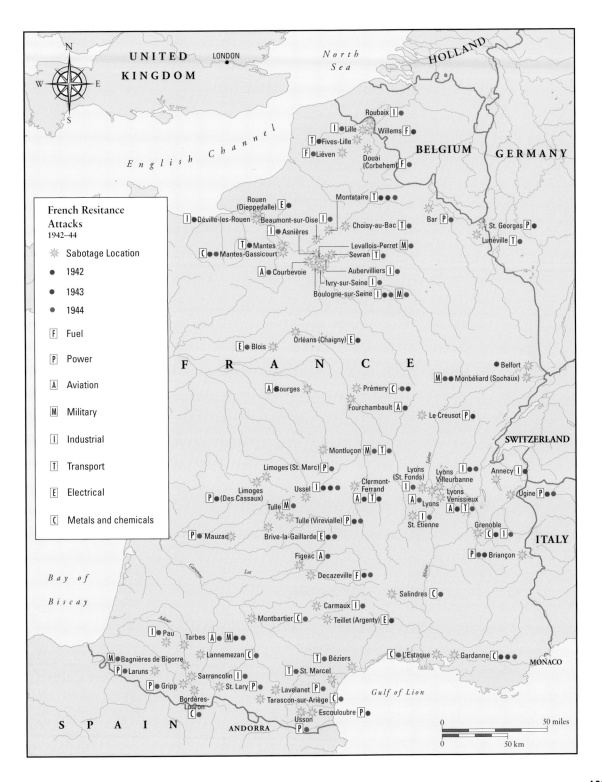

French Resistance
Attacks
1942–44

✳ Sabotage Location

● 1942

● 1943

● 1944

F Fuel

P Power

A Aviation

M Military

I Industrial

T Transport

E Electrical

C Metals and chemicals

UNITED KINGDOM

LONDON

North Sea

HOLLAND

English Channel

BELGIUM

GERMANY

Roubaix I
Lille I
Willems F
Fives-Lille T
Liéven F
Douai (Corbehem) F
Montataire T ● ● ●
Bar P
St. Georges P
Lunéville T

Rouen (Dieppedalle) E
Déville-les-Rouen I
Beaumont-sur-Oise I
Asnières I
Choisy-au-Bac T
Levallois-Perret M
Mantes T
Sevran T
Mantes-Gassicourt C
Courbevoie A
Aubervilliers I
Ivry-sur-Seine I
Boulogne-sur-Seine I ● M

F R A N C E

Blois E
Orléans (Chaigny) E
Belfort ●
Monbéliard (Sochaux) M ● ●
Bourges A
Prémery C ● ●
Fourchambault A
Le Creusot P ●

Montluçon M T

SWITZERLAND

Limoges (St. Marc) P
Ussel I ● ● ●
Clermont-Ferrand A T
Lyons (St. Fonds) I
Lyons Villeurbanne I
Annecy I
Limoges (Des Cassaux) P ●
Tulle M
Lyons A
Lyons Venissieux A T
Ugine P ● ●
Tulle (Virevialle) P ●
Brive-la-Gaillarde E ● ●
St. Etienne A T
Grenoble C I
Mauzac P ●
Figeac A
Briançon P ● ●
Decazeville F ● ●
Salindres C ●
Carmaux I
Montbartier C
Teillet (Argenty) E
Pau I
Tarbes A M ● ●
L'Estaque C
Gardanne C ● ● ●
MONACO
Bagnières de Bigorre M
Lannemezan C
Béziers T
Laruns P
Sarrancolin I
St. Marcel T
Gripp P
St. Lary P
Lavelanet P
Gulf of Lion
Bordères-Louron C
Tarascon-sur-Ariège C
Escouloubre P
ANDORRA
Usson P

ITALY

Bay of Biscay

Adour

Garonne

Lot

Saône

Rhône

S P A I N

0   50 miles
0   50 km

OPERATION POSTAGE ABLE

As the planning for the invasion of Europe commenced it was realised that there were few accurate maps and little information on the target beaches for the proposed invasion area—the Baie de la Seine and beaches off the coast of Normandy. Aerial photographs were readily available and these were ideal for identifying road networks and the layout of towns and fields. However these photos could not give an accurate representation of the topography of the Normandy beach-heads. Low flying Spitfire reconnaissance planes taking pictures at oblique angles could supply some information but had limitations.

The BBC came to the rescue with the launch of an appeal to the general public for their picture postcards showing the entire French coast, from Dunkirk in the north east to Biarritz in the south west. The response was overwhelming and was an information coup. Planners could see what type of buildings faced the beaches where the troops planned to come ashore and could identify draws off the beach and into the countryside beyond. This would be vital in order to avoid a massacre on the beach, as this is where the majority of the German defence would be pointed.

Information on the displacements of enemy units that would be opposing the landings were supplied by members of the French resistance, who supplied thousands of written reports on troop movements and the construction of beach defence, airfields and blockhouses. This prior knowledge would be essential to the success of the campaign.

The state of the beaches had also to be assessed, as military planners needed to know if the sand would be able to support heavy tanks being unloaded, as well as low

An X-Craft similar to the type used during Operation Postage Able. The craft held three crew and two divers.

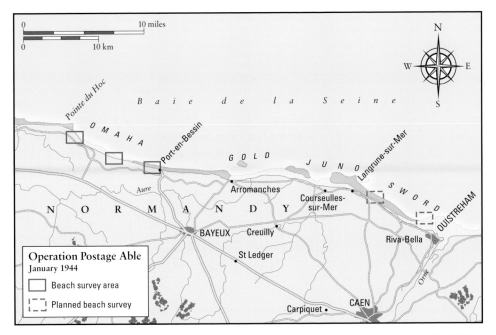

and high tide marks along with the speed of the tide. A mission to assess the beach at what would become known as GOLD beach was first carried out by two men of the Royal Engineers; Major Logan Scott-Bowden and Sergeant Bruce Ogden-Smith. On the evening of 30 December 1943/1 January 1944 the two men were taken by motor torpedo boat to the Normandy coast. From a safe distance they proceeded to swim the remaining distance to the beach. Here they took samples of the sand, which they discovered to be quite light and supported by peat bog. They also took the advantage of assessing what kind of defence the Germans had erected to defend against attack. This mission led to the British designing tanks that could lay down heavy matting and therefore not become bogged down in the soft sand.

After the success of this mission another was launched on January 16 1944. This would be known as Operation Postage Able and would be used to assess the beaches along the coast from Vierville-sur-Mer to Port-en-Bessin and off the Lion-sur-Mer area,

these beaches would be known as OMAHA and SWORD respectively.

They travelled by X-Craft, a small submersible crewed by three men of the Combined Operations Pilotage Party, along with the two divers, Scott-Bowden and Ogden-Smith. During the hours of daylight the men took soundings along the coastline to discover the depths off the coastline, at night the two divers would swim ashore and again took sand and soil samples for study. The men were working around the clock right under the noses of the enemy and with little sleep, being kept awake and alert with the use of Benzedrine tablets. The third night the operation was cancelled due to extreme exhaustion but was still considered a success due to the information gathered. Without which the invasion could have gone the other way.

Scott-Bowden and Ogden-Smith would return on the dawn of D-Day, again in an X-Craft which was used to lead the American troops into OMAHA beach, avoiding obstacles and sand bars.

OPERATION OVERLORD

After the Casablanca and Tehran conferences between the leaders of the 'Big Three', the United States, USSR and Great Britain, planning was put into place to open up a second front by the summer of 1944. The planners had to find a site in northwest Europe, between Brest in western France and the Low Countries. This area needed to have firm enough beaches to have thousands of troops, transports and armour flowing over them to reinforce the beachhead, while also being within range of the protective umbrella of Allied fighter bombers flying from airfields in southern England. It also had to be within easy reach of a major port facility that could be quickly captured and brought into use to aid in the Allied build up. The site chosen for this task that filled all those criteria was the Normandy coastline between Ste. Mare Eglise in the west to Ouistreham in the east.

The overall commander for the assault was General Dwight D. Eisenhower, an American as the majority of the forces employed after the initial assault would be from the United States. His land commander was General Bernard Montgomery of desert fame, whilst Admiral Sir Bertram Ramsey would command the naval forces and Air Chief Marshall Sir Trafford Leigh-Mallory would command the air forces.

The Beaches would be assaulted by the 1st US Army and the 2nd British Army, commanded by General Omar Bradley and General Miles Dempsey respectively. The combined British and Canadian forces, supplemented by various Free French, Polish and Dutch units would attack three beaches in the east, GOLD near Arromanches, JUNO near Courseulles-sur-Mer and SWORD at Lion-sur-Mer. The US Forces would take two beaches between Vierville and Colleville named OMAHA and opposite Ste. Mare

Eglise named UTAH. The flanks of the assault would be protected by airborne drops in and around Ste. Mare Eglise by the 101st and 82nd US Airborne Divisions and by the British and Canadian 6th Airborne Division just east of the Caen-Ouistreham Canal.

Defending against this attack was Field Marshal Gerd von Rundstedt, C-in-C West. His subordinate in the invasion area

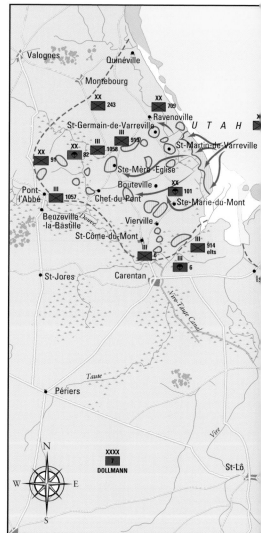

was Field Marshal Erwin Rommel, in charge of Army Group B. Rommel immediately leaped into action following his appointment in early 1944, touring the proposed invasion beaches and increasing the amount of static defences manyfold. He believed that the battle would be won or lost on the beaches, if the Allies could be stopped and driven back into the sea, without establishing a foothold then the victory would fall to the Germans, if not, Allied victory would be inevitable.

By the eve of the invasion nearly 7,000 ships of all shapes and sizes had been assembled to carry over the initial 5 Divisions that would hit the beaches in the early morning of 6 June. Many of the units would be untested, having been training for the very day in the US or Britain for over two years. A few units would be going in with experience, such as the US 1st Division, or the 'Big Red One', at OMAHA. Nearly 24,000 airborne troops would also land in the early hours of 6 June hoping to capture vital positions. This would be indeed, the Day of Days.

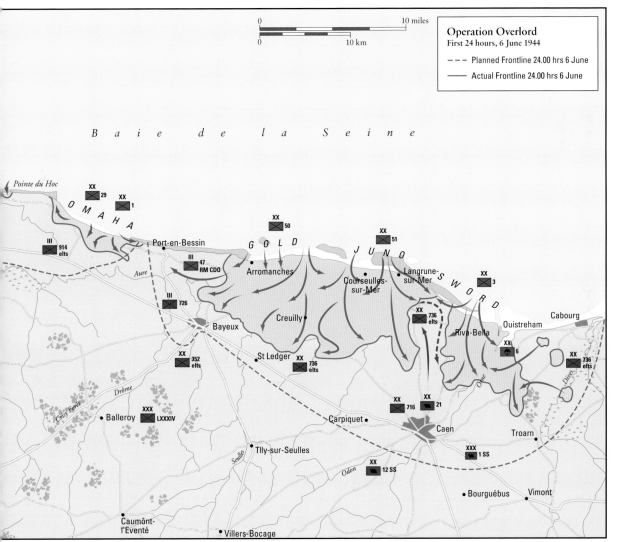

Operation Overlord
First 24 hours, 6 June 1944
- - - Planned Frontline 24.00 hrs 6 June
—— Actual Frontline 24.00 hrs 6 June

6TH AIRBORNE

The 6th Airborne Division was raised by the War Office in April of 1943, and command was given to Major General Richard 'Windy' Gale formally of the 1st Airborne Brigade. The number of the division was intentionally misleading, making the Germans believe that the British had six airborne divisions, the 6th only being in fact the second airborne division of the British Army. By early 1944 the division was up to a full strength of 12,000 men split up into three brigades, the 3rd and 5th Parachute and the 6th Airlanding. Training immediately commenced for the upcoming invasion of France.

The 6th Airborne Division was ordered to carry out a similar task to it's American cousins to the west of the invasion. They were to drop on the eastern flank of the task force and destroy or capture strategic bridges, sabotage coastal batteries and form a defensive line to halt any German reinforcement or assault on the flanks.

The first mission was for two bridges, over the Caen Canal and the Orne river, to be captured in tact, in order for the rapid dispersal of troops and armour coming off the beaches in the Sword area to consolidate the Allied eastern flank. These two bridges were to be captured in a Coup de Main operation by 6 platoons drawn from the 2nd Battalion Oxfordshire and Buckinghamshire Light Infantry. These platoons would be inserted just after midnight in six Horsa gliders, three per bridge. They would take control of the bridge, dispose of any demolition charges and wait for reinforcement from the 5th Parachute Brigade landing an hour later to the east of them.

The second mission was for the destruction of a major coastal battery at Merville consisting of four heavy casemates containing 150mm guns that could cause massive destruction amongst the invasion fleet off the Normandy coast. The destruction was tasked to Lieutenant Colonel Terence Otway's 9th Parachute Battalion.

The third and final task was for the destruction of four bridges over the River Dives and a fifth over a small stream near Varraville in order to halt or hamper any enemy advance from the east. Whilst all these operations were being undertaken the remainder of the division would be making a defensive line between the Orne and Dives rivers making preparations to halt any German movement from the south and east.

At 00.16 hours on 6 June 1944 the first glider of the coup de main party at the bridge over the Caen Canal at Benouville touched down. Piloted by Staff Sergeants Wallwork and Ainsworth, it landed within 50 yards of the bridge. Air Vice-Marshal Trafford Leigh-Mallory would later say that this was one of the most outstanding flying achievements of the war. The men, commanded by Major John Howard, soon took control of the bridge and after a brief firefight set about creating a defensive perimeter. A similar feat was achieved a few hundred yards away at the river bridge, although one of the assault parties gliders landed some miles off target. In Benouville village, west of the canal bridge, there had been some tough fighting as the paras cleared out the defenders, this led the German commander in Caen to send an armoured column to investigate. As the lead mark IV tank neared the T-junction at the bridge it was hit by an anti-tank PIAT round fired by one of the paras, setting the tank ablaze. This forced the Germans to retire for some time allowing for the bridge to be heavily reinforced by the men of 7th Parachute Battalion. Fighting in and around the bridge area would continue for the rest of 6 June, including an air attack on the bridge itself, to no effect. The men defending these important bridges were relieved by the 1st Special Service Brigade in the early afternoon of 6 June.

Meanwhile the mission to destroy the battery at Merville was not going to plan. Lieutenant Colonel Otway's 9th Battalion had been badly dispersed and by they time the had to move to his start line he had only managed to assemble 150 of the 650 men intended for the assault. Due to time constraints, if the naval commanders had not received notice that the battery had been destroyed a massive barrage from the outlying ships would be laid down at dawn, Otway had no choice but to continue. With fewer men and equipment than he anticipated, he led his men towards the battery. Here he assigned a few men to the east of the battery to put in a diversionary attack whilst the bulk of the force made an assault from the south. Two paths were cleared through the minefields using bangalore torpedoes and the men of the

9th Battalion stormed the casemates, being torn to shreds by the defenders numerous machine guns. Under this intense fire the men nevertheless managed to reach and clear out the casemates, discovering that the guns were not in fact 150mm coastal guns, but aging 100mm guns of First World War vintage. They set about disabling the guns as best they could then withdrew, not having any means in which to send the success signal. fifty men were killed in the assault with a further twenty being badly injured.

The destruction of the bridges went slightly better, with the sappers of the 8th Parachute and the 1st Canadian Parachute Battalions making their way to the various targets on jeeps that had landed with the gliders, all the bridges were destroyed before daybreak.

The bulk of the Division that was

Paratroops of the British 6th Airborne Division.

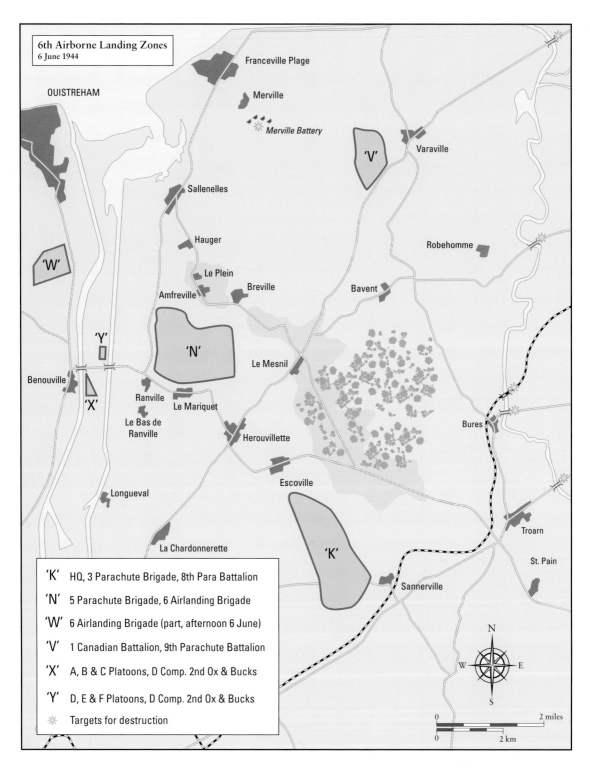

6th Airborne Landing Zones
6 June 1944

OUISTREHAM

Franceville Plage

Merville

Merville Battery

Varaville

'V'

Sallenelles

Hauger

Robehomme

Le Plein

Breville

Bavent

Amfreville

'W'

'Y'

'N'

Le Mesnil

Benouville

'X'

Ranville

Le Mariquet

Le Bas de
Ranville

Herouvillette

Bures

Longueval

Escoville

Troarn

La Chardonnerette

'K'

St. Pain

Sannerville

'K'   HQ, 3 Parachute Brigade, 8th Para Battalion

'N'   5 Parachute Brigade, 6 Airlanding Brigade

'W'   6 Airlanding Brigade (part, afternoon 6 June)

'V'   1 Canadian Battalion, 9th Parachute Battalion

'X'   A, B & C Platoons, D Comp. 2nd Ox & Bucks

'Y'   D, E & F Platoons, D Comp. 2nd Ox & Bucks

✳   Targets for destruction

N
W   E
S

0   2 miles

0   2 km

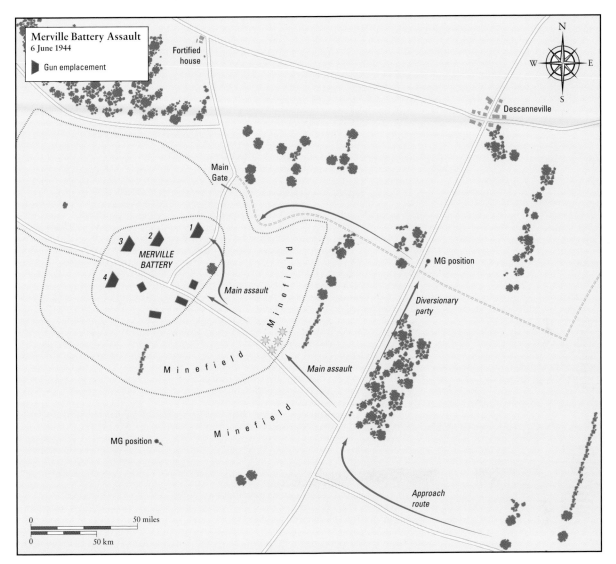

Merville Battery Assault
6 June 1944

◣ Gun emplacement

Fortified house

Descanneville

Main Gate

N
W E
S

3 2 1
MERVILLE BATTERY
4

Main assault

Minefield

Minefield

MG position

Diversionary party

Main assault

MG position

Minefield

Approach route

0   50 miles
0   50 km

landing after midnight on 6 June were badly dispersed, the Pathfinders that were dropped before them being dropped in the wrong area due to poor pilot navigation, bad weather conditions and flak. Nevertheless the men went about their tasks in small units, causing mayhem and panic within the German rear areas. By dawn all the tasks alloted to the division had been carried out with great success as the morning light not only brought the landings on the beaches but further reinforcement from the air in the form of heavy Hamilcar gliders bringing in ultra-light tanks and jeeps as well as ammunition and much needed communications equipment. For the first week after the invasion the Division defended against major assaults from the German defenders, wanting to roll up the Allied flank. The airborne troops repulsed all the assaults but with heavy losses. The men then were kept as ground troops, even though they were not equipped to fight in such a role, until the end of August when they were eventually taken out of the line.

101ST & 82ND AIRBORNE

The 101st 'Screaming Eagles' Airborne Division, commanded by Major General Maxwell Taylor was tasked with landing on the western-most flank of the Allied invasion of France. They were a green unit, having not yet seen any action in the war, but they had been training solidly in England for nearly a year to show what they were capable of and were keen to literally jump into the action.

The division was tasked with the capture of causeways between St-Martin-de-Varreville and Pouppeville leading off the invasion beach codenamed Utah, these were vital as the areas behind the beaches had been inundated by the Germans and the raised roadways were the only way of getting the armour off the beaches. The division also had to capture a large barracks area in the vicinity of St-Martin-de-Varreville known as objective XYZ which housed the troops that serviced a large coastal battery, which the paratroopers were also expected to destroy. Other units were to move further south and capture a river lock at La Barquette near Carentan to prevent

the Germans opening it and flooding the Douve river valley. Whilst carrying out these tasks the men would also set up road blocks and destroy enemy lines of communication and key bridges over the Douve river that would aid in the enemies assault on the invasion beaches and link up with the men of the 82nd Airborne Division to protect the flanks of the invasion. They would hold these positions until relieved by the men and tanks of the 4th Infantry Division coming off Utah beach.

Preceding the three Parachute Infantry Regiments of the division would be pathfinders, landing on three designated drop zones, equipped with lights and 'Eureka' radio transponders that would communicate with the 'Rebecca' receivers located on the transport planes bringing in the division. The Troop Carrier wings flying the division in would fly south from England towards the Channel islands, from here they would turn east and cross the Cotentin coast at Portbail, leaving themselves less susceptible to flak concentrated over the east Normandy coast.

In the first few minutes of June 6 the Troop Carrier C-47s approached the coast of Normandy to find a heavy cloud bank. This made navigation almost impossible, many of the pilots navigating themselves as there was a lack of trained navigators aboard the transports. The pilots flew lower and were met with extremely heavy flak, this combined with not being able to locate the pathfinders meant that the drop was badly scattered, most men did not land within a mile of their designated drop zone, some as far as twenty or thirty miles as the pilots of the transports desperately dodged the incoming flak. Some poor paratroopers were disgorged above the English Channel where they had little chance of survival with the amount of kit they were carrying. The first battle in those early hours was the hunt by individuals to find their parent unit as they dodged German patrols.

Men of the 101st Airborne Division sit in their C-47 transport aircraft en route to Normandy. The man on the right is armed with an M1 'Bazooka'.

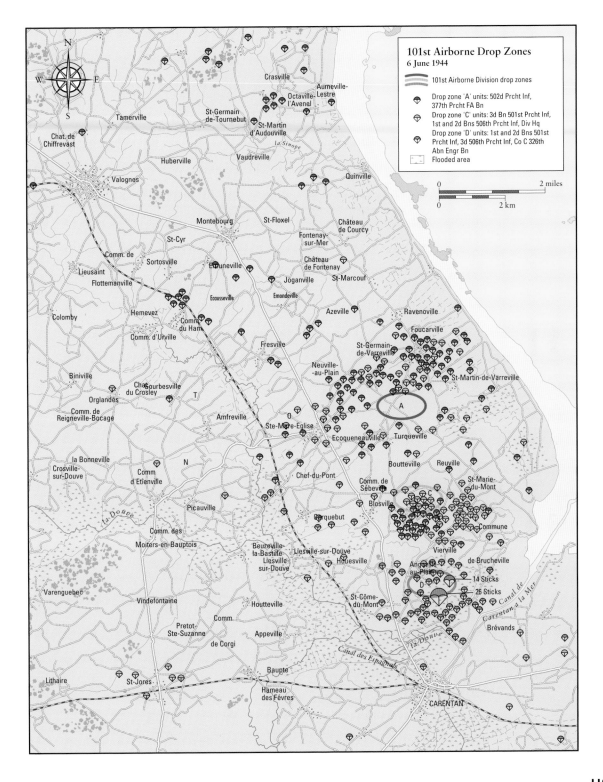

101st Airborne Drop Zones
6 June 1944

101st Airborne Division drop zones

Drop zone 'A' units: 502d Prcht Inf, 377th Prcht FA Bn

Drop zone 'C' units: 3d Bn 501st Prcht Inf, 1st and 2d Bns 506th Prcht Inf, Div Hq

Drop zone 'D' units: 1st and 2d Bns 501st Prcht Inf, 3d 506th Prcht Inf, Co C 326th Abn Engr Bn

Flooded area

0   2 miles

0   2 km

The 502nd PIR were badly dispersed but still managed to go about their missions of capturing exits off Utah and seizing the XYZ objective. The XYZ assault was carried out by a small group of men led by a staff sergeant Harrison Summers. He led fifteen men against much larger enemy force, moving through the complex of buildings and eventually clearing out over 100 German soldiers. It was thanks to the training and courageous spirit along with personnel initiative indoctrinated into these fighting men that these tasks were completed.

The men of the 506th PIR were again badly dispersed, many falling in the 82nd's area and vice versa. Again these men went about the tasks given them despite their lack of numbers and coherent command structure, they still managed to secure causeways near le Chemin. The men of the 501st also managed to capture La Barquette lock before the Germans could realise it's potential for disruption. However the men could not destroy the bridges over the Douve.

Though the men of the division were badly scattered during the drop, they managed to cause the upmost of destruction and panic in the German area, the Germans believing that they where under attack from a much larger force in some areas, whilst some believing that it was just a small commando raid of some sort. Chaos was total.

By dawn of June 6 the regiments

US paratroopers advance into a Norman village.

would only grow in strength as stragglers made their way to their units and reinforcements came in in the form of the two glider regiments. These two regiments suffered badly in the landings as many of their Waco gliders were overladen and were difficult to fly after they cast off from their tow aricraft. Combined with the high hedges of the Norman countryside, known as 'Bocage', the crews and their passengers suffered high casualties. Nevertheless the survivors constituted vital reinforcement to a precarious position.

The 82nd Airborne Division had already seen action in the Mediterranean theatre and were to drop one hour after the arrival of the 101st Airborne. The division was tasked with dropping either side of the Merderet river to capture causeways across the river to block any German reinforcement from the west to the invasion beaches at Utah and Omaha. They also had to capture the important crossroads town of Saint Mare Eglise, holding it until relieved by the infantry and tanks coming off the beaches.

The 505th Parachute Infantry Regiment had the most accurate drop of the invasion whilst landing on DZ 'O' just to the west of their target, Saint Mare Eglise. Unfortunately some of the men of this unit fell into the town as the townsfolk and the German garrison troops were fighting a house fire. This served to illuminate the falling troopers and many were killed as they descended. Two troopers were caught up on the church spire of the town, and though wounded and sitting targets, they both survived the battle. After sparodic street fighting the town was taken by the 505th, the men being ordered to protect its southern flank whilst a strengthened platoon was sent north to the village of Neuville-au-Plain to prevent counter-attacks from that direction. This platoon beat off concerted counter-attacks from a much larger German force for two days, with only a few 57mm anti-tank guns, Bazookas and personnel weapons.

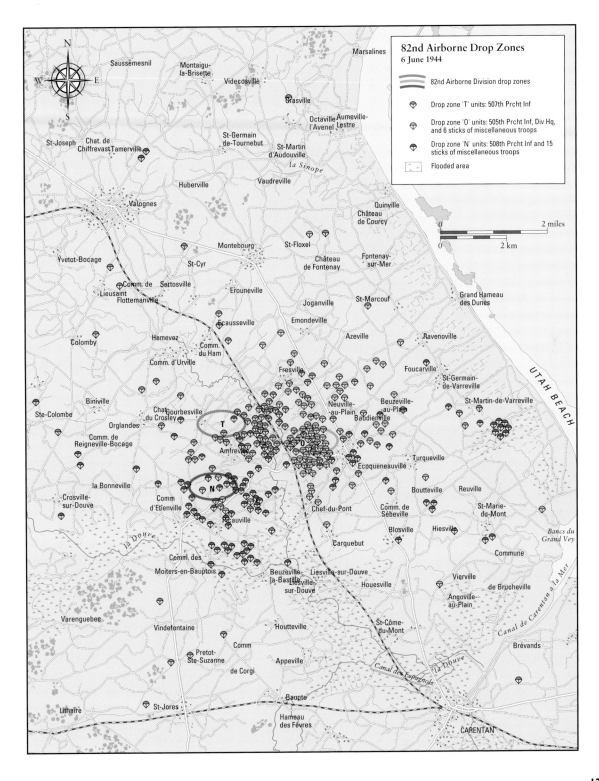

82nd Airborne Drop Zones
6 June 1944

≡≡≡ 82nd Airborne Division drop zones

⊕ Drop zone 'T' units: 507th Prcht Inf

⊕ Drop zone 'O' units: 505th Prcht Inf, Div Hq, and 6 sticks of miscellaneous troops

⊕ Drop zone 'N' units: 508th Prcht Inf and 15 sticks of miscellaneous troops

▱ Flooded area

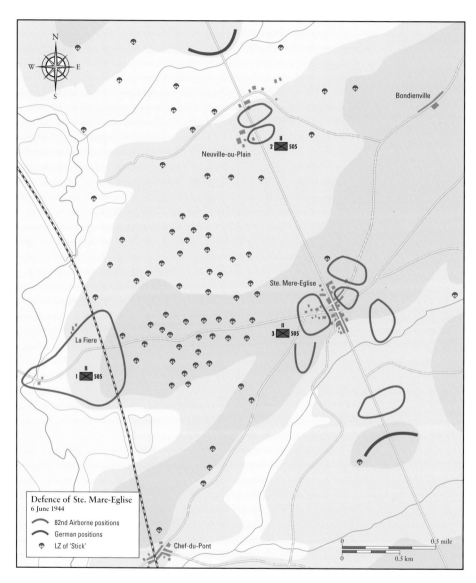

Defence of Ste. Mare-Eglise
6 June 1944

⌒ 82nd Airborne positions

⌒ German positions

⊕ LZ of 'Stick'

To the west the 507th and 508th PIR faired much worse, with badly scattered drops, many falling into the flood plain of the Merderet river, resulting in many men drowning. Much of the 507th came down in the 101st Divisions area of operations so were temporarily attached to units of that division during the initial fighting of the invasion. Many troops of the 508th led by the deputy divisional comander General James Gavin utilised the Railway embankment to orientate themselves and converged on the 1st Battalion, 505th positions around La Fiere Bridge. This unit was attempting to cross the causeway and prevent its use to the Germans, but were beaten back with heavy losses several times, despite managing to make a small lodgement on the western bank. Gavin dispatched troops further south to capture the causeway opposite the village of Chef du Pont whilst further attacks were made to cross the bridge at La Fiere. The Germans counter-attacked the paratroopers' positions around this causeway for several days, with extremely high losses on both sides. With the discovery of a sunken roadway to the north of the causeway Gavin ordered the glidermen of the 327th GIR to flank the position following a major artillery bombardment, with men of the 508th making a direct assault across the causeway. On 9 June, following this very bloody engagement the bridge was in Allied hands.

Further to the south the 2nd Battalion of the 508th, led by Lieutenant Colonel Thomas Shanley had captured a strategic point known as Hill 30. This overlooked the approach to the Chef du Pont causeway

and thanks to the unit's actions prevented the Germans from making any concerted attacks on the bridge. This unit held out for two days, despite numerous German attempts to dislodge them until relieved.

Elsewhere on D-Day a small unit action took place near Brecourt Manor in the 101st sector. Lieutenant Dick Winters along with 'E' Company of the 506th PIR was tasked with the destruction of a German battery that was firing on the causeways to Utah beach. Winters set up two machine guns to lay down covering fire whilst a section attacked the first gun with grenades. This was then destroyed with TNT set off by German stick grenades. The men then moved systematically down the battery, utilising the Germans own trench system to cover their advance. The last gun was taken by reinforcements from 'D' Company.

One of the worst mis-drops of the invasion happened to the men of 3rd Battalion, 507th PIR along with a platoon of the 501st PIR.

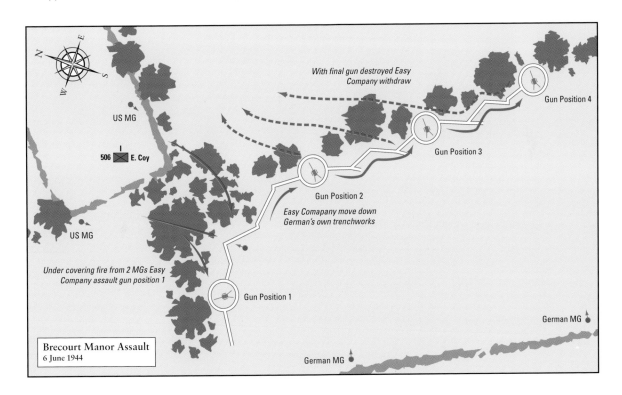

Brecourt Manor Assault
6 June 1944

US MG

506 E. Coy

US MG

Under covering fire from 2 MGs Easy Company assault gun position 1

Gun Position 1

German MG

With final gun destroyed Easy Company withdraw

Gun Position 4

Gun Position 3

Gun Position 2

Easy Comapany move down German's own trenchworks

German MG

They were to be dropped near to Amfreville but due to the heavy fog and flak they landed some 20 miles to the south near the small village of Graignes. The men converged on the village and it was decided by the groups leader, Major Charles Johnston, that the unit should remain in the village and defend it until a link up could be made with troops coming off the beaches. By the morning of 6 June the men defending the village numbered some 180. The men, being aided by the villagers set about creating feilds of fire in all directions. Contact with a lead element of the 17th SS Panzergrenadier Division was made on 10 June. The following day two attacks were held off by the paratroopers, however Johnston was killed in an artillery barrage that preceeded the final German assault. During this assault, with ammunition dangerously low the surviving paratroopers evacuated the village with the hope of making American lines. The German troops who then took over the village took horrific reprisals on the local population, executing wounded paratroopers and the villagers suspected of aiding the defenders. This action did slow the advance of the 17th SS Division, that could have made the fighting around the town of Carentan much harder for the men of the 101st tasked with its capture.

The capture of Carentan was vital in the linking up of the two American beacheads being a major crossroads town. The Germans held it with two battalions from the 6th Fallschirmjaeger Regiment along with what remaianed of the 91st Airlanding Division. Tasked with the town's capture were the men of the 101st. The attack started on 10 June with a double envelopment, the 327th GIR approaching the town from the north east whilst the 502nd approached from the north west. Both had to negotiate several water obstacles under intense fire before reaching the outskirts of the town the 502nd taking part in a bayonet charge to break the defensive line.

Men of the US Airborne pose for a photo with a souvenir picked up during the fighting in Normandy.

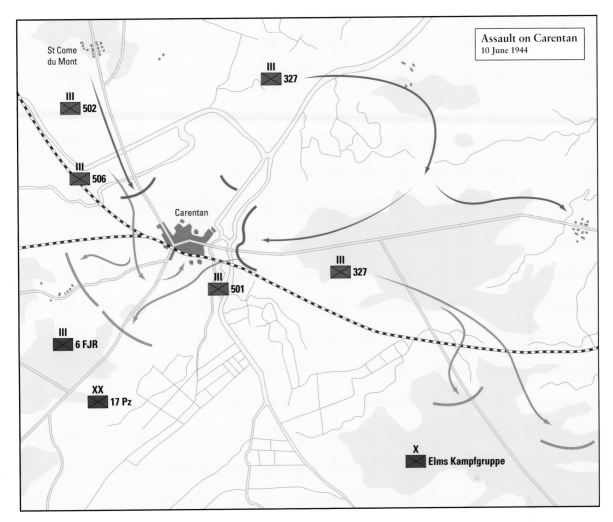

St Come du Mont

III 327

III 502

III 506

Carentan

III 501

III 327

III 6 FJR

XX 17 Pz

X Elms Kampfgruppe

Assault on Carentan
10 June 1944

The town was eventually taken on 12 June when the remainder of the Fallschirmjaeger withdrew under the cover of darkness. The 501st and 506th then moved into a defensive line covering the southern approaches to Carentan in preparation for the inevitable German counter-attack. This came with the arrival of the 17th Panzergrenadier Division in the early hours of 13 June. The tanks and armoured vehicles of the division nearly broke through the lightly armed defensive line in what would become known as the Battle of Bloody Gulch. The tide was turned in the Americans favour with the arrival of a combat command from the US 2nd Armoured Division along with troops from the 29th Infantry Division. They inflicted heavy casualties on the Germans and secured Carentan from further attacks. This meant that the two American beachheads were now linked and the Allies had a firm foothold in Normandy.

The men of the two American airborne divisions had fought tenaciously and with great intelligence. Though almost all units were badly mis-dropped they still managed to successfully carry out all their tasks with great distinction which greatly aided in the success of the invasion as a whole.

THE RANGERS AT POINTE DU HOC

Whilst 1st Battalion were fighting through the North African campaign the War Office back in the United States decided to raise another Battalion of Rangers, after what Darby and his Rangers had proved what could be achieved. Armed with the knowledge acquired from their British counterparts, the Commandos training commenced in Tennessee, where command of 2nd Ranger Battalion was eventually given to Major James Rudder. In late 1943 this unit sailed for England, to be followed shortly by 5th Ranger Battalion commanded by Major Max Schneider.

In Britian the men of the Ranger Force were to be given a special task, that of scaling a 100ft cliff under enemy fire, subduing the defence and then destroying the 155mm artillery guns thought to be emplaced in six large casemates. These weapons, if not taken out of commission could cause widespread destruction to the invasion flotilla off the Normandy coast, covering Utah and Omaha beaches. Specialist training, especially in scaling cliffs took place at the Commando Training School at Achnacarry in Scotland as well as the cliffs on the Isle of Wight. Specialist equipment was also acquired, grappling ropes that could be fired from the approaching landing craft, collapsable ladders as well as ladders borrowed from the London Fire Brigade which were bolted into two DUKWs (amphibious trucks).

The initial assault team was made up of three companies drawn from the 2nd Rangers. They would be carried to the foot of the cliffs in ten landing craft plus the four DUKWs, timed to arrive as the naval barrage from two supporting destroyers lifted. The men were to scale the cliffs by 07.00 and launch a coloured flare. If this was not achieved it was to be assumed that the assault had not been successful and the follow up force, the remainder of 2nd Ranger and all of 5th Rangers, were to land on Omaha beach with the 29th Infantry Division. Timing was imperative.

On the morning of 6 June 1944, things got off to a bad start. Rudder had relieved the officer intended to lead the assault earlier in a briefing and decided to lead it himself. On the run in on the landing craft the weather was poor and the British coxswain accidently sailed to the wrong promontory. This meant that the craft had to run parallel to the coastline and as they clawed westward they came under enemy fire. They arrived at the base of the cliffs some 40 minutes late, the naval barrage had lifted and the enemy were alert and ready for the assault. Things got worse when many of the grappling ropes would not fire high enough due to being drenched in sea water during the run in. The London Fire Brigade ladders wouldn't reach the cliff top either as the DUKWs could not get in close enough to the cliffs. The Rangers however persisted, many free climbing the cliff. Under intense gunfire and showers of grenades the Rangers reached the top where they met a new challenge of clearing out the extensive trench system, made into even more of a maze by the air and naval bombardments. However the complex was eventually cleared, but by this time the follow up Rangers had assumed failure and had gone into Omaha. To add insult to injury it was discovered that the 155mm guns were not in situ. Nevertheless a small section of Rangers went on an aggressive patrol and found them situated in an orchard a kilometre from the battery. They were duly destroyed with thermite grenades.

With what was happening on Omaha beach the Rangers had to contend with several heavy counter-attacks during the rest of 6 June. Respite did not come until the afternoon of 7 June when a company of 5th Rangers managed to break through. Out of the initial 255 men who made the assault, ninety remained able to fight.

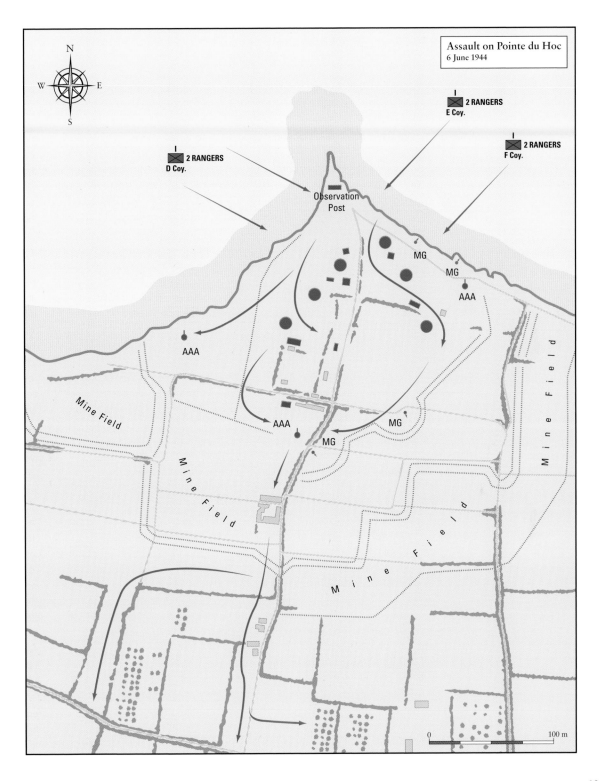

Assault on Pointe du Hoc
6 June 1944

2 RANGERS
E Coy.

2 RANGERS
F Coy.

2 RANGERS
D Coy.

Observation
Post

MG

MG

AAA

AAA

AAA

MG

MG

Mine Field

Mine Field

Mine Field

Mine Field

Mine Field

0   100 m

OMAHA BEACH

Of all the beach landings on D-Day Omaha Beach was to be the most difficult and costly. The beach itself was a wide crescent shelf, 5 miles long, flanked either side by steep cliffs. The low water mark was some 250 metres from the low sea wall that ran 50 metres in front of a steep grassy ridge that rose up to 150 feet. The only way off the beach was through five draws, and it was around these that the Germans would lay the majority of their defences. The German units given the task of repelling the invasion on this beach had been changed at the last minute from the relatively weak 716th Division, which was made up of press-ganged soldiers from the east, to the veteran 352nd Infantry Division, with the 916th Grenadier Regiment manning the immediate beach defences and the batteries of the 716th Regiment in support. There were numerous heavy emplacements, almost impenetrable to air and sea bombardment, interconnecting trenches, fire pits and machine-gun pits that had enfilading fire along the entire beach. In front of these lay the passive defences of logs with antitank mines attached, tetrahedrons (or 'Hedgehogs'), mines, anti-tank ditches and barbed wire entanglements.

Assaulting the beachhead would be two divisions, the 1st 'Big Red One' which had fought in North Africa and Sicily and the 29th, which had not yet seen action. In the van would be a Regimental Combat Team from either division, supported by a tank battalion and the C Company 2nd Rangers landing on the far-right flank.

H-Hour was to be 06.30 preceded by an hour long bombardment from the sea and air. It was hoped that these attacks would leave craters in the beach, but the airmen, fearful of hitting their own men aimed further inland, missing the beach and the majority of the defences completely. Many of the tanks, which

were amphibious 'DD' Shermans, floundered in the high seas, only a few of them making it to shore, so when the first wave of infantry hit the beaches they were met by a highly alerted defence and a wall of fire with no heavy fire support. There was nowhere to hide on the vast expanse of Omaha beach, confusion reigned as men landed on the incorrect sector

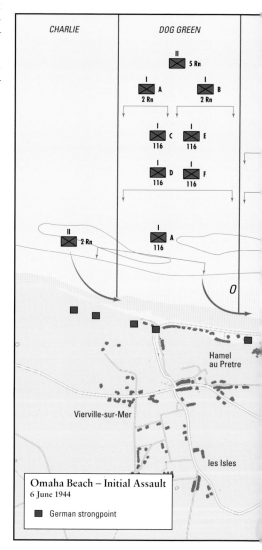

Omaha Beach – Initial Assault
6 June 1944

■ German strongpoint

and men crawled for their lives up to the sea wall where the assault soon stalled. The second wave met with much the same result, with a high loss rate particularly with officers it was down to the junior NCOs to instil some initiative and drive.

The 5th Rangers, having been diverted from Pointe du Hoc, arrived an hour after the initial assault. On seeing this unit the assistant commander of the 29th, Brigadier General Norman Cota, issued the now famous line, 'Rangers, lead the way'. It was these men

of the Rangers, mixed with the men of the assault divisions that managed to fight their way up the draws and into the rear of the German defences in the Vierville sector known as Dog Green and Dog White.

By mid afternoon a near disaster had been averted and heavy vehicles could begin to be landed on the Normandy shore. The cost had been high, the highest of all the assaults on D-Day, with over 3,000 casualties and a link up with the other beaches still to be achieved.

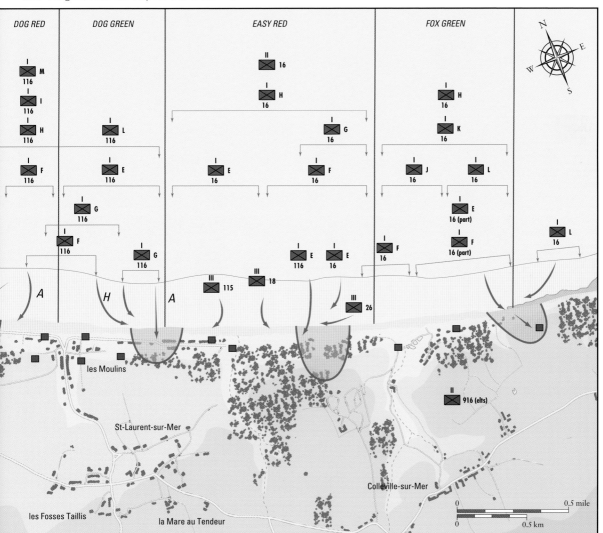

1st Special Service Brigade

Sword beach was situated on the the far left flank of the seaborne invasion of Normandy. With the port town of Ouistreham on the east and the village of Luc-sur-Mer on the west. It was defended by 716th Infantry Division which was made up of regular elements along with Ost battalions, men conscripted from the occupied east. This unit was not particularly well equipped but to their rear in the Caen area was the 21st Panzer Division, which was placed to make an immediate counter-attack.

The 3rd Division of the British Army was tasked with taking the beach and the surrounding areas, the landings concentrating over a relatively small area of beach known as Queen Sector. 8th Brigade would assault the beach followed by the 1st Special Service Brigade who would peel off to the east and take the town of Ouistreham, several strong points and then advance to relieve the men of the 6th Airborne who had captured the bridges over the Caen Canal and Orne river. Meanwhile 3rd Division would continue the advance to the city of Caen itself as well as capture the airfield at Carpiquet to its west. The 1st Special Service Brigade was made up of No. 4 Commando, supplemented by two troops of French commandos drawn from No. 10 (Inter Allied) Commando, these men would make the first landing and swing to the east, the French attacking strongholds within Ouistreham at the casino, whilst No. 4 would attack two batteries and its garrison. No. 3, No. 6 and 45 (RM) Commando would be the follow up force, the entire brigade would be commanded by Brigadier Lord Lovat.

No. 4 Commando and the French troops came ashore with the second wave and quickly moved on the town of Ouistreham. Here they met vicious street fighting, the French meeting particularly stubborn defences around the casino area. Captain Kieffer, commanding the French, ordered an assault which was beaten

back. Luckily a tank coming off the beach came to the aid of the commandos and the defence of the casino came to an abrupt end. The men of No. 4 Commando reached the batteries on the outskirts of Ouistreham to find they were heavily defended with deep anti-tank ditches, wire and numerous machine-gun posts. These guns were silenced and the defences breached, only to find that the guns had been removed some time before the invasion and been replaced with dummies. No. 4 Commando, having secured the area then went to rejoin the rest of the brigade that had come ashore half an hour after their arrival.

On the beach the remainder of the brigade was piped ashore by piper Bill Millin, taking some casualties in the process from artillery fire that was still raining down on the beaches from further inland. However, having formed up, the march to the bridges began. Lovat led the brigade taking a cross country route, not wanting to hit any major German resistance. This would be mopped up by the advancing 3rd Division, the priority being to relieve the paratroopers on the bridges. Any strongpoints the Commandos did come across were quickly dealt with.

No. 6 Commando was in the vanguard of the approach to the bridges and at the village of St Auban d'Arqunay they were fired upon by an Italian manned battery. Being less than two miles from the battery Lovat ordered a troop to neutralise the battery whilst the remainder continued to the bridge at double time. Arriving at the bridge two minutes late from the prescribed time. Here the Commandos took numerous casualties crossing the newly named Pegasus Bridge due to sniper fire, afterwards Lovat would order that all men crossing were to wear their helmets rather than their berets. The Commandos then went on to take up defensive positions around the Ranville area.

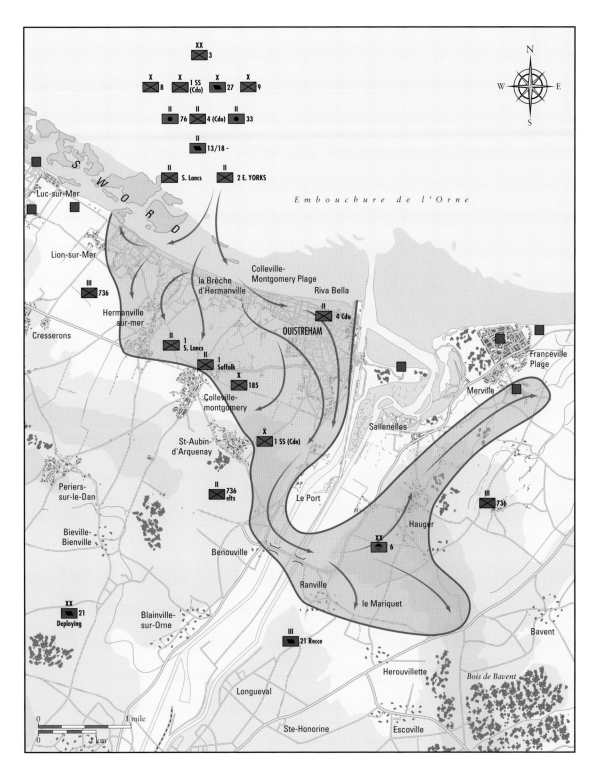

VILLERS-BOCAGE

Following the landings of 6 June the British continued to attack the city of Caen, hoping to capture it and it's airfields to the east as this would open up the countryside from tight hedgerow bocage to open field systems much more suited to mobile armoured warfare favoured by the 2nd British Army's commanders. This aim was continually thwarted by the German defenders who threw in more units to defend the city, including the powerful Panzer Lehr Division. However as the Germans awaited the arrival of 2nd Panzer Division from the south a gap in the lines opened up on the boundary between British 2nd Army and US 1st Army which would become known as the 'Caumont Gap'. The 7th Armoured Division, who were fighting around Tilly-sur-Suelles was ordered to disengage and exploit the gap and flank Panzer Lehr. This would take time so 22 Armoured Brigade was sent in advance. In the lead of this unit was the 4th County of London Yeomanry supported by infantry of the 1st Rifle Brigade.

This mixed unit of armour and motorised infantry arrived at the town of Villers-Bocage on the morning of 13 June. Entering from the west, the infantry continued through the town and came to a halt on the ridgeline leading up to Point 213. A Squadron of the Yeomanry then continued past these troops to reconnoitre the hill.

Watching these proceedings just out of sight to the south of the ridgeline was a company from the 101st SS heavy Panzer Battalion, newly arrived into the battlezone, commanded by SS-Obersturmfuhrer Michael Wittmann. With only six tanks Wittmann made an audacious decision. At 09.00 he ordered his company to engage A Squadron Yeomanry on Point 213 whilst he drove his tank onto the road and immediately destroyed two tanks. These tanks blocked the road for A Squadron to make a retreat back to the Villers-Bocage.

He then drove his Tiger tank, armed with the powerful 88mm gun, down the road, engaging 1st Rifles' Universal carriers, the infantry impotent to do anything but take cover. On arrival at the outskirts of the town he was met by 3 M5 Stuart tanks, lightly armed and armoured, they were no match for the Tiger and destroyed.

Wittmann and his crew then entered the town as the British floundered in panic. A half-track and a Cromwell tank were next to be hit and destroyed with the crews of the brewed up tanks, those that survived, engaged by German snipers that were hidden around the town.

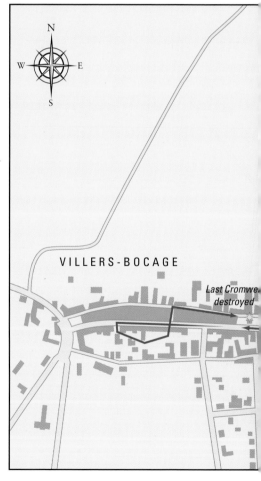

VILLERS-BOCAGE

*Last Cromwel
destroyed*

Meanwhile, a Cromwell tank, that had managed to reverse into a garden and remain unseen as the Tiger drove past, now began a pursuit, trying to aim for the weaker armour towards the rear of Wittmann's tank. The Cromwell took a shot to no effect, but was greeted by return fire from Wittmann, the Cromwell destroyed. Having reached the eastern end of the town Wittmann then turned west to make his withdrawal and rejoin his company. Before he could exit the town his Tiger was hit by a shell fired from a 6-pounder anti-tank gun disabling the giant tank. Wittmann and his crew bailed out of the crippled tank and escaped northward to the headquarters of Panzer Lehr some 4 miles north at Chateau d'Orbis.

The remaining forces left in Villers-Bocage went into all round defence whilst A Company of the Yeomanry, stuck on Point 213, tried to make a breakout but eventually surrendered as more German forces arrived in the area. Fighting continued in and around the town for the rest of the day, with tank duels taking place amongst the back streets and rubble of the ruined town. By late evening the British decided to withdraw and were covered by a smoke screen as they did so.

The town of Villers-Bocage would be continually contested, with massive RAF bombing raids on 15 and 30 June completing the total destruction. The town would not be liberated until 4 August 1944.

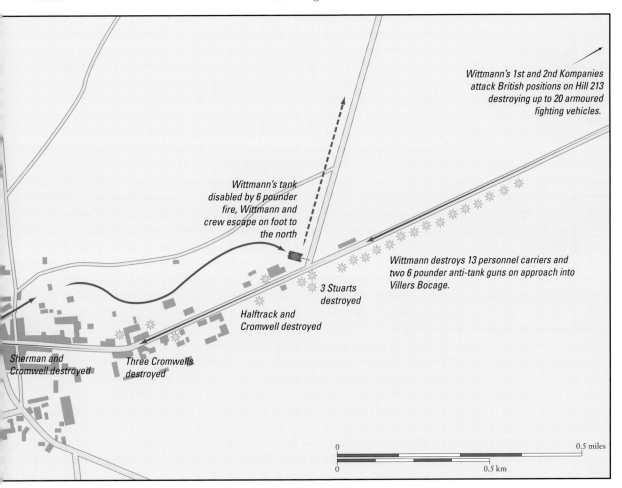

Wittmann's 1st and 2nd Kompanies attack British positions on Hill 213 destroying up to 20 armoured fighting vehicles.

Wittmann's tank disabled by 6 pounder fire, Wittmann and crew escape on foot to the north

Wittmann destroys 13 personnel carriers and two 6 pounder anti-tank guns on approach into Villers Bocage.

3 Stuarts destroyed

Halftrack and Cromwell destroyed

Sherman and Cromwell destroyed

Three Cromwells destroyed

0   0.5 miles

0   0.5 km

133

TALLBOY AND GRAND SLAM MISSIONS

During raids carried out by the RAF it was noticed that there larger blast bombs were ineffective against large or reinforced targets as these lost most of their destructive power through the air, so heavy constructions like bridges and viaducts could stay standing against anything other than a direct hit. Barnes Wallis, of Bouncing Bomb fame, had been working on 'earthquake' bombs since the early forties. This meant that an extremely heavy bomb would be dropped from a great height, penetrate the earth and then fire, causing a local 'earthquake' and thus destroying the structure that was being targeted.

Problems arose for Wallis in that the casing of the bomb had to be extra strong in order to survive the initial impact with the earth. Most bombs of the period had very thin casing, so experiments were put in place to find a suitable metal. Accuracy was also a problem as the bomb was dropped it went through the sound barrier. This immense speed meant that the bomb wobbled in flight and therefore went off course. This was rectified by the angle of the tailplanes being altered inducing a spin and therefore keeping the bomb on a steady flight.

The first bomb of the type to be introduced into combat was named Tallboy and weighed in at 12,000lbs, about 6 tons. The first target for the Tallboy bombs was the rail tunnel at Saumur in the Loire Valley. This was one of only a few routes the Wehrmacht could use to move reinforcements north to the Normandy battlefront. The mission was given to 617 Squadron of the RAF, made famous by their raid on the Dams in 1943, they were now retained by Bomber Command as a specialist unit. Twenty-five aircraft flew on the raid, nineteen of which were armed with the Tallboy. The bomb was so

large that the bomb-bay doors had to be removed, with the lower portion of the bomb open to the elements. The raid was a success, a direct hit blocking the tunnel completely.

The next use of the bomb was during Operation Crossbow, which was to destroy V1 and V2 launch and storage facilities in northern Europe. The bunker at Watten under construction to house the V2 was completely destroyed on 19 June followed by seven other attacks on similar facilities throughout June and July, undermining the German Vengeance weapon programme.

Sorties were then flown against enemy-occupied ports, especially those with reinforced U-boat pens, hitherto inpregnable to standard bombs. These targets were hit from the beginning of June 1944 to the end of the war.

Tallboys were also employed in the attacks on the *Tirpitz*, sheltering in the fjords of Norway. Three missions were flown between September and November 1944, the final mission eventually sinking the battleship with two direct hits.

With the success of the Tallboy the next bomb to be delivered for operational use by the RAF was the 22,000lbs, 10 ton, 'Grand Slam' bomb. However these did not come into operation until late in the war. Used to great effect against bridges, viaducts and U-boat pens much like it's little sister, it was used in nine missions, the last being flown to attack coastal batteries on Heligoland on 19 April 1945.

It was mooted that they should be used in the Pacific theatre to attack Japanese island strongholds, but the Atomic bomb brought the conflict to an end before they could be operationally used in theatre.

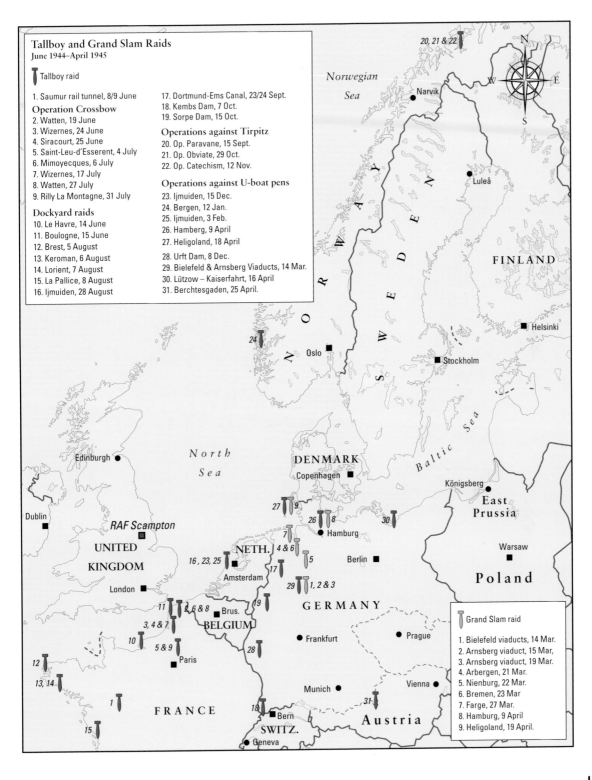

Tallboy and Grand Slam Raids
June 1944–April 1945

Tallboy raid

1. Saumur rail tunnel, 8/9 June

Operation Crossbow
2. Watten, 19 June
3. Wizernes, 24 June
4. Siracourt, 25 June
5. Saint-Leu-d'Esserent, 4 July
6. Mimoyecques, 6 July
7. Wizernes, 17 July
8. Watten, 27 July
9. Rilly La Montagne, 31 July

Dockyard raids
10. Le Havre, 14 June
11. Boulogne, 15 June
12. Brest, 5 August
13. Keroman, 6 August
14. Lorient, 7 August
15. La Pallice, 8 August
16. Ijmuiden, 28 August

17. Dortmund-Ems Canal, 23/24 Sept.
18. Kembs Dam, 7 Oct.
19. Sorpe Dam, 15 Oct.

Operations against Tirpitz
20. Op. Paravane, 15 Sept.
21. Op. Obviate, 29 Oct.
22. Op. Catechism, 12 Nov.

Operations against U-boat pens
23. Ijmuiden, 15 Dec.
24. Bergen, 12 Jan.
25. Ijmuiden, 3 Feb.
26. Hamberg, 9 April
27. Heligoland, 18 April

28. Urft Dam, 8 Dec.
29. Bielefeld & Arnsberg Viaducts, 14 Mar.
30. Lützow – Kaiserfahrt, 16 April
31. Berchtesgaden, 25 April.

Grand Slam raid

1. Bielefeld viaducts, 14 Mar.
2. Arnsberg viaduct, 15 Mar,
3. Arnsberg viaduct, 19 Mar.
4. Arbergen, 21 Mar.
5. Nienburg, 22 Mar.
6. Bremen, 23 Mar
7. Farge, 27 Mar.
8. Hamburg, 9 April
9. Heligoland, 19 April.

VENGEANCE WEAPONS

Even before the war Germany had been at the forefront of rocket production, so it was not surprising when this wealth of knowledge was tapped to produce a devastating, almost unstoppable weapon. The main area for the development of these Vergeltungswaffen, or vengeance weapons, was at Peenemunde on the German Baltic coast. Here Scientists such as Wernher von Braun, who would later go onto have a major part in NASA's rocket programme, worked tirelessly to perfect these new devices.

The first of these devices to be rolled off the production line was the Fieseler Fi 103 flying bomb, or better known as the V1, it was powered by Argus pulse jet giving it a range of 160 miles and was pilotless, using a primitive autopilot . Looking like a small stubby aeroplane but without a cockpit for the pilot the missile made a distinctive throbbing sound as it flew which would later give it its nickname of 'Buzz Bomb' or 'Doodlebug'. Launch of the missile could be made from a static ramp or air dropped from a modified bomber, usually a Heinkel He. 111. Development of the missile was moved to East Prussia after a major raid on Peenemunde by the RAF in August 1943. After tests were run and it was proved to be effective production went into full swing, moving to underground facilities to avoid destruction from

The V1 'Buzz Bomb' was the first effective cruise missile. It had a range of 160 miles and carried a warhead of over 800 kg.

the Allied air forces.

Launch sites were constructed all along the northern French coast allowing the missile to be able to hit its primary target: London. The first combat launch was made on the morning of 13 June 1944, the first of the bombs falling near Gravesend. Within two weeks over 2,000 had been launched towards Britain, the RAF and USAAFs attempts at bombing the launch sites were proved to be ineffective as the targets were so small.

Defence against the missiles lay in the RAF and Army anti-aircraft units of Southern England. The RAF would fly fighter cover over the Channel and inland whilst the Army AA units covered the coastline, anything flying into either zone would be considered a threat and engaged. The V1 was able to fly at 400 mph, this meant that only the newest aircraft in the RAF's armoury could be utilised, later versions of the Spitfire and the Hawker Tempest falling into this category. Their tactic would be to fly a few thousand feet above the operational height of the V1, then when sighted would go into a shallow dive behind the bomb, catch it up and destroy it with relative ease, as the bomb was not advanced enough to take evasive manoeuvres.

Those that did get through the defence caused great shock and worry amongst Londoners. The sound of the pulse jet alerted the public but it was the silence that followed the engine cutting and its inevitable dive into the ground was what really tore at the nerves of the public. In total over 9,200 V1s were launched at Britain, 2,500 reaching their target. Total civilians killed were 6,139, with over 17,000 injured by the raids.

The launch sites for the V1 were overrun after the breakout in Normandy, ending the short but terrible reign of this new type of weapon, but it would not mean the end of Germany's vengeance weapons.

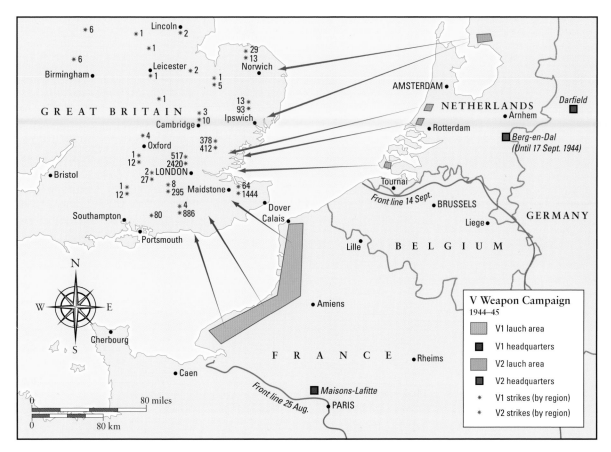

Development of a rocket powered missile had been on the table since the mid-thirties, but the end result was not apparent until 1944 when the V2 was eventually ready for combat. This posed a severe threat as it could be launched from a mobile unit that towed it to a launch site, fired, then withdrew, making spotting the units incredibly difficult. Also once it was launched there was no stopping it as it flew at speeds up to 3,000 mph, a speed unobtainable by aircraft of the period.

The first target for the missile was Paris on 8 September 1944, followed by sustained attacks on London. It was a truly terrifying weapon as there was no warning of its impact, there would be a quick 'whoosh' sound then a massive explosion, causing mass casualties and destruction wherever it hit. As

the Allies rolled through northern Europe the Wehrmacht aimed the majority of the missiles at the port of Antwerp, over 1,200 landing on the city to cause as much damage as possible to deny its use to the approaching forces.

Due to the Allied advance the weapons were eventually out of effective range for attacks on London by March 1945, having killed nearly 3,000 British civilians as well as 1,700 dead due to attacks on Antwerp.

As the war came to an end the scientists that had been responsible for missile programme were much sought after as the Allies realised that this technology would be of great importance in the future, many being relocated to the USSR and USA at the end of the conflict and going on to work in both the civilian and military rocket programmes.

The V1 and V2 attacks on southern England gave the nation a second 'Blitz'. A terrible toll was taken on the civilians living in the area and had the weapons been deployed earlier could have changed the outcome of the war altogether.

SAS Behind The Lines in France

The SAS was by 1944 a veteran unit, having served throughout the campaign in the north African desert and through the battles for Sicily and Southern Italy, it would now take part in the largest invasion in history. Units would be called upon to link up with the French Resistance and aid in the sabotage of the German transport infrastructure, gather intelligence as well as create chaos and misdirection, causing potential enemy reinforcements to chase shadows.

During the build up to Operation Overlord there had been numerous campaigns to deceive German military intelligence as to where the imminent invasion was going to come. To add to this would be special SAS units that would drop just before the main parachute drops of the three Allied airborne divisions. Known as Operation Titanic, small groups of SAS troopers would drop over 500 dummy parachutists along the French coast north of the Seine river and inland from the landing zones in Normandy, east of the Dives river and south of St Lo. To these dummies where attached gun-fire simulators and explosives, with the express intention of drawing German troops away from the real landing zones. To a certain degree these drops were successful with the Germans thinking they were being attacked towards their rear, sending troops to hunt down non-existent soldiers that could have been used in the defence of the invasion on the beaches.

In Brittany several drops across the region would take place on the night of 5 June, members of the 4th SAS, all Free French troopers, landed in Brittany, Operation Samwest landing near St Brieuc, Operation Dingson towards the south of Brittany near Vannes and Operation Cooney in the north near St Malo. These units numbering between 100–180 troops were to link up with the local resistance fighters and interdict any troop movements made towards the battlefront in Normandy.

This included the sabotage of rail lines as well as ambushing convoys. 4th SAS established a base near Saint-Marcel and on 18 June this was assaulted by German troops forcing the SAS troopers to disperse.

A similar action was taken by men of 'B' Squadron 1st SAS during Operation Bulbasket. An advance team landed on 6 June in the Vienne department south west of Tours. the rest of the squadron dropped in on 7 and 11 June, bringing with them armoured Jeeps armed with twin Vickers 'K' guns and the heavier US .50cal machine gun as they had used in the desert as well as explosives and personnel weapons. Their aim was to hinder the advance of the 2nd SS Panzer Division that had been stationed in south west France up to Normandy. They made over twenty individual attacks on transport links, but on 3 July their camp was discovered and attacked by a large German force. A few men managed to escape, but thirty men, with a shot-down USAAF pilot and members of the resistance were captured, a further three injured SAS troopers being taken to hospital. A few days later these men would be forced to dig their own graves and then were executed. A similar fate befell the men in hospital.

After the breakout from Normandy another mission was launched by ninety-one men of 2nd SAS into the Vosges mountains in eastern France, known as Operation Loyton. These men were to harass the Germans as they retreated back into Germany then expect to link up with Patton's 3rd Army advancing on the area. However, 3rd Army came to a standstill due to fuel shortages and the SAS team faced a Panzergrenadier division that had just moved into the area. After several months intelligence gathering the unit was to make its way back to Allied lines. However, thirty-one men were captured en route to safety and along with men of the resistance they were also executed.

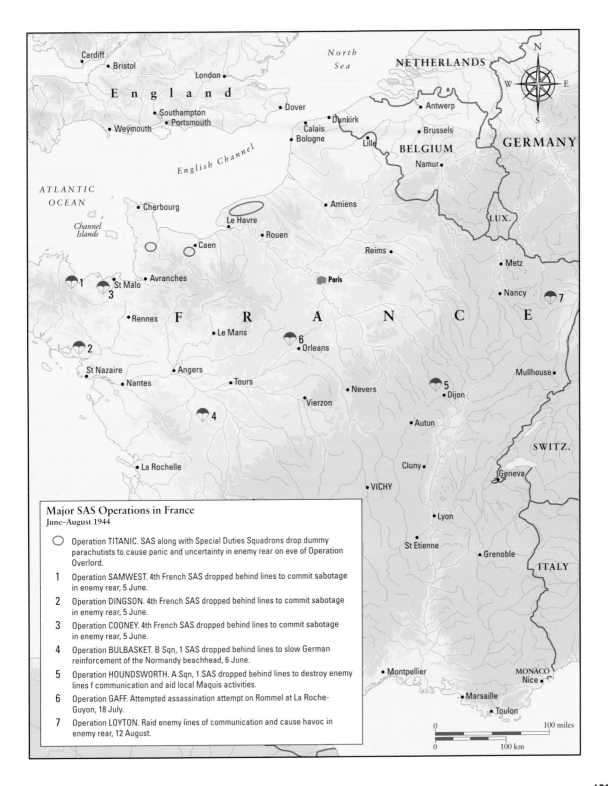

Major SAS Operations in France
June–August 1944

○   Operation TITANIC. SAS along with Special Duties Squadrons drop dummy parachutists to cause panic and uncertainty in enemy rear on eve of Operation Overlord.

1   Operation SAMWEST. 4th French SAS dropped behind lines to commit sabotage in enemy rear, 5 June.

2   Operation DINGSON. 4th French SAS dropped behind lines to commit sabotage in enemy rear, 5 June.

3   Operation COONEY. 4th French SAS dropped behind lines to commit sabotage in enemy rear, 5 June.

4   Operation BULBASKET. B Sqn, 1 SAS dropped behind lines to slow German reinforcement of the Normandy beachhead, 6 June.

5   Operation HOUNDSWORTH. A Sqn, 1 SAS dropped behind lines to destroy enemy lines f communication and aid local Maquis activities.

6   Operation GAFF. Attempted assassination attempt on Rommel at La Roche-Guyon, 18 July.

7   Operation LOYTON. Raid enemy lines of communication and cause havoc in enemy rear, 12 August.

SOVIET PARTISANS

The German invasion of Soviet Russia in June 1941 was a shock to the Russian high command, the advance on such a wide front at such speed left many units of the Red Army surrounded, the majority falling into incarceration. However a few small units managed to escape to the thick forests and deep marshes of Belarus and Ukraine. It would be these units, mixed with members of the population loyal to the communist cause that would form the nucleus of the Soviet partisan movement.

During the first winter these units carried out small raids on convoys and rail lines but to little effect as they lacked any formal command structure and knowledge of sabotage and intelligence gathering. However in 1942 the gap between the German North and Centre armies, known as the Vitsyebsk Gate, was exploited, giving the Russians a chance to send in trained leaders, specialists who could teach the use of explosive and how to make ambush attacks and commissars to keep the men and women loyal to the Stalinist cause.

Over the next year these revitalised partisans would completely disrupt the German rear areas, as well as taking heavy handed reprisals against those who collaborated with the enemy occupiers. This would include assassinations of those involved along with the killing of their families and the burning down of the family home. By 1943 these actions were discouraged by the high command back in Moscow as being counter-productive. It was the Germans that created more partisans with their own reprisals on the innocent soviet population. If an installation was attacked or a rail line sabotaged the Germans would often round up entire villages and slaughter them, the rules of engagement being completely different to those seen in the deserts of North Africa or fields of North West Europe. The Germans would also 'employ' the local populace to 'guard' installations, if the alarm was not raised to any attack from the partisans it would result in death for them and their famillies. The occupied population flocked to the partisans cause.

During 1943 the actions of the partisans were being controlled in conjunction with actions on the battlefront. This included the partisan attacks on the railroads of western Russia in order to slow the build up and then the re-supply of the Germans attack on the Kursk salient. These attacks on the vast rail network cut the German supply line by a third, severely hampering any chances of their success. As the Germans sent troops through to the front they would often have to fight their way to it. Being attacked from the forests by sniper fire and men throwing grenades, before the attackers would melt back into the woods. As the Germans were pushed back the various partisan units would invariably join the regular Red Army and continue the fight.

The contribution made by the Soviet partisans is inestimable but from a relatively modest beginning they rose to number over 500,000 personnel.

Partisans pose for a photograph with a typical assortment of weapons.

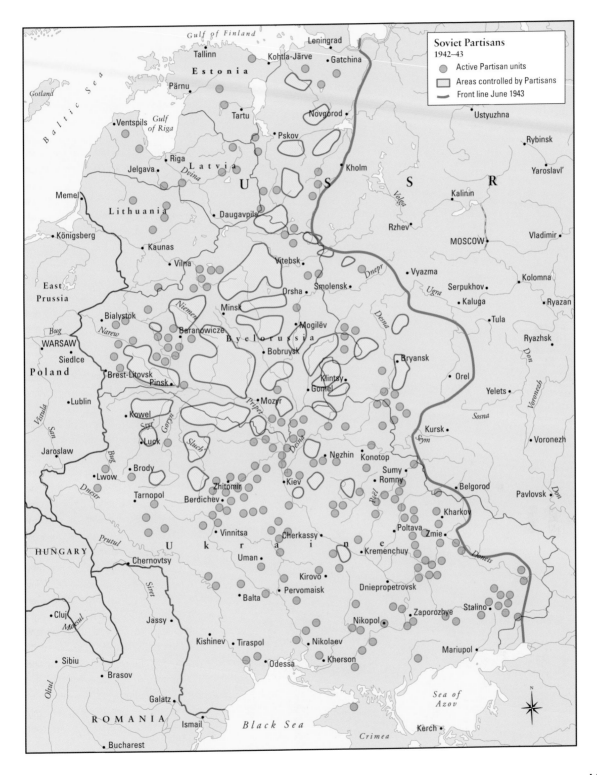

Soviet Partisans
1942–43

- Active Partisan units
- Areas controlled by Partisans
- Front line June 1943

WARSAW UPRISING

With the Allies in the west starting to break out of the beachhead fighting in Normandy and the Russian military behemoth approaching the Vistula river, the Armia Krajowa, the Polish Home Army, saw an opportunity to finally rise up after five years under the Nazi yoke and liberate their capital city, Warsaw.

The uprising would be led by General 'Bor' Komorowski following instructions from the Polish government in exile in London leading a total of some 40,000 insurgents against an occupation force of 15,000 German troops starting on 1 August. The Germans were in the process of reinforcing Warsaw as the Russians approached, turning the city into a fortress, this meant that a large number of soldiers were within easy reach of the city, including a panzer division. The Poles were also under-armed, possessing only 1,000 rifles and a similar number of sub machine guns and pistols. The uprising would depend heavily on the capture of arms and ammunition from the Germans.

Strategic targets for the uprising were bridges across the Vistula to help the approaching Russians, who would never arrive, as well as police stations, train stations the tallest building in Warsaw, the Prudential Building.

In the first days of the uprising the Home Army managed to capture most of the Old City and City Centre areas, along with the Wola district to the west as well as Zoliborz in the north and Mokotow district in the south of the city. Though there were strongholds of German troops within these areas. The various captured parts of the city also had no means of communication and were reliant on runners and the sewer system to keep each other informed, though they mostly fought as independent entities.

On 2 August Obergruppenfuhrer Erich von dem Bach-Zelewski was given command of all military units tasked with the crushing of the uprising, with direct orders from Heinrich Himmler to kill all within the city, whether they were fighters or not, along with the complete flattening of the city so as to act as an example to all other European cities under the control of the Nazis. The Germans moved into the Wola district on 5 August and systematically went about clearing houses, killing all within and committing some of the worst atrocities of the war.

With Stalin refusing to help the Poles in their fight against their oppressors Churchill ordered the supply of the insurgents. Flying from airfields in southern Italy, Polish, South African and British along with USAAF aircraft flew over 200 sorties and dropped much-needed arms and medical supplies, though the majority landed in the German sectors.

Despite this the Germans made a slow and costly advance through the city, destroying entire blocks to quell the uprising. It took almost two months before the Poles capitulated, it is thought that over 150,000 Polish civilians died in the fighting, with a further 20,000 insurgents killed.

Members of the Polish Home Army escort a prisoner into captivity.

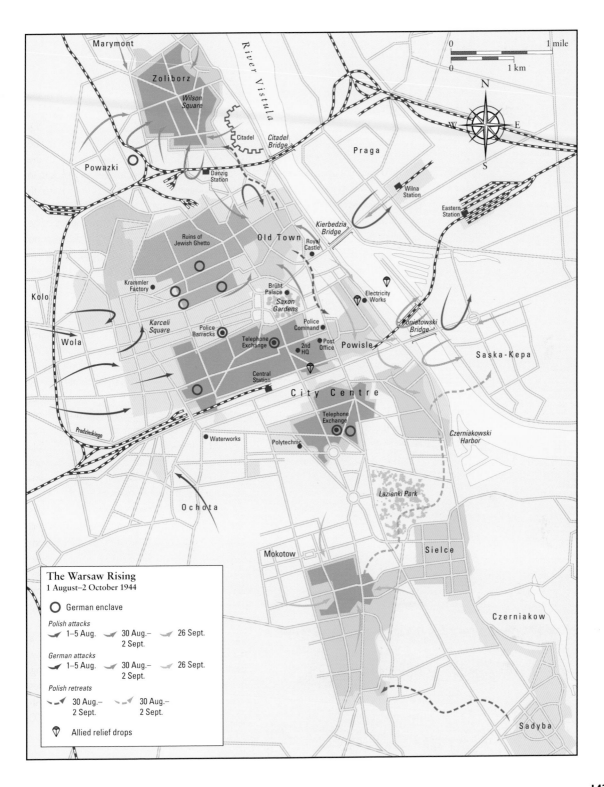

Marymont

Zoliborz

Wilson Square

River Vistula

Citadel

Citadel Bridge

Praga

Powazki

Danzig Station

Wilna Station

Eastern Station

Kierbedzia Bridge

Old Town

Ruins of Jewish Ghetto

Royal Castle

Electricity Works

Krammler Factory

Brühl Palace

Saxon Gardens

Kolo

Poniatowski Bridge

Karceli Square

Police Command

Saska-Kepa

Wola

Police Barracks

Telephone Exchange

2nd HQ

Post Office

Powisle

Central Station

City Centre

Czerniakowski Harbor

Pradzinskiego

Telephone Exchange

Waterworks

Polytechnic

Lazienki Park

Ochota

Mokotow

Sielce

Czerniakow

The Warsaw Rising
1 August–2 October 1944

◯   German enclave

Polish attacks

1–5 Aug.   30 Aug.–   26 Sept.
            2 Sept.

German attacks

1–5 Aug.   30 Aug.–   26 Sept.
            2 Sept.

Polish retreats

30 Aug.–   30 Aug.–
2 Sept.   2 Sept.

▽   Allied relief drops

Sadyba

SPECIAL DUTIES FLIGHTS

The need to supply the various resistance units around Europe, particularly in France and Yugoslavia, with weapons, radios and equipment led to the formation of a specialised RAF unit known as No. 1419 (Special Duties) Flight. This small unit utilised the Westland Lysander and the Armstrong Whitworth Whitley, aircraft that Bomber Command were happy to part with as they were considered obsolete.

This unit would then go on to form the nucleus of a much larger operation as SOE came in to prominence, forming No. 138 and No. 161 Squadrons. The former would use large bomber type aircraft to drop agents, known as 'Joes', and stores into occupied territory whilst the latter would specialise in the ferrying of agents in and out of occupied territory. The formation of these units went against the wishes of the head of Bomber Command, Arthur Harris, who thought that every available aircraft and aircrew should be involved in the night bombing campaign of Germany's industry. The importance of SOE and the supply of resistance fighters around occupied Europe made his wishes redundant and were overruled.

This did however mean that the supply of aircraft to the units came in a trickle. The first aircraft was the Lysander, initially used as an Army cooperation aircraft, spotting for artillery. The aircraft had one major advantage. It had an incredibly short take off and landing capability and with the addition of a ladder attached to the rear cockpit this was used as a fantastic 'taxi' for agents without parachute training to enter or leave occupied territory. In the months leading up to D-Day 101 agents were inserted whilst 128 were recovered by the Lysander flights. The RAF also used the American designed Lockheed Hudson, a twin-engined aircraft with a much greater range than that of the Lysander but with a landing and take off run twice that of the smaller aircraft. However, this was capable of carrying a far greater number of agents, ten as opposed to a maximum of three, and was used when suitable landing sites could be found. The Whitley, was a two-engined bomber that was quickly replaced by the much larger Handley Page Halifax. This aircraft was a four-engined bomber and capable of carrying a vast amount of stores that could be parachuted down in containers, it also had a fantastic range, managing to reach as far east as Poland, whilst flying from bases in southern Italy.

The squadrons were based mostly in southern England, for ease of flying their missions to France, Belgium, the Netherlands and Italy, their main bases being at RAF Tempsford and Newmarket. However, if they were required to fly to Norway Scottish airbases were used as were North African bases or Italian bases used when flying to Eastern Europe.

The USAAF also introduced specialised squadrons of aircraft for the delivery of stores to the resistance fighters of Europe. Their first operation, flying heavily modified Consolidated B-24 bombers, was Operation Carpetbagger which began in early January 1944 and would continue until September of

The Westland Lysander was capable of a very short take off and landing, making it ideal for the insertion and extraction of agents into the fields of Europe.

that year. From then on the units would be known as the 'Carpetbaggers'.

Supply missions would mostly be carried out on nights where there was a full moon to aid in navigation. The aircraft would fly alone and at the relatively low level of 500–1,000 feet. This would also help in navigation as river, rail and road networks could be clearly seen from that height. On the ground the resistance fighters awaiting the arrival of a drop would mark the drop zone with torches or fires or later on the introduction of Eureka and Rebecca radio direction finding sets, these were rare and often failed. In total tens of thousands of weapons and supplies were dropped by these units throughout the war, without these missions many of the resistance units would have found it impossible to take the fight to the enemy.

MARKET GARDEN

As the Allies broke out of Normandy a rapid advance took place across the entire front as the Germans withdrew eastwards. By September almost all of France and Belgium had been liberated and the Allied commanders wanted to keep the pressure on the Germans all along the wide front, from the port of Antwerp in the north to the Swiss border. This was hampered by the severe lack of supplies to the troops and tanks at the front. Fuel, ammunition and supplies were still coming over the beaches of Normandy and the newly opened port of Cherbourg, hundreds of miles to the rear. These supplies had to reach the front via the 'Red Ball Express', a convoy system of trucks, though successful it lacked enough quantity to feed all the Allied armies. This led to various plans from the main commanders, Montgomery, Bradley and Patton, all vying for the much need supplies in order to fulfil their different strategies.

XXX Corps was tasked with advancing to the bridges on a single road. This left them open to constant ambush from either flank.

The one strategy that did strike a chord with the Supreme Commander, General Eisenhower, was that of Field Marshal Montgomery's. It would involve an audacious plan to drop three airborne divisions from the Allied First Airborne Army, to capture eight bridges over numerous rivers, with the British 1st Airborne Division capturing the furthest bridge over the River Rhine, the gateway into Germany's industrial heartland, the Ruhr. It could potentially end the war by Christmas, or so the commanders boasted.

Dropping as part of the airborne element known as 'Market' north of the town of Eindhoven would be the 101st Airborne Division, commanded by General Maxwell Taylor. His troops would secure the bridges at Son and Veghel. North of the 101st would land the 82nd Airborne Division under General James Gavin, capturing the bridges at Grave and Nijmegen. Just north of the Americans would land the British 1st Airborne Division under Major General Roy Urquhart capturing the main prize of the bridge over the Rhine at Arnhem. The 1st Airborne would be reinforced by the Polish 1st Independent Parachute Brigade. The men of these units were only tasked to hold these bridges until relieved by the ground element known as 'Garden'. The thrust through the German lines starting just inside of Belgium would be made by Lieutenant General Brian Horrocks' XXX Corps, led by the Irish Guards, part of the Guards Armoured Division. They were to advance through the captured towns and over the bridges along one exposed highway to eventually relieve the 1st Airborne well within five days.

The Germans by this period had began to create a defensive line following the crushing defeat in Normandy. The withdrawal toward the western border of Germany, though quick, had been successful. By 16 September

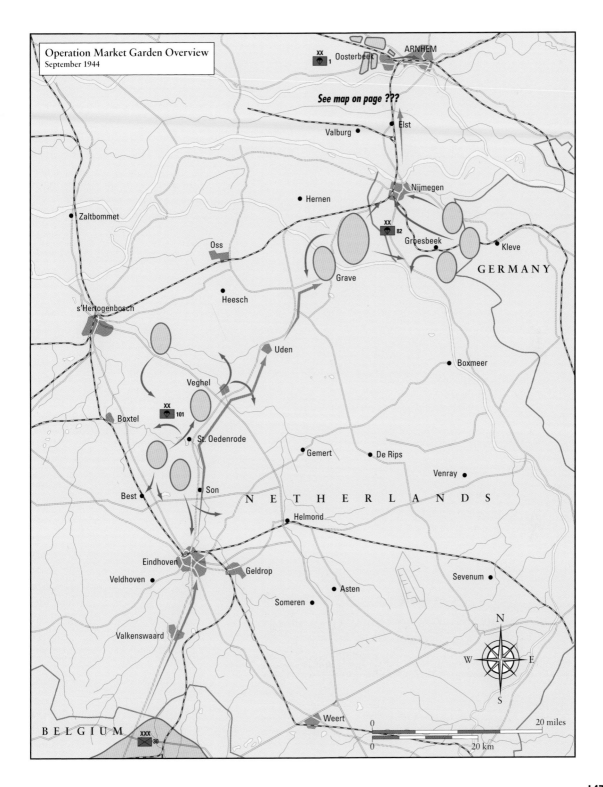

US paras inspect the wreck of a Waco glider for survivors and supplies.

the rout had stopped and the Germans were preparing to hold the line from Antwerp to Metz then onto the Siegfried Line, Germany's western most defensive line. This line was especially strong in the Arnhem Nijmegen sector, with Allied decrypts, Dutch Resistance and aerial photography all showing that the 9th and 10th Panzer Divisions, along with supporting infantry were re-grouping in the area. Despite this intelligence the Allied commanders decided to still go head with the plan.

In the early afternoon of 17 September the air over the southern Netherlands was filled with the deafening sound of over 2,800 troop transports along with 1,600 gliders, all stuffed to the gills with paratroopers, Jeeps, artillery and supplies along with a fighter escort of 1,200 aircraft.

The 101st landed without resistance, quickly moving on their objectives. However as they approached the bridge over the Wilhelmina Canal it was destroyed by the German defenders. Elements of the 506th

PIR would continue to move south and reach the outskirts of Eindhoven, here in the late afternoon they would meet the lead elements of XXX Corps arriving amongst much jubilation from the local population.

Further north the 82nd landed again facing little initial resistance. They secured the bridges at Grave and over the Maas-Waal Canal, and moved to secure the eastern flank from counter-attacks that could be launched from the German Reichswald, securing the high-ground around Groesbeek. Movement on the main bridge across the Waal river to the north of Nijmegen was slow and by the time the 82nd arrived elements of the German defence had arrived, halting the Americans in the suburbs of the town.

At Arnhem only half the Division could be landed due to a lack of transport aircraft. This meant that only the 1st Parachute Brigade landed just after lunch time. This unit again had to be halved as one was tasked to capture the bridge some five miles from the

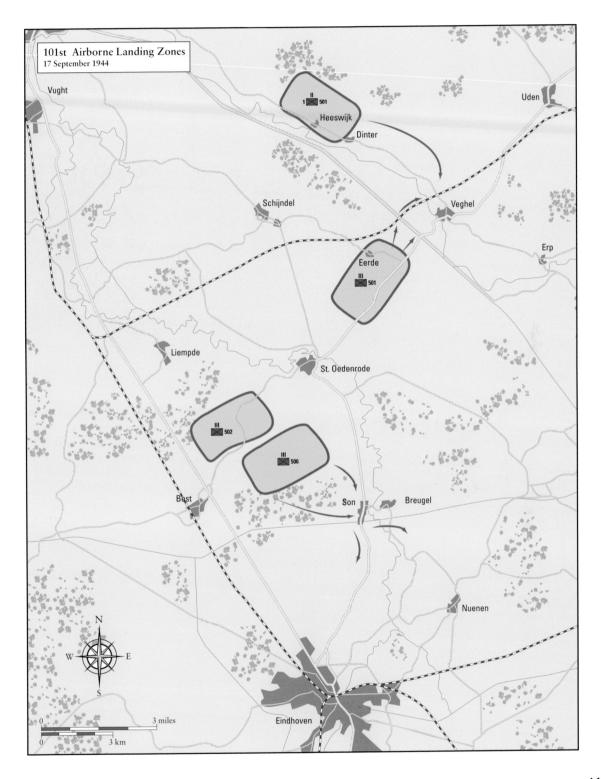

101st Airborne Landing Zones
17 September 1944

Vught

Uden

II
1 ⊠ 501

Heeswijk

Dinter

Veghel

Schijndel

Erp

Eerde

III ⊠ 501

Liempde

St. Oedenrode

III ⊠ 502

III ⊠ 506

Best

Son

Breugel

Nuenen

N
W   E
S

0   3 miles

0   3 km

Eindhoven

landing zones whilst the other secured the landing zones for the follow up landings the next day. The reconnaissance platoon, armed with Jeeps to race to the bridge was halted by spirited defence in the suburbs of Arnhem, this was also met by the majority of the British paras. However 2nd Battalion under Lieutenant Colonel John Frost managed to find a route following the north bank of the Rhine and arrived at the north end of the bridge in the late evening. The battalion set up an all round defence then attempted to capture the south-

ern end, failing twice. Around this time it was discovered that communications between all the units spread across the battle zone and with supporting RAF fighter-bombers had failed, the radio sets not having the sufficient strength to communicate with one another. Unable to communicate with his dispersed brigade Urquhart set about reaching his men at the bridge on foot, this led to him having to hide in a loft whilst dodging German patrols, and to him being out of touch with his troops for many hours during a crucial period of the battle.

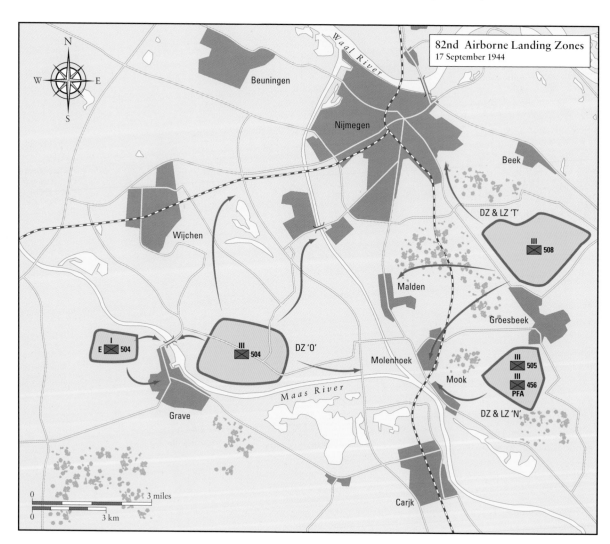

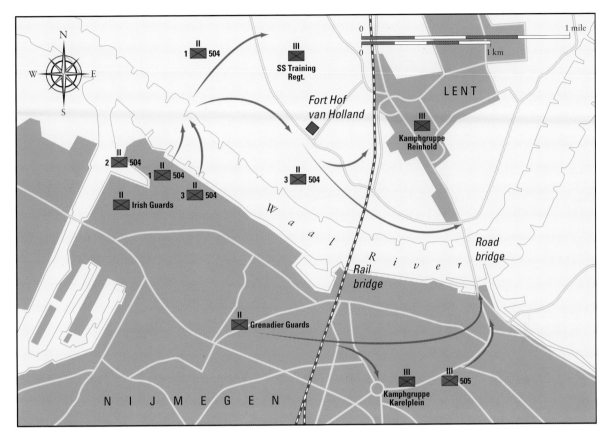

Field Marshal Walter Model, commanding the defences in the sector soon surmised what the aim of the Allied plan was and set about mobilising a strong retaliation. Sending 9th SS Panzer Divisions reconnaissance company to secure Nijmegen whilst counter-attacking the British forces now stuck in street fighting in the suburbs of Arnhem and around the landing zones.

XXX Corps left their start line at the Meuse-Escaut Canal and crossed into the Netherlands behind a rolling barrage a mile wide. They were met by strong resistance on either flank which took time to silence, with artillery and ground attack aircraft. By nightfall they had yet to reach Eindhoven in strength.

Day two saw the 9th SS Reconnaissance Battalion returning from Nijmegen to assault the northern end of the

Arnhem bridge, which was held off by the men of 2nd Battalion, inflicting heavy losses on the Germans. Meanwhile at the landing zones the second airlift arrived very late due to poor weather conditions back in England. The men landed under heavy fire from the Germans surrounding the area, but moved up to support the paras in the Arnhem suburbs who were now less than a mile from the bridge.

In the 82nd sector they were facing concerted attacks from the Germans especially around the drop zones, one of which the Germans managed to capture. This was immediately retaken by the paratroopers who were expecting the Glider Infantry to arrive later that afternoon. The men of the 101st completely secured Eindhoven and saw off local counter-attacks and after meeting with the main thrust of XXX Corps went about building

British paras in a fighting position in the Arnhem area

a bailey bridge at Son which was completed in the early hours of the third day, XXX Corps were now severely behind schedule.

The third day saw the majority of 1st Airborne unable to break through to the men stuck at the north end of the bridge, Urquhart decided to withdraw to the small town of Oosterbeek. Meanwhile at the bridge, 2nd Battalion were being heavily shelled and mortared from all sides, demolishing many of the buildings used by the defenders. Ammunition and especially medical supplies for the mounting casualties were beginning to run dangerously low.

At Nijmegen the Grenadier Guards of XXX Corps made contact with the 82nd, using their tanks the men made a combined attack on the bridge. This failed so a plan was drawn up to assault the bridge in a similar way whilst a battalion of paras made an assault

crossing a mile upstream. This was delayed severely by the wait as the assault boats were brought up from the rear. This task was made all the harder by the single roadway that was used by the entire Corps, which could easily be attacked from both sides by the Germans.

The fourth day saw the fighting around the bridge at Arnhem reach its climax, the men of 2nd Battalion fighting from the rubble at point blank range, skirmishing with German infantry heavily supported by armour. It was during these battles that Frost was badly injured, passing on command to Freddie Gough. A ceasefire was arranged so the casualties of both sides could be evacuated into German care. The men of 2nd Battalion, with little or no ammunition had little choice but to surrender, with many attempting to escape, these being taken in by the Dutch population until an opportunity arose to escape. The remainder of 1st Airborne were now within a perimeter in Oosterbeek, with their southern flank to the Rhine. This was attacked by the Germans with the intention of cutting their only route of escape, this was held off.

In Nijmegen the assault boats had arrived and the men of 3rd Battalion, 504th PIR went about constructing the flimsy craft made from canvas and wood. A barrage was laid down by the Guards' tanks as well as a smoke screen, which soon lifted due to high winds. The men paddled for all their lives under intense fire from the defenders. Half the battalion arrived on the north bank of the Waal only to have to then cover 200 metres of open ground, the boats then returning to bring in the rest of the battalion. This unit overcame what would become known as 'Little Omaha' and stormed the northern end of the bridge. With men from the 82nd also taking the southern end the Bridge was now in Allied hands. Much

to the disgust of the American troopers that had taken the bridge at such a heavy cost XXX Corps then stopped the advance for the day, not wanting to drive into an area known to be heavily infested with anti-tank guns. Time was also needed to re-form the leading unit as most of the Guards Armoured Division was still heavily engaged in the clearing of Nijmegen with the men of the 82nd.

On the fifth day the surviving men of the 1st Airborne, numbering under 4,000 out of 10,000 originally inserted, continued to hold the Oosterbeek perimeter, holding back infantry assaults often with bayonets. Supplies continued to be another source of despair, as without radio contact many of the containers dropped by the RAF simply fell into the Germans hands. Radio contact was established with artillery that had advanced with XXX Corps, and this offered vital firepower to the dwindling paratrooper defence. In the late afternoon the Polish parachute brig-

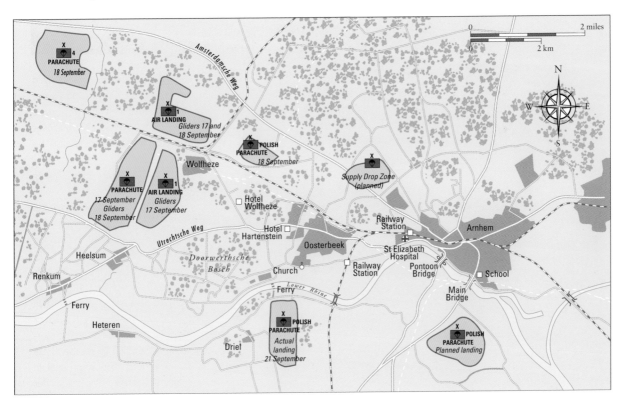

ade was dropped under heavy fire opposite the British bridgehead at Driel. Hoping to utilise a ferry to reinforce the British, it was found to be missing, with the opposite side being held by the Germans in any case. The Poles withdrew to the village of Driel for the night whilst contact was established with the British and a plan could be made.

The Poles at Driel caused the Germans to move some of the forces attacking the Oosterbeek perimeter to assault the the village south of the river. The Poles attempted to reinforce the British by sending men via rubber dinghies, this movement was spotted by the enemy, who opened fire with machine guns, causing some casualties and for the reinforce-

British paras prepare for another attack during the defence of the Oosterbeek perimeter.

ment to stop. Meanwhile further to the south the Guards Armoured Division had become bogged down in the marsh ground north of Nijmegen, and were held up by well placed anti-tank guns. 43rd Division was ordered into the lead, but this was again delayed by the jams on what had become known as 'Hell's Highway'.

Repeated attempts were made to reinforce 1st Airborne on 23 and 24 September following the link up of XXX Corps with the Poles holding Driel, however all these failed with the Germans taking more prisoners than troops making it into the airborne perimeter. That evening it was decided to pull what remained of the 1st Airborne Division out. The withdrawal was ordered for the following evening of 25 September.

Sensing the British were close to defeat the Germans pushed the defenders, especially on the eastern perimeter, the assaults only being held off thanks to artillery called in from Allied emplacement to the south of the Rhine. The British began to withdraw before midnight with men of the Royal Engineers ferrying the men across the river. They left behind wounded, medical staff and volunteers to man the perimeter whilst the withdrawal took place. Of the 10,000 men that went in to Arnhem on 17 September, only some 2,400 made it back to Allied lines. 1,485 men lost their lives fighting for the bridge at Arnhem whist the remaining 6,200 men were taken prisoner, most were injured in some way. The frontline just north of Nijmegen would remain much the same until early 1945 with the launch of Operation Veritable.

Planning for the operation was deemed to be far too optimistic, with the need to capture all the bridges along the single-road highway almost an impossibility, especially with the men of the 1st Airborne being dropped up to ten miles from their target. Combined with the communication breakdown of the 1st Airbornes and the expectation that the German resistance would be weaker than it actually was, despite intelligence warnings to the contrary, the operation was doomed to failure.

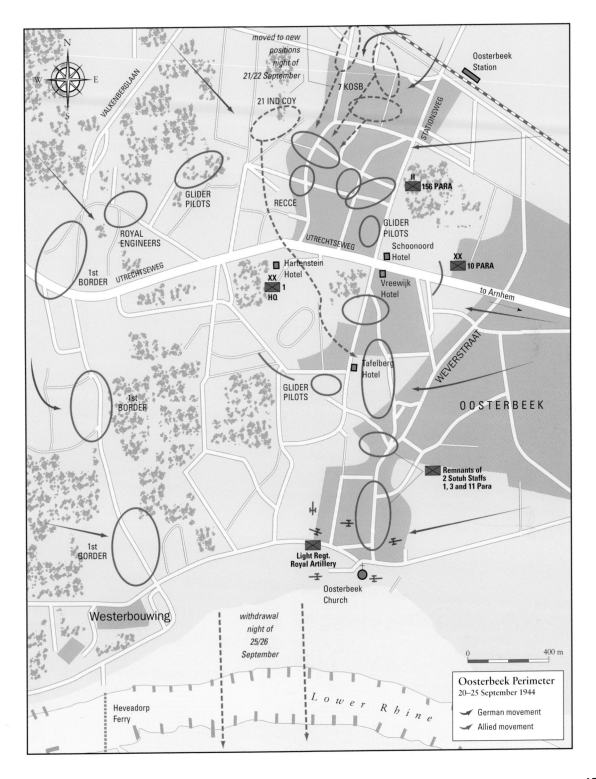

N

W · E
S

moved to new
positions
night of
21/22 September

Oosterbeek
Station

21 IND COY

7 KOSB

VALKENBERGLAAN

STATIONSWEG

GLIDER
PILOTS

RECCE

II ⊠ 156 PARA

ROYAL
ENGINEERS

UTRECHTSEWEG

GLIDER
PILOTS

Schoonoord
Hotel

XX ⊠ 10 PARA

1st
BORDER

UTRECHTSEWEG

Hartenstein
Hotel

XX ⊠ 1
HQ

Vreewijk
Hotel

to Arnhem

1st
BORDER

GLIDER
PILOTS

Tafelberg
Hotel

WEVERSTRAAT

OOSTERBEEK

Remnants of
2 Sotuh Staffs
1, 3 and 11 Para

1st
BORDER

Light Regt.
Royal Artillery

Oosterbeek
Church

Westerbouwing

withdrawal
night of
25/26
September

0   400 m

Oosterbeek Perimeter
20–25 September 1944

🛩 German movement

🛩 Allied movement

Heveadorp
Ferry

L o w e r   R h i n e

THE BATTLE OF THE BULGE

Supply problems still dogged the Allied advance into Nazi Germany. By October 1944, following the failed attempt to break into the Ruhr during Operation Market Garden, the situation was worse then ever. Fuel, food and ammunition still had to be transported all the way from Cherbourg and the beaches of Normandy, the French Channel ports still remained in German hands, and would remain until May 1945. To add to this all supplies had to come via trucks as the French rail network had been systematically destroyed by the Allies prior to the invasion of northern France. With Eisenhower wanting to stick to his broad front advance on Germany, the front would have to remain static whilst supplies were built up sufficiently and the recently captured port of Antwerp could be bought up to full working condition.

A German soldier, wrapped up against the extreme weather, poses for a photograph during the German surprise attack through the Ardennes.

Hitler saw this lull in the fighting as a chance to launch a final, decisive assault. One that would split the western Allies and force them to sue for peace, thus allowing Hitler to pull all his forces eastward to defend against the Russian onslaught. Hitler wanted to use his strategic reserves in an attack through the Ardennes forest, seizing bridgeheads over the Meuse then continue up to Antwerp, in the process cutting off and surrounding four Allied armies. This ambitious plan was advised against by Hitler's highest commanders, nevertheless he gave the orders for it to proceed.

Overall command of operation 'Wacht am Rhein' (Watch on the Rhine) would come under Field Marshal Gerd von Rundstedt, commander in the west, and Field Marshal Walter Model, commander of Army Group B. At their disposal were three armies. Attacking in the northern sector, with the aim of capturing the city of Antwerp, was the most powerful of these armies, 6th Panzer Army, commanded by General Sepp Dietrich. This incorporated 1st SS and 12th SS Panzer Divisions and would advance along the Elsborn Ridge, capture Liege, then roll onto Antwerp. In the centre would be 5th Panzer Army, under General Hasso von Manteuffel. 5th Panzer would secure the important crossroad towns of St Vith and Bastogne before pushing on to capture Brussels. Furthest south was 7th Army, the only army without a panzer division, commanded by General Erich Brandenberger, they would secure the southern flank from American counter-attacks.

Along with these regular units would be two special units tasked with specific objectives. Operation Greif under Otto Skorzeny would infiltrate the American lines wearing US uniforms and driving US vehicles, secure bridges on the Meuse river and spread disinformation in the American rear. Operation Stosser, would entail a Kampfgruppe of Fallschirmjaeger com-

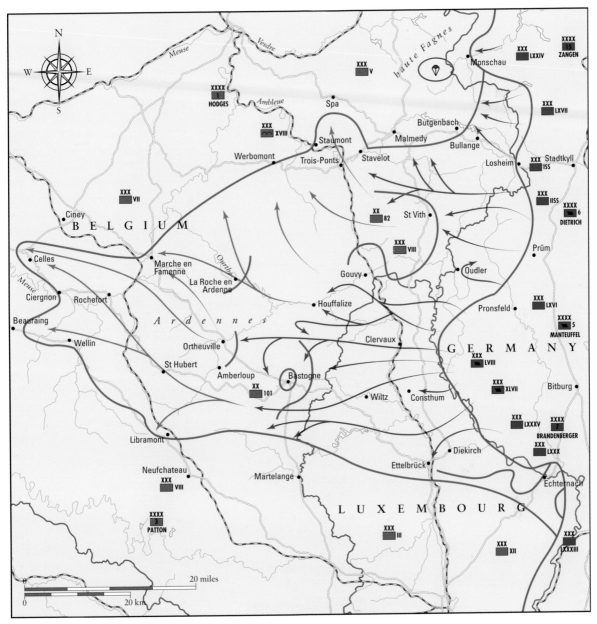

manded by Oberst Friedrich von der Heydte, a veteran of Crete, to land just north of the main thrust to capture a vital crossroads at Baroque Michel for 24 hours before being relieved by the 12th SS Panzer Division.

All this would require the utmost surprise and would require the capture of Allied fuel supplies along the way. The German Army at this time had severe fuel shortages and would start the battle with only enough fuel to reach half way to their final objectives. All radio traffic was kept to a minimum, with the Allies having little knowledge of any assault due to the Germans now using the telephone network and bad weather impeding any aerial reconnaissance. Many of the German units would not be made aware of the upcoming attack until the very last minute to keep operational security. The Allies were so complacent that the Germans were all but defeated expected no counter-attack at all, the commanders assumed that Germany was too weak to launch any major offensive. The Allies used the Ardennes forest, scene of the spectacular German assault on France four years earlier, as a resting point for units that had been in recent combat as well as a training area for units newly arrived to the front. The last major assault of the German Army was ready to go in.

A bombardment from 1,500 guns along a front of some 80 miles opened up on the American frontline at 05.30 on 16 December 1944. Skorzeny's commando unit was just behind the lead elements of assault, and soon overtook them to reach their objectives. However, the majority of his men were captured before reaching too far into the

American rear. They did have an adverse effect on the Americans by causing fear and confusion, with rumours spreading rapidly. This was remedied by the troops asking questions that only an American citizen would know the answer to.

Operation Stosser met with a similar result, having been delayed by 24 hours. The 1,500 men of the kampfgruppe were badly scattered due to poor flying conditions and badly trained pilots, many never having flown the Ju52 transport plane before. This would also be the first night drop made by the Fallschirmjaeger. Von der Heydte only managed to rally 300 of his troops by the morning of 17 December. Deciding his force was not large enough to capture the crossroads at Baroque Michel, he carried out a reconnaissance patrol. Again his intentions were hampered when none of the unit's radios were found to be serviceable. Not being able to send the information he gathered he ordered his troops to disperse and make their way back to the German lines. He himself was badly injured with a broken arm and would

Men of the 101st Airborne stand triumphant next to the sign of the town they so stoutly defended.

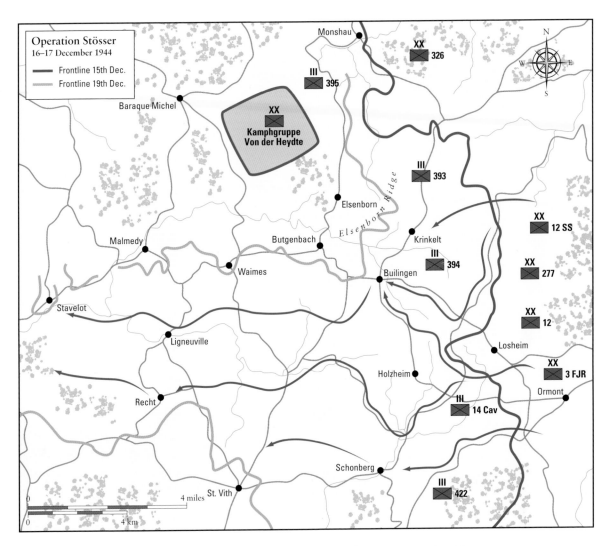

Operation Stösser
16–17 December 1944

Frontline 15th Dec.
Frontline 19th Dec.

Monshau

326

395

Kamphgruppe
Von der Heydte

Baraque Michel

393

Elsenborn

Elsenborn Ridge

12 SS

Krinkelt

Malmedy

Butgenbach

394

277

Waimes

Builingen

12

Stavelot

Losheim

Ligneuville

3 FJR

Holzheim

Ormont

Recht

14 Cav

Schonberg

422

St. Vith

0   4 miles
0   4 km

eventually surrender to US forces.

In the northern sector the 6th Panzer Army advanced along the Elsborn Ridge to meet dogged resistance from the US 99th and 2nd Infantry Divisions. The advance unit of the German northern thrust, Kampfgruppe Peiper, commanded by Obersturmbannfuhrer Joachim Peiper, made a rapid advance, bypassing many defending American units, on its way to the crossroads town of Malmedy. Outside of this town it came across the lead elements of the 7th Armoured Division, the 285th Field Artillery Observation Battalion. The men of this unit put

up an initial defence but soon surrendered in the face of overwhelming odds. Over 150 men of the unit were ushered into a field under guard. The Germans in charge of the POWs then opened fire. Some US personnel managed to escape into the surrounding forest, however, eighty-four men were slaughtered. The Malmedy Massacre, as it would become known as, only strengthened the Americans' resolve to halt the German assault. By 19 December Peiper's unit had reached Stavelot and were advancing on Trois Ponts as the Allied response to the German assault began to take shape.

In the centre sector 5th Panzer Army had made slow progress due more to the weather and the effects it had on the road conditions than to the US forces facing it. The veteran 28th Infantry Division managed to avert total disaster whilst many 'green' US units tended to panic and retreat, causing more confusion and clogging up the road system. All this allowed time for the Allied commanders to make decisions on how to counter the German offensive. Eisenhower decided to send in the strategic reserve, which was the 82nd and 101st Airborne Divisions, resting and refitting in the rear after the fighting in the Netherlands and Huertgen Forest. These units moved rapidly to the frontline, the 82nd heading to the St Vith area and the 101st to Bastogne. Whilst these forces bolstered the defence and helped deny the Germans the important crossroad towns, the British XXX Corps in the north and US third Army in the south changed their axis of advance and cut off what was fast becoming a 'bulge' in the Allied frontline.

The 101st Airborne Division supported by Combat Command B of the 10th Armoured Division moved into Bastogne on 19 December. By this time the lead German units of Panzer Lehr and 2nd Panzer Division had bypassed the town to the north and south, and along with the 26th Volksgrenadier Division, had effectively surrounded the defenders. The Americans went about shoring up an all round defence, covering all the main routes into town with what little they had, the speed of their deployment meaning that many of the men fighting would do so without proper winter clothing. Nevertheless the Division acquitted itself well, holding off determined German assaults. On 21 December the majority of Panzer Lehr and 2nd Panzer Division continued on with the advance west. By 22 December the supporting US artillery were down to firing ten rounds per gun. The Germans, sensing victory sent in a messenger under a white flag to ask for the defenders' surrender. The acting commander of the 101st, General Anthony McAuliffe

gave the simple reply, 'NUTS!' This fired up the resolve of the embattled airborne troops. By Christmas Eve the weather had begun to open up and the men could be supplied by air, bringing in much needed medical supplies and ammunition. On 26 December the lead elements of 3rd Army entered the town square, the siege had been lifted and the town had been denied to the Germans.

Meanwhile further north the 82nd Airborne Division had been deployed along

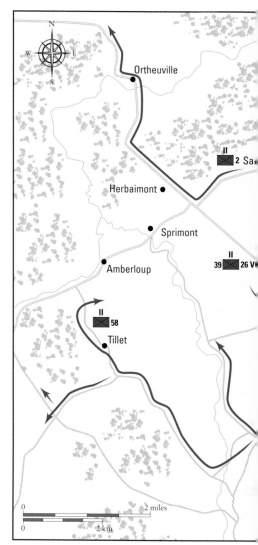

the Salm river, south of Trois Ponts to block the advance of the 9th SS, 21st and 1st SS Panzer Divisions. It was important to deny the Germans passage over the river to prevent St Vith to be completely cut off. Major General James Gavin made sure all his units had anti-tank guns and had made preparations for all crossings to be destroyed if the enemy came close to making a crossing. The men held the line as the US 3rd Armoured Division pulled out through its positions. By Christmas Eve

the 82nd had now come under the command of Field Marshal Montgomery's 21st Army Group, and was ordered to make a retreat to shorten its lines of defence, something the airborne troops were not used to making. On 27 December they held off a last concerted effort by the 9th SS Panzer Division to break through, it was now the turn of the Allies to take the offensive.

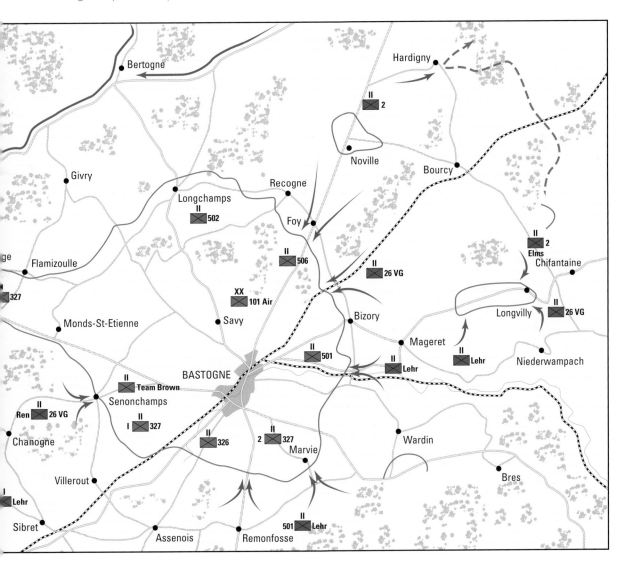

US troops man an artillery position in a village in the Ardennes.

By Christmas the weather was beginning to clear and the Allies could again employ their superiority in air power. The Allied air forces attacked the German supply lines to the rear whilst fighter bombers began targeting German armour and vehicles on the roads. This led to a critical shortage of fuel for the leading elements and all advances came to an abrupt halt.

Eisenhower saw a chance to trap the Germans in the pocket that they themselves had created. He ordered an advance to start

on 1 January 1945 so that Montgomery's forces in the north could advance on Houffalize to meet up with Patton's forces advancing from the south. This was thrown into disarray whilst Montgomery prepared his troops for the assault in a heavy snowstorm, not launching until 3 December. This was all the Germans required to start a withdrawal of their men.

Meanwhile on 1 January Operation Bodenplatte, a last gasp by the Luftwaffe to destroy as many Allied aircraft on the ground as possible, was launched. This ended in complete disaster, leading to the complete loss of the Luftwaffe as a fighting force.

The Germans put up a successful rear guard action, but due to the lack of fuel much of the army's heavy fighting vehicles would remain. On 7 January Hitler eventually relented and agreed to a general withdrawal to the original lines. This was completed on 25 January. The Battle of the Bulge would be the bloodiest battle ever fought by the US in the Second World War.

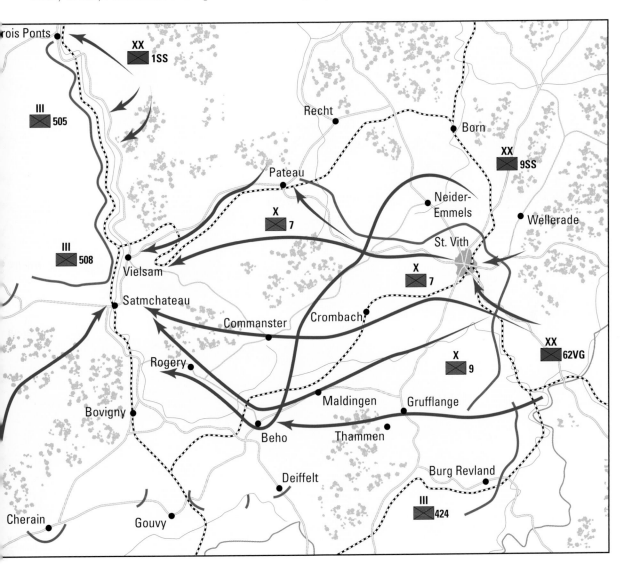

OPERATION BODENPLATTE

Operation Bodenplatte (far right) was a last ditch attempt by the Luftwaffe to halt the superiority of the Allied air forces in western Europe, though tactically a success it sounded the death knell for the once mighty Luftwaffe.

By the end of 1944 the Luftwaffe was in severe decline. A lack of fuel and trained pilots, as well as operational machines was severely depleted. On the Allied side the opposite was true. They held overwhelming air superiority and with the capture of most of Belgium and the Netherlands they could now move their tactical air forces closer to the front lines to assist in ground operations. Flying freely above the German positions they could identify targets and attack them themselves or call in artillery or heavy bomber support.

With the planning of Operation Wacht am Rhein it was conceived that a large force of aircraft would be put into the air to support the ground operation. But the poor weather conditions that limited the Allied flying operations during December also led to the Luftwaffe holding off the attack until conditions improved.

The idea of Operation Bodenplatte (Base plate) was to attack Allied airfields in North East France, Belgium and the Netherlands. Flying at low level to deceive Allied Radar they were to pounce on the airfields early in the morning and destroy as many aircraft on the ground as possible. However, operational secrecy was at the forefront and this led to few people being fully aware of the entire operation. Even squadron commanders were kept in the dark until as late as possible, these men were then not allowed to tell their pilots under their command what was expected of them until they were almost in their cockpits. This led to much confusion and loss of potential.

With the battle on the ground in the Ardennes forest all but stalled there was to be one last push called Operation Nordwind to be launched on the morning of 1 January 1945, this would be combined with Bodenplatte. Every available fighter and fighter-bomber unit had been moved with the utmost secrecy west for the attack. Just after first light the Luftwaffe's last major offensive took to the air.

The units were made up of Messerschmitt 109s and Focke Wulf 190s with a few Me 262 fast jet-fighter bombers also taking part, all great aircraft, the problem lay in the vastly inexperienced crews.

Led to their respective targets by units drawn from the night fighter squadrons the German pilots flew low and fast. However, instructions had not been filtered through to the German flak units who, used to Allied air superiority, immediately started firing on their comrades. The inexperienced pilots, flying higher and slower than there veteran counterparts, were easy targets for the anti-aircraft crews of both sides.

On arrival over the targets the Allies were caught by surprise, many aircraft being caught on the ground and destroyed. The timing of the attack perhaps owing much to the fact that it had been New Years Eve the previous night and few patrols being launched.

However, many allied squadrons did take to the air and when they met their German foe they held the advantage of being over friendly territory. By the end of the attack some 500 Allied aircraft lay destroyed or beyond repair, Luftwaffe losses lay at 280 aircraft out of the 1,000 employed lost. Many of the aircrews were either killed or captured. A loss much worse than the aircraft themselves.

The Luftwaffe had played its last hand and though tactically the operation it was a success it would never again recover and would hold no major part in the rest of the conflict.

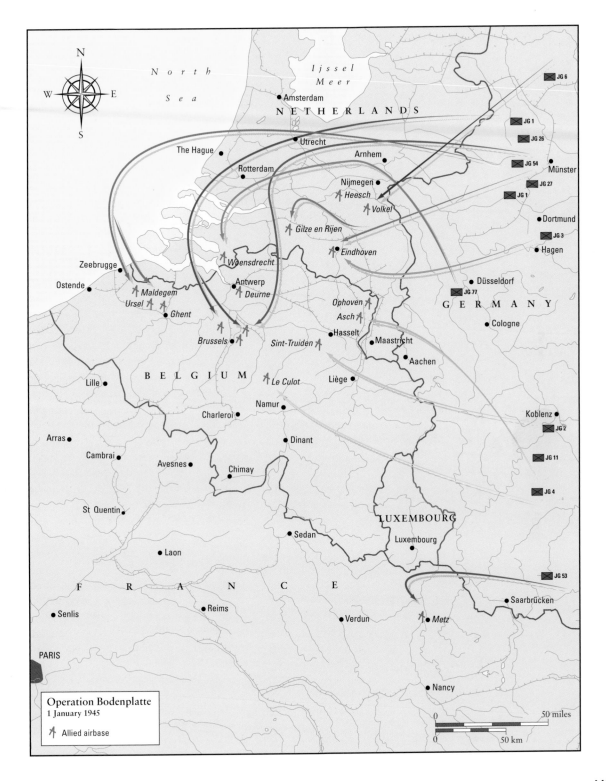

Operation Bodenplatte
1 January 1945

✈ Allied airbase

RAID ON CANABATUAN

In September of 1944 the 6th Ranger Battalion was an newly activated unit. Having converted from a artillery battalion to a special force whilst training for action near Port Moresby on Papua New Guinea, by October of that year it was ready to take part in the US invasion of the Philippines. The men of the unit, though lightly armed captured outlying islands off the coast of Leyte and aided in the navigation of the main invasion force to the beaches on Leyte. The next few months saw the men of the 6th Ranger Battalion act as a protective force for construction battalions around the Leyte, then Luzon beacheads.

On 27 January 1945 the commander of the 6th, Lieutenant Colonel Henry Mucci received orders to infiltrate a force of his Rangers behind enemy lines to liberate 500 captured US soldiers being held in a camp some miles outside of the town of Canabatuan. These men had been incarcerated since the Bataan Death March of early 1942 and were in a desperate state, the US commanders assumed that they would be moved, which meant death for many of them or killed outright.

Mucci chose C Company, plus a platoon from D Company, commanded by a young captain: Robert Prince, for the raid. These men would slip behind the lines and meet with Filipino guerillas who would lead them to the camp. Here they would link up with a small number of Alamo scouts, a specialised reconnaissance unit, who had kept the prison under observation for a final brief, before making the assault.

The Ranger company's approach to the camp was succesful but not without incident, narrowly avoiding detection by a passing Japanese convoy, they trekked across open grassland, avoiding all major roadways. Once near the camp the Rangers were dispersed whilst Mucci and Prince conferred with the Alamo scouts and the guerillas. The scouts confirmed that the approach to the camp was over a flat open area, kept this way to deter guerilla attacks and to be able to easily indentify escaped prisoners. The guerillas also confirmed that a large number of troops were stationed at Canabatuan town, which was a few miles away and could easily fall on the camp at a moments notice. Faced with these problems the men set about forming a plan.

The men of the Rangers would crawl over the open ground towards the camp whilst a USAAF P-61 Black Widow reconnaissance aircraft flew low passes over the camp. This was hoped to draw the attention of the Japanese guards skywards, aiding the Rangers' approach. Once near the camp, timed to be at dusk, Company 'F' of thirty men would move around the camp's side and rear. On their signal, which would be covering fire opened up on the Japanese part of the camp, the main force of 90 men would assault the camp's main gate. Units would move up and cover the tank shed with a bazooka whilst elements broke into the POW cage and aided the prisoners to the rear. Whilst all this was happening men of the Filippino guerillas would be covering a force of Japanese encamped over the nearby Cabo river.

All of this went to plan, the guerillas blowing a hole in the Cabo river bridge preventing any tanks moving on the camp and successfully holding off successive Japanese assaults. In the camp itself much of the Japanese contingent were killed or wounded in the mass of gunfire. The prisoners, though disorientated were quickly liberated, those too weak placed apon local carts for the march back to US lines.

Nearly 500 POWs were successfully liberated during the raid for the loss of two Rangers, one being the chief medical officer dispatched to aid the prisoners. It is estimated that over 500 Japanese were killed.

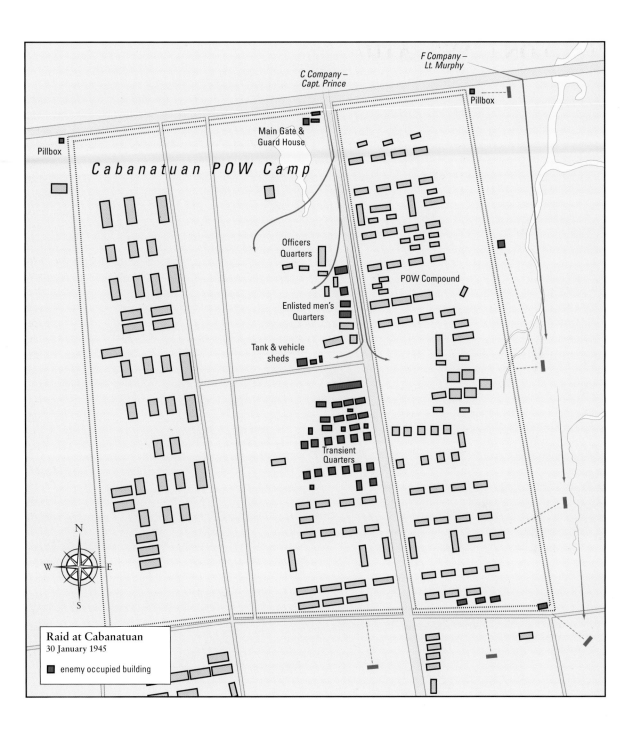

F Company –
Lt. Murphy

Pillbox

C Company –
Capt. Prince

Main Gate &
Guard House

Pillbox

Cabanatuan POW Camp

Officers
Quarters

POW Compound

Enlisted men's
Quarters

Tank & vehicle
sheds

Transient
Quarters

N
W   E
S

Raid at Cabanatuan
30 January 1945

■ enemy occupied building

RETURN TO CORREGIDOR

Corregidor was the final bastion of the American defence of the Philippines after the invasion by the Japanese in December 1941. On 11 March 1942 General MacArthur, commanding the defence of the islands, left under the cover of darkness to Australia. Under a month later the island fortress, known as the 'Gibralter of the East', fell to the Japanese. The US and Filipino defenders taking a terrible toll on the Japanese before surrendering. In 1945 the island still stood as an imposing defensive obstacle to Manila, the capital of the Philippines, it was decided that it would be assaulted from the air and sea and re-captured by the tried and tested 503rd Parachute Regimental Combat Team along with 3rd Battalion, 34th Infantry Regiment of the 24th Infantry Division.

The assault was preceded by a naval bombardment from US warships in Manila Bay that would last two weeks, battering at the formidable defences of Corregidor, which included a vast network of tunnels under the main hills known as Topside and Malinta Hill. An aerial bombardment commenced on 13 February which would continue right up to the time the men of the 503rd dropped, on 16 February 1945 at 08.30. The combat team landed on the Topside feature and were faced with a fanatical defence, the men barely able to dig foxholes before the Japanese were counter-attacking.

Meanwhile the 3rd Battalion, 34th Infantry landed at San Jose Point. The men of this unit would move to secure the harbour and the entrances to the Malinta Hill tunnel complex. These men would be faced with almost continual banzai charges by the Japanese emerging from the tunnels, invariably these assaults would be cut down with great loss of life on the Japanese side.

On Topside ferocious fighting would continue for two days as the Paratroops struggled to take control of key points. It was during these battles that Private First Class Lloyd McCarter would display exceptional bravery. McCarter single-handedly silenced an enemy machine gun by covering 30 yards of open ground under fire, before destroying the position with grenades. Two days later he would account for six enemy snipers, before attacking an enemy column that was preparing to attack the paratroopers. He would draw the fire of the Japanese whilst his comrades made ready the defences. He continued to harass the Japanese until his machine gun jammed. Grabbing a Browning Automatic Rifle, he continued this fire

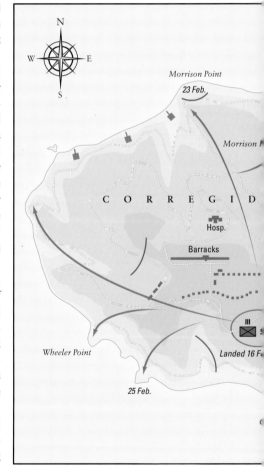

until it too jammed. Finally, whilst exposing himself to enemy fire to pin down where the enemy was he was wounded badly. Even still he refused to be evacuated to the rear areas before passing on this vital information. He would later be awarded the Congressional Medal of Honour, America's highest award for bravery.

On the night of 18–19 January the Japanese made a banzai charge on the paratroopers positions around Wheeler Point. 500 Japanese soldiers flung themselves at fifty defenders. They met a hail of fire and in the aftermath 250 dead were found strewn across the battlefield, for the loss of fifteen dead paratroopers.

On 21 February around Malinta Hill the men of the 3rd Battalion, were alarmed by

a massive explosion from within the hill. Some of the garrison inside had blown themselves up. Still banzai charges followed and realising that the Japanese garrison were not going to surrender 3rd Battalion sealed all the entrances to the complex. Engineers then poured gasoline into the tunnels and set them alight, killing all within.

Sporadic fighting continued all over the island until 26 February when the island was finally declared secure. The combined losses for the American units was over 320 men killed or severely wounded, whilst out of the Japanese garrison numbering almost 7,000 only some fifty men survived.

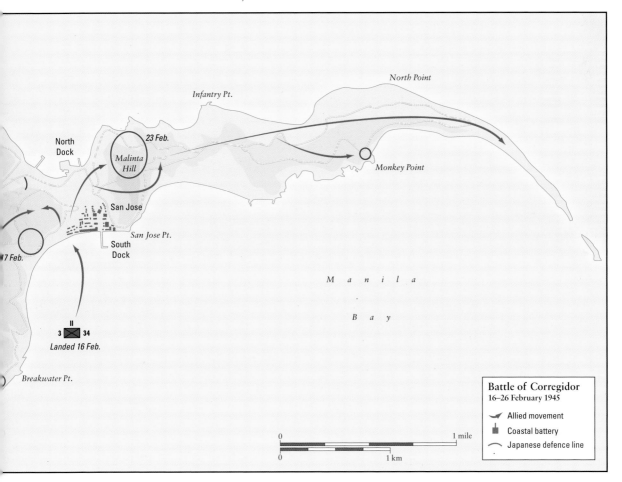

OPERATION VARSITY

*General Bernard Law
Montgomery, architect
of Operation Varsity.*

By March 1945 the Allies had advanced up to
the River Rhine, the last great defensive barrier
against the western armies. The Canadians had
fought through the Reichswald whilst the British
had assisted in the restoring of the lines in the
northern sector of the Ardennes following
the Battle of the Bulge. Further to the south
Hodge's US 1st Army was at Koblenz on the
Rhine and Patton's 3rd Army was opposite
Mainz. Montgomery, seeing a chance to cross
the Rhine in the area of Wesel utilising his
21st Army Group put forward the plan for
Operation Plunder. This would incorporate
1st Canadian, 2nd British and 9th US Armies.
Crossing the Rhine they could then advance
into the German industrial heartland, the Ruhr
and on to the North German Plain, which was
ideal ground for a rapid armoured advance.
Montgomery would also include airborne forces
in his plan. Dropping just behind the river crossings to secure towns on the intended route of

advance as well as disrupting the German reac-
tion to the crossings and halting reinforcements
into the area. Learning lessons from the Market
Garden debacle, the airborne troops would
expect to link up with the ground forces within
24 hours.

The plan was for the Canadian 1st
Army to hold the left flank of the assault whilst
also making feint attacks across the river to
draw the defenders' attention from the main
assault. The British 2nd Army was to make
an assault crossing opposite Rees with the
1st Commando Brigade crossing just north of
Wesel itself. The US 9th Army would cross
further to the south with the aim of advancing
on Munster whilst protecting the right flank.
The airborne element would utilise the 17th
US and 6th British Airborne Divisions. The 6th,
made up of 3rd Parachute Brigade commanded
by Brigadier James Hill, 5th Parachute Brigade
commanded by Brigadier Nigel Poett and 6th
Airlanding Brigade commanded by Brigadier
Hugh Bellamy would drop around the towns
of Hamminkeln and Schnappenberg and the
Diersfordter Wald, a forested area east of the
Rhine, secure the towns and the surrounding
area and await for the arrival of the ground
forces. They would also capture several crossings over the smaller Issel river to the east
of the Rhine. The 17th, made up of 507th
Parachute Infantry Regiment commanded by
Colonel Edson Raff, 513th PIR commanded by
Colonel James Coutts and 194th Glider Infantry
Regiment commanded by Colonel James Pierce
would drop just south of the 6th but north of
Wesel, again securing areas of the Diersfordter
Wald and disrupt any attempts by the enemy
to reinforce the battle zone. The plan was also
made to include the 13th US Airborne Division
but due to a lack of transport aircraft this division was left behind.

Preparations for the crossing com-

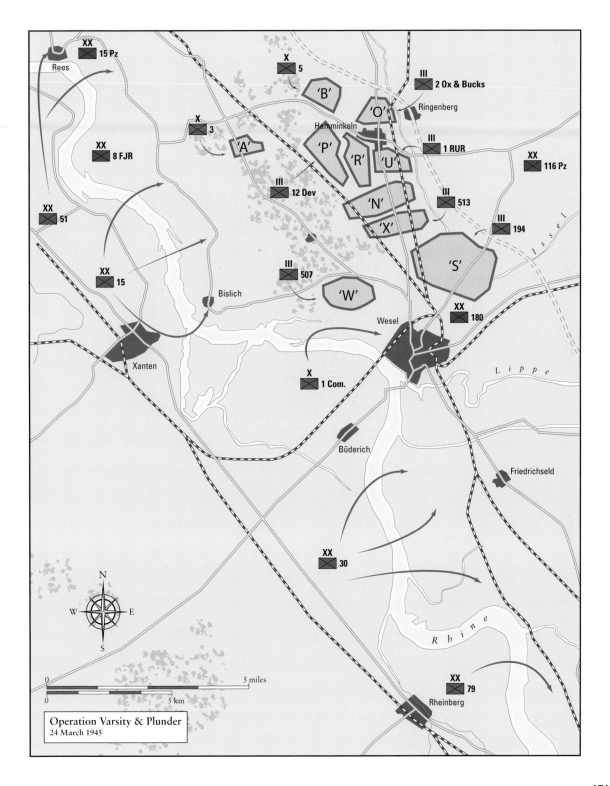

Rees

XX 15 Pz

X 5

III 2 Ox & Bucks

'B'

'O'

Ringenberg

X 3

Hamminkeln

'A'

'P'

III 1 RUR

XX 8 FJR

'R'

'U'

XX 116 Pz

III 12 Dev

III 513

'N'

III 194

XX 51

'X'

Issel

'S'

XX 15

III 507

Bislich

'W'

Wesel

XX 180

Xanten

X 1 Com.

Lippe

Büderich

Friedrichseld

XX 30

N

W E

S

Rhine

XX 79

Rheinberg

0 ————— 5 miles
0 ————— 5 km

Operation Varsity & Plunder
24 March 1945

171

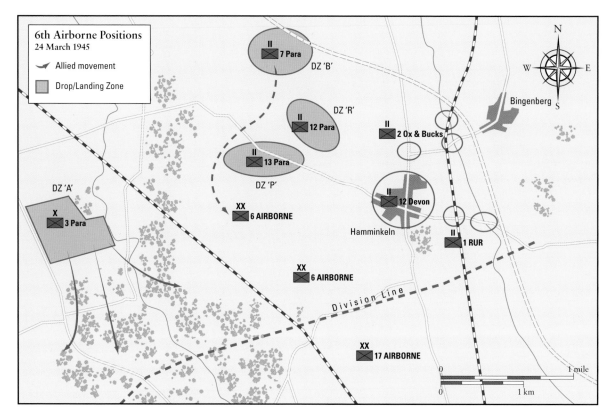

menced on 16 March with the laying of a massive smoke screen to cover the Allied build up and deployment of the supporting artillery, which would total over 5,000 guns. Facing the upcoming assault were elements of the German 86th Corps and 2nd Parachute Corps, with the brunt of the attack been taken by 7th Parachute Division and the 84th Infantry Division. Further to the rear on the east side of the Issel river were the severely depleted but still threatening 116th Panzer Division, with a total of some seventy tanks. The area surrounding Wesel was also thick with anti-aircraft batteries.

During the afternoon of the 23 March 1945 a massive air raid on Wesel was followed by a four hour bombardment from the allied artillery covering the entire 21st Army Group front but concentrating on the town of Wesel. Late that evening the first elements of 2nd Army, the 51st Highland Division made

its crossing in amphibious Buffalo vehicles, the crossing taking less than three minutes. The path was laid by an array of searchlights and tracer fire firing from the west to the east bank. Just after midnight the 15th (Scottish) Division would land on the east bank too. The 1st Commando Brigade would do the same landing just north of Wesel. No. 46 (RM) Commando were in the lead and managed to create a bridgehead, despite tough resistance. No. 6 Commando then passed through their positions and began entering the outskirts of the town before they were met by local counter-attacks. The Germans, alerted for days by the smoke screen and the preliminary bombardment were dazed, but soon began to put up a solid defence all along the eastern bank of the Rhine, the 51st Division did not manage to capture the northern town of Rees by the end of the first day, whilst the 15th Division was facing Fallschirmjaeger well emplaced with machine guns and numerous anti-tank ditches.

To the south the Americans were meeting less stubborn resistance but were still taking casualties. The lead unit, 30th Infantry Division managed to gain a strong foothold on the eastern bank whilst the 79th Division did the same to their south.

On the morning of 24 March 1,600 transports, mostly C-47 Dakotas but with some newly arrived C-46 Commando and C-54 transports, began to form up above Belgium. Being towed by these aircraft were a total of 1,300 gliders, made up of Horsa, Waco and the heavy lift Hamilcar. The vast armada stretched for some 200 miles and was heavily protected by fighter aircraft. This was to be the largest airborne drop in military history.

The 3rd Parachute Brigade were the first over their drop zone, DZ 'A', and were met with ferocious anit-aircraft fire. The unit did however manage to land as a cohesive unit on the drop zone ten minutes before their H-Hour

of 10.00. Once on the ground they held off local counter-attacks and went about clearing their area of the Diersfordter as well as moving on the village of Schnappenberg, which was captured by 14.00.

Closely following the 3rd were the men of 5th Parachute Brigade, landing on DZ 'B'. Here the men again landed within their designated area but were met with intense artillery fire onto the drop zone. This had to be neutralised before the Brigade could then go about its tasks.

The 6th Airlanding Brigade was separated into companys for its assault. The 2nd Oxfordshire and Buckinghamshire Light infantry landed to the north on LZ 'O'. Their task being to secure the two bridges over the River Issel. The 1st Royal Ulster Rifles landed just south on LZ 'U' to secure the main road bridge whilst 12th Battalion of Devonshire Regiment landed LZ 'P' tasked with the capture of Hamminkeln. By now the German defenders were fully alerted and the slow moving gliders, along with the

A Bren-gunner leads a patrol through the streets of Hamminkeln.

towing aircraft were met with heavy flak. This took an extreme toll on the glidermen with many casualties from aircraft crashing or making emergency landings. These same flak cannons were then lowered to the horizontal where they enegaged the brigade as they formed up on their respective landing zones. 2 Ox and Bucks captured the two bridges and established footholds on the eastern bank of the Issel. I RUR also captured their bridge. 12 Devons took the most casualties on landing but despite this moved on Hamminkeln and took it with the aid of the misdropped men of 513th PIR. As the glidermen dug in to defend their positions local counter-attacks by the Germans, supported by armour were made, these being fought off. However the area around 2 Ox and Bucks positions at the road bridge was severely threatened and they were pushed from the east bank. This was taken with an immediate counter-attack, but when enemy armour approached the bridge it was decided to blow it.

First of the American units to drop was the 507th PIR. They were to drop on DZ 'W' but due to a thick haze low to the ground half of the regiment landed further north of the town of Diersfordt. Nevertheless the men made their way to the rest of the regiment, engaging any enemy they saw on their way, again all the regiments tanks were fulfilled by the early afternoon.

Next to drop were the 517th PIR. En route to the drop their aircraft hit a particularly bad belt of flak, taking a huge toll on the transports, especially the C-46 Commando aircraft. The C-47s with which the paras were familiar with had been fitted with self-sealing fuel tanks, however the C-46s did not have this facility and were very susceptible to explode due to the high volume of flak. General Matthew Ridgway would later forbid the use of the type in future operations. To add to the drama the ground haze caused the 507th to be misdropped on the 6th Airlanding Brigades area. Typically of paratroopers they dealt with the problem quickly and adapted their plans accordingly.

C-47s flying in formation after dropping during Operation Varsity.

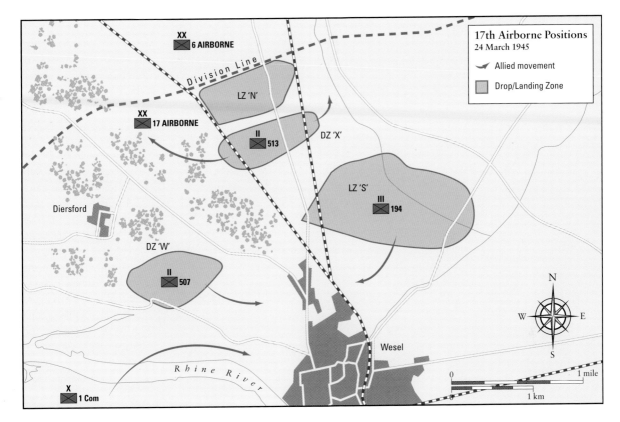

They joined forces with their British counterparts and aided in the capture of Hamminkeln.

West of the 507th the 194th GIR came down on LZ 'S'. Again the gliders and transports took heavy casualties, the glidermen actually landing amongst an artillery emplacement engaging targets on the western bank of the Rhine. This was duly silenced by the glidermen.

As 24 March came to a close all the tasks given to the men of the various airborne units had been accomplished. The German rear had been thrown into disarray and allowed for the consolidation of the bridgehead over the Rhine by the land forces. The routes taken by any potential counter-attack from the German panzer units stationed further to the rear were held and the town of Hamminkeln had been captured. By midnight of 24 March the 15th Division had made contact with the 6th

Airborne and armour was starting to come across the river to further reinforce the bridgehead. By the following day twelve pontoon bridges were laid across the Rhine to aid the stream of Allied forces east of the river. The attack had been costly on the airborne forces, with the 6th Airborne suffering 1,300 casualties and the 17th Airborne suffering a similar amount. However the lessons learned from Market Garden had proved to be fruitful, with an airborne army landing in the enemy's direct rear area a swift victory could be achieved. The German defences in the west had been cracked and now the road was open for 21st Army Group to exploit the gap and continue on to the Elbe river, swinging south to join with the American counterparts, who had forced various crossings along the southern part of the Rhine. Within six weeks the war in Europe would come to an end .

INDEX